Y0-BVO-603

DEMOCRATIC CONSOLIDATION IN EAST-CENTRAL EUROPE

Democratic Consolidation in East-Central Europe

Fritz Plasser
Professor of Political Science
University of Innsbruck

Peter A. Ulram
Head, Social Research Department
Fessel-GfK Austria

and

Harald Waldrauch
Research Assistant
Department of Political Science
Institute for Advanced Studies
Vienna

First published in Great Britain 1998 by
MACMILLAN PRESS LTD
Houndmills, Basingstoke, Hampshire RG21 6XS and London
Companies and representatives throughout the world

A catalogue record for this book is available from the British Library.

ISBN 0–333–73366–5

First published in the United States of America 1998 by
ST. MARTIN'S PRESS, INC.,
Scholarly and Reference Division,
175 Fifth Avenue, New York, N.Y. 10010

ISBN 0–312–21495–2

Library of Congress Cataloging-in-Publication Data
Plasser, Fritz, 1948–
[Politischer Kulturwandel in Ost-Mitteleuropa. English]
Democratic consolidation in East-Central Europe / Fritz Plasser, Peter A. Ulram and Harald Waldrauch.
p. cm.
This book is a revised, updated and substantially expanded version of our study 'Politischer Kulturwandel in Ost-Mitteleuropa' published in German in 1997.
Includes bibliographical references (p.) and index.
ISBN 0–312–21495–2 (cloth)
1. Political culture—Europe, Eastern. 2. Political culture––Europe, Central. 3. Europe, Eastern—Politics and government—1989– 4. Europe, Central—Politics and government—1989– I. Ulram, Peter A. (Peter Adolf), 1951– II. Waldrauch, Harald. III. Title.
JN96.A91P5813 1998
306.2'094'091717—dc21 98–13607
CIP

The work is a revised, updated and substantially expanded translation of *Politischer Kulturwandel in Ost-Mitteleuropa*, published in German by Leske+Budrich-Verlag, 1997.

This book is printed on paper suitable for recycling and made from fully managed and sustained forest sources.

10 9 8 7 6 5 4 3 2 1
07 06 05 04 03 02 01 00 99 98

Printed and bound in Great Britain by Antony Rowe Ltd, Chippenham, Wiltshire

Contents

Preface

This book is a revised, updated and substantially expanded version of our study *Politischer Kulturwandel in Ost-Mitteleuropa*, published in German by Leske & Budrich (Opladen, 1997). It condenses the data and results of a comparative research project initiated in 1990 and carried out over several years. Against the backdrop of the collapse of communism, the opening of the 'Iron Curtain', and both the liberalization and democratization of East-Central European countries, issues of transition and consolidation suddenly attracted the attention of political scientists everywhere, especially those working in the field of comparative politics. Two factors were decisive in the launching of the 'Politischer Kulturwandel in Ost-Mitteleuropa' project: first, the decision of public institutions to provide funding for a comparative research project of this scope; and secondly, the professional, international opinion research infrastructure provided by Fessel+GfK in Vienna, Prague, Bratislava, Budapest and Warsaw. A number of institutions and individuals active in the fields of academia or politics have lent inestimable and indispensable support, both financial and logistic, to 'Politischer Kulturwandel in Ost-Mitteleuropa' over the years.

In particular, we are grateful to Professor Rudolf Bretschneider of Fessel+GfK, who has taken a keen personal interest in the project and generously supported it from its earliest stages. Thanks to the cooperation, logistic support and professional competence of GfK's management in Austria and its research directors in the four East-Central European capitals, it has been possible to conduct regular annual representative opinion surveys with comparable variables and questions since 1990.

This volume would not have been possible without the support of colleagues and partners of many years' standing. We wish to thank Marianne Zawilensky (Center for Applied Political Research), who has been in charge of the organizational and secretarial aspects of the project since fund raising began in 1990. Wolfgang Meixner (Center for Applied Political Research) proofread and copy-edited the German manuscript with particular care. Arike Handsur of Fessel+GfK assisted with parts of the manuscript. Ellen Palli (Department of Political Science, University of Innsbruck) and Wolfgang Palli (Innsbruck) typeset both the German and English manuscripts. We are grateful to Herwig Engelmann (Berlin) for his competent

English translation of our text and to Lee Anne Oberhofer (Social Sciences Language Center, University of Innsbruck), who copy-edited the present version of our study. Last but not least, we thank Macmillan Publishers and commissioning editor Sunder Katwala for their obliging cooperation.

The publishing of this book was made possible through the financial support of the Austrian Federal Ministries for Foreign Affairs, Economic Affairs, and Science and Transport.

Vienna, March 1998

List of Tables and Figures

Tables

Appendix of data

Figures

1

Introduction

In the eight years since regime transition, there has been a virtual flood of publications on reform processes in East-Central Europe (Poland, the Czech Republic, Slovakia, Hungary, Slovenia and Croatia), Southeastern Europe, and the new states formed in the wake of Soviet collapse. Most contributions to date have been descriptive. Conceptual approaches and theoretical explanations of social, political and economic transformation in the former Eastern bloc got off to a rather slow start, but are now so vast in number that it is increasingly difficult to keep up with the debate. Some authors (cf. Sandschneider, 1995) try to establish a comprehensive theory of political, social and economic system change. Most, however, use existing theories to explain the changes occurring in their field without losing sight of the impact of other spheres of postcommunist society.

Any comprehensive theory of system change, however, pays for its scope and vision by sacrificing attention to detail. Political scientists are of course primarily interested in the political implications of the system changes in East-Central Europe; they tend to consider other developments only insofar as they can be integrated into a theoretical model describing and explaining political change.

In the *theoretical* section of our study, we outline consolidation research and its concepts. This approach concentrates on political change and was originally developed for regime transformations to democracy in other parts of the world. With some modifications, its concepts are nevertheless applicable to Central and Eastern Europe. We are primarily interested in the many ways of understanding democratic consolidation. We discuss the most important and currently debated concepts and compare them to our own approach, especially in order to draw attention to the relevance and status of political culture – the main focus of this book – within the context of consolidation research. Linkages between theories and concepts of political culture, legitimacy and democratic consolidation have often been neglected in the literature. Our goal here is to take a few first steps in this direction, even though we could not always consider the theoretical imperatives derived from our ideal types of regime change and consolidation research in the *empirical* part of our study.

In the latter section, we analyze the most important patterns and developments in the change of political culture in postcommunist societies and substantiate the analysis by using trend data from comparative, representative surveys conducted in the Czech and Slovak Republics, Hungary and Poland between 1990 and 1997. Within the framework of our project 'Politischer Kulturwandel in Ost-Mitteleuropa' (The Transformation of Political Culture in East-Central Europe) (Plasser and Ulram 1992a, b; 1993a; 1994b; 1996), we concentrated on an analysis of trends in democratic orientation and of selected indicators of political culture over time.

We mainly consider concepts of and attitudes towards politics in general and democracy in particular, as well as concepts of legitimacy, potentials of political support, and trust in the political institutions of postcommunist societies. Subsequent sections deal with the degree and extent of political involvement, with attitudes towards political efficacy, and with relations between voters and parties. We identify patterns of party preference and voter coalitions and then analyze the potential for conflict inherent in social and political tensions in the four postcommunist societies selected for study, maintaining a political culture approach throughout these analyses. In the final chapters, we investigate attitudes towards economic transformation and the expectations of citizens affected by it. We then link socioeconomic factors to those of political culture.

2

The Concept of Consolidation in Regime Change Research

Democratization research has long been characterized by an ongoing battle over the paradigms of *structure* and *actor*, with purists on both sides attributing exclusive powers of explanation to their variable. This conflict must be resolved, and the regime change approach seems to present us with an opportunity to do so, provided we place "actors and their choices in the broader context within which transitions occur" (Munck, 1994a: 371). We thus not only continue to give actors and their performance the significance they are due, but also ensure that structural and historical contexts receive adequate consideration.[1]

We start from the assumption that in any analysis of regime change, at least four aspects must be studied empirically and/or theoretically:

1) the regime being replaced
2) reasons for the replacement
3) modalities of regime change
4) the new regime envisaged and desired.

Ideally, regime change research should never lose sight of the fact that the characteristics of the old regime and the reasons for its replacement (inability to achieve goals, political or socioeconomic failure, disintegration of its repressive potential, etc.) are of great importance for every aspect or process of regime change, including type, instigating factors, pace, actors involved, strategies applied, degree of violence, and problems to be solved. The way in which a particular regime is replaced plays a role in shaping the new regime, but the "mode of transition" alone (Karl and Schmitter, 1991) cannot determine the future of an emerging democracy. It is the various characteristics of the old regime which narrow the choices of the emerging one. A direct cause-and-effect relationship between "modes of transition" and "types of democracy emerging" (Schmitter and Karl, 1992) therefore seems too simple for our purposes (cf. Waldrauch, 1996a, b). By giving each of the four aspects of regime change mentioned above balanced consideration, however, it should be possible to abandon the *transitology* approach which all too often neglects context variables in favor of a *regime change* or modified "path dependent" (Linz and Stepan, 1996: xiv) approach to democracy.

2.1. The Concept of Regime

We need, first of all, to be more precise about our understanding of the term "regime".[2] Definitions abound, of course, but Munck's (1995) effort to clarify the matter is particularly useful for our purposes. He begins by distinguishing between the "formal" and "behavioral" dimensions of a regime and then identifies the three components of the formal dimension: "1) the type of actors who are allowed to gain access to principal governmental positions; 2) the methods of access to such positions; and 3) the rules followed in the making of publicly binding decisions" (ibid.: 4). No regime, however, can be complete without the behavioral dimension: "This second dimension concerns the link between actor and formal rules and draws upon a quite simple but extremely consequential point: that formal rules structure and shape the conduct of politics only inasmuch as actors accept these rules and strategize accordingly" (ibid.: 5).[3] We will show, however, that in the case of democracy, the behavioral dimension is insufficient and must be supplemented with an *attitudinal* dimension based on the acceptance of democratic procedures.

Although Munck's concept of regime is one of the best proposed, it has a rather limited capacity to direct our attention to crucial aspects of regime changes. To simplify somewhat, we will assume that a regime consists of two main elements: on the one hand, Munck's "principal governmental positions" and, on the other hand, the population as well as political and civil society.[4] These two elements may relate to each other in four different dimensions:

1. *Intra-social relations,* referring to the presence or absence of openly negotiated conflict within society insofar as it is politically relevant, and thus to political competition and pluralism.

2. *Influence relations between society (active) and government institutions (passive).* This refers to the scope and potential of both the population and civil and political society to exert pressure on political institutions and the decision-making processes. Such influence may be wielded directly (eligibility, channels of recruitment, procedures of participation by citizens), by means of participation (any form of direct inclusion of citizens or social groups into decision-making processes), through informal pressure (strikes, rallies, lobbying), or by means of formal but indirect influence (active right to vote).

3. *Influence relations between government institutions (active) and society (passive).* This term designates any action or method that government institutions deem necessary and carry out in order to stabilize existing regime structures. Non-democratic regimes employ tactics such as repression, terror, threats and surveillance; restriction of the autonomy of societal subsystems; traditional or ideological "legitimation from the top" (Di Palma, 1991); or substantial legitimation (i.e., increasing material welfare). Democracies, in contrast, can draw on substantial as well as procedural legitimation, the latter comprising the granting of basic rights and liberties.

4. *Influence relations among government institutions.* What matters here are the rules which govern the decision making of these institutions; in other words, whether an institution decides arbitrarily and at its own discretion or whether it is guided by a basic set of institutional checks and balances provided by law.

While Munck's definition covers items 1, 2 and 4, it ignores item 3, or rather, breaks it up and distributes it among the other three. But this particular relationship is necessary to stabilize all the others, a fact especially obvious in non-democratic regimes.[5] The four dimensions of influence relations may overlap in various ways, depending on the type of regime. The means or forms found in one type of relationship may have a considerable impact on the others. In totalitarian regimes, for example, the single party is also the governing institution, while in democracies, parties are an expression of societal pluralism. Similarly, the lack of pluralism in totalitarian regimes is the result of repression from above.[6]

The characteristics of the four regime relations, the way they were created, the means used, and their intensity, are decisive factors in any regime change and the many difficulties to be solved in its various stages. How much and what kind of pluralism was possible under the old regime? How firmly established were institutions of political decision making? Were the armed forces included in decision making, and if so, how? Was there a strong ideology, and were attempts at shaping society in accordance with it successful? To what extent did repression, arbitrariness and surveillance contribute to the depoliticization of society? Was the regime supported by external hegemonic pressure? To what extent was the autonomy of societal subsystems curtailed? And so on. It is of course also important to know what type of government preceded the non-democratic regime about to be replaced. If it was democratic, then its institutions, parties and organized interests can serve as valuable elements of continuity during regime change. This is particularly true if the earlier regime was successful, if it was not too far in the past, and if its political organizations were able to survive the period of non-democratic government by going either underground or into exile.

2.2. Democratic Regime Change: Transition and Consolidation

In regime change research which focuses on actors, there is now a firmly established distinction between two phases of transformation: transition and consolidation. Defining and contrasting these two phases has often created considerable confusion. O'Donnell and Schmitter (1986: 6) used the term "transition" to denote the interval between two regimes. Six years later, O'Donnell defined the same term as the stage of regime change that ends with the establishment of democratic government (1992: 18), saying that a changeover to democracy is not complete until consolidation has taken place. The concept of consolidation suffers from the same lack of clarity.[7]

One way of avoiding some of this confusion is to combine the concept of regime with a procedural minimal definition of democracy. Such minimal definitions of democracy have gained acceptance in regime change research and are now largely uncontested. To expand on Robert Dahl's concept of polyarchy (1971), they emphasize competition, participation and a set of basic rights.[8] Thus, according to this definition and our four sets of relations, a regime can be considered democratic if it fulfills the following minimal criteria:

1. There is competition for access to central political institutions and, as a prerequisite, pluralism in political and civil society (Dimension 1).

2. Competing individuals or parties are granted access to central government institutions through competitive, regular, fair, free, and universal elections by secret ballot and with the comprehensive participation of adult citizens. This is designed to ensure vertical accountability (Dimension 2).

3. The state does not restrict societal pluralism; rather it supports it by governing according to basic political and civil rights and liberties and the rule of law. This implies that the scope for restraining the autonomy of societal subsystems is narrow and that autonomous subsystems or institutions, e.g., the judiciary or, to some extent, the economy, can exist (cf. Rüb, 1996)[9] (Dimension 3).

4. Decision making in government institutions takes place within the framework of a system of separate and balanced powers (especially between the judiciary and the executive and legislative institutions) established by law. A system of checks and balances ensures the horizontal accountability of democratic institutions, and there are neither 'tutelary powers' (Valenzuela, 1992) which lack democratic legitimacy, nor areas which are not explicitly subject to the sovereignty of democratically legitimized institutions (Dimension 4).

This definition therefore also implies an efficient *rechtsstaat*, since it is difficult to imagine a democracy functioning without an administration governed by the rule of law. According to the principal of universal legality, the law must also constrain political and state institutions. By definition, a democracy must have a set of basic citizens' rights; these are, however, worthless if insufficiently protected and not fully guaranteed by state institutions. "As a political form effective over a given territory, democracy is necessarily connected with citizenship, and the latter can only exist within the legality of a democratic state" (O'Donnell, 1993: 1361). Even though it is important to separate the concepts of regime and state, there seems to be an intrinsic convergence or causal relation between them in the case of democracy. Yet this interrelationship between democracy and *rechtsstaat* contrasts sharply with the following scenarios:

> Where political structures are less democratic (or more authoritarian), the distinctions among state, regime and government become increasingly blurred and, in the case of totalitarianism, virtually disappear altogether. Where regime change is occurring in the direction of democratization, then, an important indicator is the extent to which state/regime/government distinctions have become clearer (Lawson, 1993: 201).

The above definition of regime can now be applied to distinguish between transition and consolidation. By definition, then, transition centers around the establishment of the formal, minimal criteria of a democratic regime. It requires the abolishment of non-democratic institutions and the establishment of central, democratic ones in their place. Transition is complete once free elections, universal suffrage and basic rights and liberties are formally secured, that is, anchored in a constitution, and an elected, unconstrained government is in office.[10] The transition process can therefore not rely on the relative security of a stable structure of institutions, a fact which has resulted in the often-quoted "uncertainty" or "*under*determination of the transition" (Schmitter and Karl, 1994: 176).

Democratic consolidation, on the other hand, aims at completing regime change by stabilizing the behavioral and attitudinal foundations of democracy. Consolidation thus denotes the continuous marginalization or elimination of behavior patterns or attitudes incompatible with the base line of democracy and the stabilizing of those in harmony with it. Pridham (1995) termed this negative and positive consolidation, respectively. The distinction between transition and consolidation is also evident, though less rigorously maintained, in the arguments of O'Donnell (1992)[11], Linz, Stepan and Gunther (1995) as well as Linz and Stepan (1996a, b) and Munck (1995). The definition found in Gunther, Puhle and Diamandouros (1995) basically proceeds from the same criteria of distinction, but they consider a regime to be defined solely by its formal aspects, which then need to be stabilized as part of consolidation.

Democratic consolidation describes adaptations of perfomance and attitude such as contributing to the effective functioning and stabilization of the basic principles of democracy. Its goal is to safeguard democratic institutions under conditions of democratic competition and thus reduce insecurity. Decisions as to the type and character of political institutions to be formed as part of transition are, however, based on the current or anticipated power relationships of political actors. Colomer (1995) suggests that representatives of the regime to be replaced will insist on *majoritarian institutions* (majority vote system, unicameral parliament, centralization) if they feel strong and confident of winning at the polls. In all other cases, according to Colomer there will be a blend of majoritarian and *pluralist institutions* (proportional representation, directly elected president, bicameral parliament) or an even more pronouncedly pluralist system of *checks and balances*. If these expectations prove false, those unhappy with the election results may well question the legitimacy of the new institutions. The more insecurity there is about future power relations, the more likely institutions are to be contested even after the founding elections. And since transition often involves the head-on opposition of two heterogeneous blocs that begin to disintegrate once elections have been held, majoritarian institutions which favor a limited number of actors will probably undergo some form of change.[12] Colomer (1995: 81; cf. Kasapovic and Nohlen, 1996) finds ample evidence to support this hypothesis for Eastern Europe. As long as institutional change remains within the boundaries of democratic solutions, however, it should not be regarded as a step backwards into the transition stage, but merely as the substitution of one set of democratic rules for another. Frequent alterations of political rules, on the contrary, may indeed indicate defaults in consolidation which make it difficult for political actors to adapt their behavior and attitudes so as to comply with democratic rules.

Following (or accompanying) consolidation, there may still be process of *extending and deepening*[13] the basic principles of democracy and of other important democratic institutions, and democratic principles may be expanded beyond the minimum of competition for central positions in the system of government. This may happen, for example, through federalization, through increasing the forms and applications of direct democratic participation, through broadening and enforcing civil rights, or in a number of other ways. More simply, this could be termed an improvement in the quality of democracy.

If we distinguish stages of regime change according to their defining features, i.e., establish an "analytical sequence" (Merkel, 1996a: 40), we no longer have to assume a temporal sequence.[14] While earlier concepts of consolidation and transition implicitly assumed that the stages of regime change would succeed one another, many authors now recognize the possibility of overlapping stages. Transition, consolidation and deepening may even occur simultaneously. Logically, transition must come before consolidation and be completed either before it or at the same time. Only then can a regime change toward a democracy which satisfies minimal criteria be considered complete. If some formal minimal criteria of democracy are promptly satisfied while the fulfillment of others is postponed (though not only in such cases), there will be a prolonged overlapping of transition and consolidation. This would be the case, for example, if liberalization resulted in freedom of political association and elections were duly held, but the army retained its stronghold as a monitoring force. Another example is Poland in 1989, where the first elections were only semicompetitive. In such cases, the tendency was often to regard transition as complete but to speak of "diminished subtypes of democracy" (Collier and Levitsky, 1995) which adhere to the concept of democracy but do not satisfy all of its (formal) minimal requirements. As Gunther, Diamandouros and Puhle (1996: 52) remind us, "the concept of democratic consolidation is necessarily double-barreled – it joins two distinct dimensions that must be assessed separately in analyzing the status of political regimes." According to our conceptualization, transition is about making sure that the behavioral and attitudinal adaptations of consolidation actually relate to the basic rules of democracy. If transition remains incomplete and some minimal criteria are not met, democratic consolidation cannot, in theory, be accomplished without further changes in the basic rules. Whatever is being consolidated must also conform to the minimal criteria of democracy (cf. Linz and Stepan, 1996: 3f.).

2.3. The Concept of Democratic Consolidation

Though we have given a rudimentary definition of consolidation, we certainly do not wish to create the impression that it is uncontested on a conceptual level. In the following sections, we therefore compare and contrast our present version[15] with others in order to specify its content in greater detail and point out possible coincidences with other processes, patterns of development or "democratization trajectories" (Gunther, Diamandouros and Puhle, 1995), factors influencing the course of consolidation, and indicators of its progress.

Definitions of consolidation emphasize various processes, levels, dimensions, locations or areas of political change. One and the same term therefore often denotes a great variety of aspects. In order to differentiate among the many concepts of consolidation and examine the content of each, we refer to the following set of dichotomies:

1) Evolutionary processes versus political solutions of problems during consolidation
2) Behavioral versus attitudinal dimensions of consolidation
3) Elite level versus "mass" level of consolidation
4) Consolidation of democracy whole and entire or of its "partial regimes" (Schmitter)
5) Minimalist versus maximalist concepts.

2.3.1. Evolution or Direction in Consolidation

The literature contains a long list of processes and problems to be solved, which, depending on the respective author, represent the essence of consolidation or at least a major influence on its course:

Processes include: habituation; socialization; institutionalization; structuring; internalization of rules; integration; stabilizing patterns of peaceful conflict resolution; legalization; diminishing transitional insecurities; increasing spontaneous adherence to rules out of self-interest; legitimation of democracy and both its procedures and institutions, along with delegitimization of non-democratic options; rapprochement, reconciliation and depolarization; developing mutual trust, cooperation and consensus as well as reproducing this democratic consensus; the emergence and stabilization of democratic political culture.

Tasks and problems to be solved include: formation of an autonomous political and civil society; drafting, revising and ratifying a constitution; establishing representative legislative and executive institutions; economic, social, cultural, ethnic and other contextual problems; segregation of societal spheres, primarily those of politics, economy and law; punishing human rights violations committed under the old regime; neutralizing undemocratic actors and eliminating their power to install governments without an electoral mandate; establishing civilian control over the armed forces; eliminating powers of surveillance and veto insofar as they are not answerable to elected governments; eliminating undemocratic discrimination in voting laws; clear-cut separation of public and private spheres; creation of an efficient state administration which adheres to the rule of law, satisfies professional norms and guarantees the rights of citizens; ridding the state bureaucracy of politically tainted individuals; extending democratic principles to other spheres of social life; providing for the necessary parallel processes of democratic deepening.

The purpose of distinguishing between processes and targets is to point out that consolidation may be seen either as a primarily evolutionary process of various adaptations on an (inter) subjective level, or as the sum of all attempts and directed initiatives to solve problems and thereby promote such evolutionary processes.

2.3.1.1. Institutionalization and the Intersubjective Core of Consolidation

Many of these tasks and processes refer to identical or similar developments, and consolidation research is looking for a subcategory for them. In keeping with the trend towards *new institutionalism,* the concept of institutionalization is the favorite choice.[16] According to Goodin (1995), power is the key variable of new institutionalism. He concentrates on the ways institutions channel access to power and structure collective decision making:

> The existence of institutions makes certain things easier to do and other things harder to do. Holding positions within or control over those institutions gives some people greater capacity to work their own will upon the world, at the expense of others lacking access to such institutionalized power resources (Goodin, 1995: 16).

Institutions may be defined as societally stabilized patterns of behavior and interaction.[17] Institutions stabilize the predictability of actions (cognitive dimension) by narrowing the choice of actions possible or permitted. In so doing, they make actions possible in the first place; without institutions, meaningful and directed action would be difficult because anything would be possible and anything could happen. This dual function of providing for actions and limiting options in democracies can only be effective, however, if all the actors involved generally adhere to, support, and allow themselves to be governed by the rules, procedures and structures (objective dimension). Their actions must be in accordance with decisions reached with the help of these institutions; they must support them both normatively (normative dimension) and in their political action (behavioral dimension). But there is also a *functional or instrumental* side to institutions: predictability and normative acceptance do not, in themselves, turn rules, procedures and structures into institutions. "They must also function properly, i.e., accomplish the task or mission set for them, or be compatible with the supply of resources they must extract from their environment" (Offe, 1994b: 1). Institutionalization, therefore, is a process which refers to three levels: 1) establishing norms, rules and structures, 2) supporting them through behavior, expectations and normative attitudes, and 3) reinforcing them functionally and instrumentally.

How can we integrate this institutional approach into consolidation research? Obviously, institutionalization is central to the entire process of democratization. During transition, we witness the formal establishment of the minimal criteria for democracy: the ratification of rules relating to a set of inalienable basic rights and liberties, the competition for central positions of political power through the channel of participation in elections, and the submission of government institutions to rules of political accountability and *rechtsstaat*. Thus the foundations are laid for the objective of dimension government institutions.

Strengthening their normative and behavioral dimensions subsequently requires that all important political actors learn to act according to the procedures and rules established by the new institutions. Actors must learn not to undermine the rules, but to adjust to them, internalize them and ultimately see them as legitimate. The same compliance can also reasonably be expected from other actors involved in the political process (cognitive dimension). This stabilization of institutions on the intersubjective level is precisely what we have been referring to as the behavioral, normative and cognitive part of regime change; in other words, as consolidation.

If political institutions created during transition prove untenable in the consolidation phase because they lack consensus, they will (or should) be changed. Even if cooperation and concerted agreement, i.e., pact making, established the formal principles of central political institutions during transition, it does not automatically follow that attempts to adapt or strengthen these institutions will enjoy a similar basis of consensus and compromise. Therefore, if the institutionalization of democracy hopes to make changes in the objective dimension of its institutions or their intersubjective support, it must often rely on evolving and hard-to-control processes instigated by decentralized actors. More often than not, such actors can no longer agree to trust a relatively uninvolved body or even centralized round table negotiations to decide on a concrete design for institutions.[18]

If institutions are created by actors involved in direct democratic competition, the "logic of consequentionality" (March and Olson, 1989: 160) will dominate, i.e., each side will push for solutions that are in its own best interest. Defusing the conflict over institutional arrangements calls for mutual trust, compromise, cooperation and consensus. These not only facilitate negotiations concerning the institutional design; they can also stabilize existing institutions in their cognitive and normative dimensions. In the final analysis, we are dealing with a paradox: trust and voluntary political deradicalization facilitate the ratification of workable institutions, but only wisely conceived and workable institutions can contribute to increasing trust and voluntary compliance with rules. There is no short cut into what appears to be a closed "circle of virtuous institutionalization" (Valenzuela, 1992); institutionalization can only come about one step at a time. The more polarized and wary political opponents are, the more vital the role of institutions in which communicative interaction gradually establishes trust. Participation in these institutions must be linked to rewards even for those who are not election winners or directly responsible for political decisions. Such rewards may be symbolic (scope for political self-representation) or material (financial rewards, key positions, organizational resources, access to information, etc.). Przeworski (1991: 33) puts it this way:

> In conclusion, from the static point of view democratic institutions must be "fair". They must give all the relevant political forces a chance to win from time to time in the competition of interests and values. From the dynamic point of view, they must be "effective": They must make even losing under democracy more attractive than a future under nondemocratic alternatives.

2.3.1.2. Consolidation as a Goal-oriented Political Action

We have defined consolidation on the levels of intersubjective behavior and attitude. But how do the problems listed above relate to the process of consolidation? Are they to be seen as integral part of consolidation, or do they merely influence its progress?[19] In order to specify exactly what consolidation is and what promotes or hinders it, one must distinguish between dependent and independent variables. Without that distinction, we can never be confident in determining what needs to be done and what ought to be avoided, since any action would be part of the general process anyway. Consolidation would then quickly become an overloaded and analytically useless concept. We can easily identify a tendency to overload consolidation in the work of Huntington (1991: 208-279), Morlino (1994) or Merkel (1996b), and even in some passages by Linz and Stepan, authors of one of the most influential definitions of consolidation. They claim, for instance, that "consolidated democracies need to have in place five interacting arenas to reinforce one another in order for such consolidation to exist" (1996: 7) namely, "a free and lively civil society, a relatively autonomous and valued political society, a rule of law, a state bureaucracy that is usable and an institutionalized economic society" (ibid.). They do not state clearly, however, whether the creation and stabilization of these five arenas are elements of consolidation or indispensable prerequisites for it (cf. Schmitter, 1997).

Let us first turn to those items which, in our view, clearly do not constitute consolidation *per se*. In particular, this applies to the constitutional stipulation of the minimal criteria for a democratic regime, which, as we have argued, is really the core of transition. This may come about either through the revision of an existing constitution (as in Poland, 1989-1992, or Hungary, 1989-1990; cf. Sokolowicz, 1995; Ágh, 1995c; Bos, 1994), or the ratification of a newly drafted one (as in Slovakia and the Czech Republic in 1992; cf. Elster, 1995; Hendrych, 1995). What matters is that democratic rules do indeed exist. If democratically adapted constitutions are replaced by new ones or if genuinely democratic constitutions are amended, this should no longer be viewed as part of transition, but as an inherently democratic process which might have an impact on the progress of consolidation. Elimination of constitutionally stipulated "tutelary powers", of "reserved domains of authority and policy making" or of unfair electoral laws are obviously similar in that they are all integral elements of consolidation as defined by Valenzuela (1992).[20] If there are institutions which lack democratic legitimation or for which such legitimation is impossible, then that democracy does not yet satisfy minimal requirements. Therefore, eliminating such constraints of democracy is, in principle, a part of transition, even if it happens simultaneously with the consolidation of democracy.

Since transition and consolidation usually overlap, decisions on the formal structure of core democratic institutions influence most other behavioral and attitudinal components of consolidation, especially among elites. Many theorists therefore emphasize the importance of paying attention not only to the content of decisions on the structure of institutions, but also to the ways in which decisions are reached. A consensual resolution, they argue, is much more likely to produce attitudes and behaviors compatible with democracy than any unilaterally imposed solution, since it favors identification with new institutions (cf. Schmitter, 1988: 50-3). Theorists disagree, however, on how and to what extent exemplary democratic processes influence constitution building. Ackerman (1993) calls for a maximalist approach: a constituent assembly elected directly by the people specifically for the purpose of drafting a proposal, subsequently to be ratified in a referendum. Merkel (1996b) and Sandschneider and Segert (1996b), on the other hand, doubt whether such a paragon of formal legitimacy can produce the "empirical legitimacy" of a democratic constitutional arrangement in the context of what are at best rudimentary civil societies.

The problem becomes more complex when we consider the tasks which, though not part of the constitution, are obviously relevant for the minimal criteria of democracy and decisive for transforming rules of politics into structures of political action. This primarily concerns the establishment of the rule of law and norms of action. The rule of law and the principle of constitutionalism[21] which support it are absolutely necessary, since only they can guarantee basic rights and liberties.

We also need to emphasize the importance of strengthening administrative institutions in their functional-instrumental and/or organizational dimension, i.e., by allocating adequate material resources and professional staff.[22] Whatever the precise circumstances, the goal, according to Linz and Stepan (1996), must always be to create a "usable state bureaucracy". In most cases, there will be a state administration, but it may well be plagued by low professional standards, a lack of experience and a tendency to disregard the laws. This problem is aggravated, especially in postcommunist societies, when disciplinary measures are taken (or, in many cases, *not* taken) against functionaries or supporters of the former regime.[23] The thoroughness and credibility of this part of institutionalization can have a decisive impact on the course of consolidation. Political actors may tie their support for democracy to the actual efficacy (finding concrete solutions to substantial political problems) or potential efficacy (the possibility of solving such problems through adequate endowment of political and administrative institutions) of its central political and administrative institutions.

It is more difficult to pinpoint the relationship between consolidation and economic, social, and other policy problems. It is important to note that finding solutions for problems is not an inherent part of consolidation; it may at best exert a positive influence on its course. Even this is not always necessarily the case: in Southern Europe, the conscious decision to postpone social and economic reforms actually made consolidation easier (Diamandouros, Puhle and Gunther, 1995: 396). East-Central Europe never had that option: the simultaneity of political, economic and social (or, indeed, state) transformation was a foregone conclusion. The significance of these problems lies in the fact that political actors' support of democratic procedures may be contingent on the solution of substantial problems. Many authors have identified economic difficulties as the principal obstacle to democratic consolidation, basing their theories on a "tightly coupled" hypothesis which asserts a close connection between the support of economic reform and the endorsement of political change.[24] Although we should by no means underestimate the significance of economic problems and their solutions, there are justifiable doubts about its exclusive central position:

> A good number of new or recent democracies have imposed dramatic and austere reform policies and survived. Even if the reforming governments are voted out in every election, rather than only in about half of them, it would not demonstrate the vulnerability of democracy itself, so long as the regime (and popular belief in its legitimacy) held on. Furthermore, when politicians who embrace reform lose public support, we should not necessarily assume a cause-and-effect relationship, especially when discontent increases even as economic conditions improve (Diamond, 1995a: 134f.).

Linz and Stepan (1996: 76-81, 435-439) warn of the "danger of an inverted legitimacy pyramid", according to which rapid, successful economic reform must precede any attempt to reform the state and improve democracy. On the contrary, they argue, the top of the legitimacy pyramid – i.e., democracy, which has emerged as its most cherished object in countless opinion polls – should be given priority. Politics aimed exclusively at providing the foundation for economic growth will most likely lose popular support:

> [T]he endeavor to legitimate the new post-1989 democracies by the efficacy of the new capitalists and thus by increasing *by whatever means* the number of new capitalists is to invert the legitimacy pyramid. (...) We believe that, for imploded command economies, democratic polities can and must be installed and legitimized by a variety of appeals *before* the possible benefits of a market economy actually materialize fully (Linz and Stepan, 1996: 438-9).

The case of ethnic conflict is considerably more complex. The first step must always be to grant full citizenship rights to all members of ethnic minorities. If this is not done, as was the case in Latvia and Estonia,[25] the minimal criteria of democracy have not been met. Even if minorities are in principle recognized as citizens, the way in which they are actually treated can still affect consolidation. This is likely to be the case if the majority or its elites practice a policy of assimiliation along ethnicist or nationalist lines; and if, furthermore, a minority becomes conscious of such discrimination and not only reacts to it by demanding specific minority rights, but also makes its support of political reform contingent on the granting of such rights. Preuss (1995: 114-9) identifies a general trend toward exclusionary, "communitarian" concepts of citizenship in postcommunist countries which, he claims, also makes itself felt on the constitutional level. From the vantage point of consolidation theory, this is dangerous insofar as such concepts may begin to invade the sphere of everyday politics in the form of antiliberal and antipluralist sentiments. These particularly threaten young democracies with no firmly established civic tradition of political conflict.

In 1970, Rustow's pioneering studies in transitology included the rule that democracy can only flourish if the borders of the state and the community of citizens are uncontested. Although democratization research has often neglected the question of statehood, Linz and Stepan (1996: 16-37) recently drew attention to it. The rule, however, should be stated more precisely. The Czech Republic, for instance, took steps towards both formal democracy and its consolidation before the dissolution of its union with Slovakia. In Spain, consolidation proceeded despite persistent terrorist attacks by the Bask separatist movement, ETA. Linz and Stepan emphasize the importance of offering rewards for the creation of multiple, rather than exclusive, ethnic identities during regime change. The key, they contend, is to hold national elections prior to any regional ones, since only the former can stimulate the formulation of national agendas and the organization of national parties. It is then possible for a civic identity to emerge alongside ethnic ones. Unfortunately, analyses of the relationship between ethnicity and democratization lag far behind political philosophers' recent achievements in the field of minority and group rights (see, among others, Kymlicka, 1995a, b; or Bauböck, 1996).

As regards the necessity of extending democratic principles to other spheres of social life – a tenet which O'Donnell included in his definition (1992: 48f.) – and the need for a parallel process of "democratic deepening" (Diamond, 1995b), it is important to note that while both certainly aid consolidation, they are not indispensable. Electoral competition for central positions of government may be considered sufficient; federalization might simply not be an issue; more opportunities to participate could be low on the list of priorities. Extending democratic principles to other spheres of social life (e.g., democracy in the workplace) can even have a negative influence on consolidation, since conservative groups' rejection of democracy might be confirmed by firsthand experience of the way it works. For that reason, the establishment of democratic behavior and attitudes is often a prerequisite for an extension of democracy.

2.3.2. Behavioral and Attitudinal Dimensions of Consolidation

We have established that the goal of the process of consolidation is to make changes on the (inter) subjective level. So far, there seems to be general agreement on that point. When it comes to emphasizing the priority of one component of consolidation over another, however, there is a lack of consensus. Diamond (1994, 1995b) equates consolidation exclusively with the attitudinal dimension by emphasizing the creation of legitimacy and by making a sharp distinction between democratic deepening on the behavioral level and the process of consolidation. In contrast, Przeworski (1991) builds his concept of consolidation exclusively on behavior, questioning the explanatory relevance of normative convictions for the survival of democracy. In his view, the stability of democracies is the result of their having satisfied the material interests of all concerned, and depends to a great extent on successful economic reform. "To evoke compliance and participation, democracy must generate substantive outcomes: It must offer all the relevant political forces real opportunities to improve their material welfare" (ibid.: 32).

Both approaches seem inadequate. Przeworski cannot explain why certain democracies (for instance, during the interwar period) collapsed in the face of serious economic crisis while others did not; Diamond misses the crucial step between the recognition of the legitimacy of democracy in principle and its actual stabilization through democratic behavior.[26] Even if legitimacy is widely accepted, a small group can still pose a threat to democracy and its consolidation. Moreover, a broad basis of legitimacy does not necessarily mean that political actors are capable of behaving in ways compatible with the survival of democracy.

2.3.2.1. The Behavioral Dimension

In general, political practices which conform to the formal basic rules of democracy must be stabilized in order to ensure the survival of the system. At the same time, any behavior which aims at undermining democracy must be eliminated, neutralized or isolated. Often "the sheer fact that party elites have accepted, as a fundamental rule of the game, the process of alternation in power" (Pasquino, 1990: 58) is seen as an indicator of consolidation's progress or accomplishment, gauged by means of a "one-turnover test" (Przeworski, 1994: 13) or a "two-turnover test" (Huntington, 1991: 268). These tests, however, are both too unidimensional and too vague. Liebert (1995: 90f.) demonstrates this with the concept of "transfer of power", which provides the foundation for this behavioral indicator. She argues that it may only account for the exchange of a few parties within a coalition government, or the switch from a center-right to a center-left coalition. But transfer of power can also entail replacing one single-party government with another from the opposite end of the political spectrum, thus putting democracy to a much harder test. Finally, Liebert points out that this indicator fails to take into account whether or not a particular group is permanently excluded from the interplay of power.

The absence of organized groups that attempt to undermine democracy has often been called a crucial factor in consolidation.[27] These groups may be parties, individual politicians, organized interests, social groups, armed forces or terrorists. Linz's checklist of semiloyal and disloyal behavior (1978: 27-38) is especially useful in identifying forms of behavior hostile to democracy and thus, to consolidation.[28] It may be easy for outside observers to draw a clear picture of disloyalty, but it is often considerably more difficult for those involved in the political process. "It is this basic ambiguity of the definition of disloyalty, except in the case of small, highly ideological and principled antisystem antidemocratic parties, that makes it so difficult to defend an embattled democracy and to prevent a silent takeover by antidemocratic parties" (ibid.: 32). The situation is further complicated by the fact that in democracies struggling toward consolidation, semiloyal actors, rather than disloyal ones, present the real problem: in theory, they may well be convinced of the advantages of democracy, but their reaction to political crises is hard to predict.[29] Linz ultimately identifies the key task for all loyal forces as "defining the disloyal opposition clearly and at some stages isolating it politically, but this process can be successful only if there is concomitant readiness to incorporate into the system those who are perceived as at least semiloyal by some actors of the regime-building coalition." In other words, it is important to integrate as many political actors as possible, unless they adopt an unmistakably antidemocratic stance. Rewards and stimuli must be created in an effort to motivate them to articulate their concerns through the channels of democratic procedure. In postwar Italy, the country's antisystem party was a less serious obstacle to consolidation than the exclusion of the PCI, an increasingly loyal party (see Cotta, 1992; Gunther, Puhle and Diamandouros, 1995: 22-26). Many Eastern European countries face a similar dilemma: former communist and postcommunist parties are often still relegated to the sphere of semiloyalty or disloyalty despite the absence of relevant indicators. Disloyal or semiloyal groups are not likely to obstruct consolidation, according to Weil (1994: 95), unless they are in a position to tip the scales in the process of power bargaining, prevent solutions compatible with the system or incite loyal parties to engage in semiloyal or disloyal behavior. The most serious danger, however, is that voters may reward semiloyal or disloyal behavior with electoral victories or political trust.[30]

Our regime model is a schematic representation of the levels of behavioral stabilization during consolidation. Liebert's attempt at systematization is very similar, and we have tried to integrate her approach into ours. The following behavior patterns must be taken into consideration:

1. *Relations on the level of government institutions.* In general, this concerns the stabilizing of procedures in central government institutions and relationships between institutions in accordance with democratic principles.[31] During consolidation, parliament and the executive must "have acquired a stable external status and regulated their internal structures" (Schmitter, 1988: 25). While routinization and professionalization are important factors, stabilization depends primarily on marginalizing behavior which undermines the horizontal accountability between the office of the president and government, parliament, and constitutional or other courts of law. The rejection of accountability to other democratic institutions can become a serious problem especially in (semi) presidential systems; it

might also result in "delegative democracy" (O'Donnell, 1994), in which there is typically refusal to cooperate with other institutions and claims to represent the nation's "true" interests. Rudiments of delegative democracy have emerged in East-Central Europe, especially in Poland under Lech Walensa's presidency (Linz and Stepan, 1996: 269-283). Another practice of delegative democracy is the conscious breaking or bending of rules with the strategic intent of improving one's own relative position of power (Osiatynski, 1995b). In this respect, as in most others, the Slovakia of Vladimir Meciar has skirted or overstepped the boundaries.[32] In the context of delegative democracy, Liebert also mentions the inability to form a government, the attempt to boycott pertinent endeavors, the unlawful dissolution of parliament, martial law, the oppression of parliamentary opposition, and, finally, what she terms 'bureaucratic autonomy'.

2. *Influence relations between society (active) and government institutions (passive).* Both the elites and the public must get used to the fact that elections are the central and inevitable channel of influencing political decision making. Political and societal actors who refuse to accept elections as the only way to form a government must be neutralized, isolated or encouraged to participate in the political process according to the rules. The first step must naturally be to curb violence and mass mobilization with destabilizing intent as well as the blatantly obstructive politics of extremist parties, including, according to Liebert, violent political upheavals or strikes, *coups d'état* and the boycotting of elections. Less patent, though no less destructive, are practices such as electoral fraud, corruption, infiltration of the bureaucracy and government, or large-scale flight of capital.

3. *Influence relations between government institutions (active) and society.* The crucial factor here is the concrete implementation of basic rights and liberties. The focus must be on the practice of the rule of law, the real possibilities of benefiting from civil and political rights, the degree to which security forces respect human rights, and practices of state institutions which aim at curtailing societal pluralism or excluding particular parties and interest groups (O'Donnell, 1993; Poppovic and Pinheiro, 1995). In East-Central Europe – especially in Hungary prior to the

elections of 1994 and in Slovakia under Meciar – political elites in government have frequently adopted behavior clearly contradictory to democratic principles. This was particularly true with respect to the media: there were repeated attempts to restrict freedom of speech, primarily through political appointments.[33]

4. *Intrasocietal relations.* On this level, too, we find behavior patterns of political actors which attempt to hinder social organization and block the access of certain social or political groups to political decision-making processes and institutions. While it is certainly true that disloyal groups must be prevented from exerting a negative influence on democracy, the pretense of protecting the democratic-electoral process may be nothing more than a veiled attempt to exclude political competitors or organizations of civil society which hope to exert influence on the political process from outside the sphere of parties. In East-Central Europe, this manifested itself in the form of "overparticization": "new parties have actually become almost the only political actors; they 'particize' the whole political scene and try to monopolize it" (Ágh, 1994c: 296). There are also dangerous forms of intrasocietal relations, among which Liebert lists mass mobilization or incitement by extremist parties, as well as mutual support among such parties, status groups or mafia-type organizations.

2.3.2.2. The Attitudinal Dimension: Legitimacy and Political Culture

With the notable exceptions of Przeworski (1991), Di Palma (1990a, b), and Burton, Gunther and Higley (1992a, b), most theorists assume more or less explicitly that legitimacy is the "key variable in democratic consolidation" (Merkel, 1996a: 51), or even the only decisive variable (Diamond, 1994). There have been, however, only a few attempts to integrate the three dominant approaches in the field: theories of consolidation, theories of the significance of legitimacy (as a system variable of political culture) for the stability of democratic regimes in general, and empirical studies of political culture and legitimacy in emerging democracies.

Theories of political culture and institutions normally assume a degree of homogeneity between the political culture and the institutions of a society. This is what Liebert (1995: 161) has called a "mirror image hypothesis". But regime changes can either produce new incongruences[34] or expose existing ones. Tensions can result from the creation of institutions whose procedures and norms have no equivalent in the political culture of society: this "cultural lag" is a basic assumption of all political culture research on postcommunist Europe. Conflicts may also arise because certain institutions no longer correspond to the transformed political culture. It is difficult to substantiate this explanation of political regime change, however, since nondemocratic regimes do not normally allow surveys in which the methodological requirements of a free-speech situation are respected.[35]

Easton's distinction (1975; 1979) between *objects* and *types* of support which can be combined to form various *dimensions* of support, has been fundamental to many theories of legitimacy. Although there is still room for improvement in Easton's concept (cf. Westle, 1989), his basic assumptions are valid. He assumes the existence of three kinds of support objects (political community, political regime, authorities) and at least two support types (*diffuse*, long-term support unrelated to output; and *specific*, short-term, output-related support). According to Easton, legitimacy (along with trust) is the main component of the diffuse support which can be given to all three objects above. His idea that there is a hierarchy of support with respect to the stability of a political system is especially important for consolidation research. Thus diffuse support is more important than specific support, and commitment to the political community ranks higher than commitment to a particular regime[36] or its representatives in power.

Przeworski (1986: 51f.) on the other hand, tries to avoid the issue of legitimacy altogether:

> What matters for the stability of any regime is not the legitimacy of this particular system of domination but the presence or absence of preferable alternatives. (...) A regime does not collapse unless and until some alternative is organized in such a way as to present a real choice for isolated individuals.

From our point of view, however, the absence of alternatives to democracy is not a sufficient guarantee of democratic stability or consolidation because it ignores the dynamics of democratic competition. If a democracy has virtually no diffuse support upon which to draw and survives only because there are no alternatives, then the lack of belief in its legitimacy will ultimately harm it. First, political actors will exploit the fact that no one still considers its democratic principles worthy of respect. This is especially true if institutions charged with punishing deviant behavior are also corrupted by a declining belief in legitimacy. Secondly, sooner or later there will be political actors who try to satisfy the demand for alternatives on the democratic market. The mere absence of alternatives to democracy is therefore only temporary, and other choices could emerge in a very short time (cf. Schmitter, 1994: 58f.).

Merkel (1996a) starts at the opposite end of the same chain of reasoning. Legitimacy, he argues, is central to consolidation. Although he distinguishes between diffuse and specific support, he does not clearly state whether he considers the former or the latter as legitimacy and thus as indispensable for consolidation. His broad understanding of legitimacy is also evident on his fourth level of consolidation (ibid.: 39): he considers the emergence of a rich civic culture as indispensable. He takes this even further than Pridham, who merely speaks of a "remaking of the political culture *in a direction* that is system-supportive for a new democracy" (1995a: 169; author's italics). Merkel also shows that even though legitimacy may be of critical importance, data on legitimacy cannot, in itself, tell us much about the progress of democratic consolidation. "Without a sufficient degree of legitimacy that varies from case to case, a democratic system remains unconsolidated and unstable" (1996a: 51). As indicated by the expression "that varies from case to case", no dependable statement on the course of consolidation can be made without reference to a concrete political context. How, if not by taking concrete political structures into account, can we specify the appropriate degree of legitimacy? We should certainly bear in mind that *democratic* legitimacy is at issue and not lose sight of the structures and institutions which are inherent to the kind of politics we wish to see stabilized. The question here is: Do they satisfy democratic requirements in their formal and/or behavioral aspects? Moreover, we could now ask whether a lack of legitimacy is *per se* equivalent to a lack of consolidation and instability, or whether the former is merely a cause of the latter (cf. O'Donnell, 1996b: 160).[37] Analytical differentiation of the stages of consolidation seems much better suited to resolving this dilemma. We have defined consolidation as the buttressing of democratic minimal criteria by means of attitudinal and behavioral adjustments. Consolidation is not in itself the equivalent of democratic stability, but leads to it. We still need to identify the concrete causal mechanisms that lead to the (de)stabilization of the democratic minimum, especially in the case of attitudes.

Morlino and Montero devised a convincing concept of relevant types of support in the context of consolidation research. They distinguish among 1) the diffuse legitimacy of democracy in general, 2) the absence of preferable alternatives, and 3) the perceived efficacy of democratic practices. Items 1 and 2 represent a dimension of legitimacy defined as a "set of positive attitudes of a society towards its democratic institutions, which are considered as the most appropriate form of government" (ibid.: 232). Perceived efficacy, on the other hand, is the equivalent of specific support as defined by Easton. Responding to demands for a contextualization of legitimacy, the authors emphasize that diffuse legitimacy matters more in countries with a recent nondemocratic past, and that the issue of alternatives is particularly crucial if the regime to be replaced is associated with successful modernization (ibid.: 233f.). The absence of preferable alternatives might temporarily compensate for insufficient diffuse legitimacy and create "legitimacy by default"; conversely, strong diffuse legitimacy could be reinforced by the absence of plausible alternatives to democratic government. They argue that a distinction between diffuse legitimacy and the perception of any plausible alternative is called for, at least in posttransitional states.

A special form of negative legitimation through the absence of alternatives might be what Valenzuela (1992: 78) has labeled "inverse legitimation". The term indicates not a rejection of all possible non-democratic options, but a surge of democratic legitimacy before, during or shortly after transition. Still-vivid memories of repression trigger a categorical rejection of the old regime, which translates into a bonus of legitimacy for the new democracy.[38] Negative legitimacy can also be induced by the perception of an international consensus which discredits all nondemocratic alternatives.[39]

If consolidation is seen as part of a process of democratic institutionalization, it becomes clear that not only evaluative, but also cognitive assessments are important on the attitudinal level. The cognitive dimension is reflected in a number of definitions of consolidation (cf. O'Donnell, 1992: 48f.; Valenzuela, 1992: 70; Schedler, 1997b).[40] Correspondingly, a stabilizing of democratic norms requires not only their positive assessment, but also the expectation that they will be permanent. Rules and principles will be able to shape the structure of actions if, and only if, they can be expected to last; and their efficacy in structuring action will in turn influence their stabilization. The cognitive dimension of consolidation very clearly reveals mutual influence relations between the spheres of actions and attitudes during the process of consolidation. If there is to be an incentive for abiding by the rules, then they must be predictable, and rules are only predictable if others obviously respect them. Linz succeeds in capturing both the evaluative and the cognitive dimensions of consolidation in one concise formula: consolidation is the process that results in democracy's being "the only game in town" (1990: 158).

The notion of predictability leads us to a key variable in political culture research: trust. Trust contributes to reducing complexity and uncertainty about the future by accepting certain aspects of it as known and familiar (Sztompka, 1995: 255). It has an integrate effect; it widens the scope of action and serves as an incentive to cooperate. Distrust, on the contrary, is dysfunctional for both parties involved in any interaction (ibid.: 259f.) Sztompka regards lack of trust as the fundamental predicament of postcommunist societies (cf. also Rose, 1994). Unlike Jowitt (1992) and others, however, he does not place the blame exclusively on the heritage of the past, but holds perceptions of inefficiency in state institutions partly responsible. In view of the above-mentioned mutual influence relations between actions and expectations, empirical analysis of the attitudinal foundations of consolidation should be especially cautious about interpreting low levels of trust as either a cause or an effect of insufficient consolidation. It would be too onedimensional to consider lack of trust exclusively in terms of a population slowing the pace of consolidation. It is quite possible that some institutions do not merit trust[41], either because of their incompetence in problem solving or because their actors fail to comply with democratic criteria. They would misconstrue any public support as encouragement.

Since consolidation theories and analyses of legitimacy must assume, in principle, that the significance of political culture for the stability of democracies is empirically measurable, the many doubts about its explanatory potential on the macro level of political regimes present cause for concern. Criticism has come from sources other than authors who reject the concept of political culture in the tradition of Almond and Verba. Gabriel (1994a: 29), for instance, says that "due to the lack of adequate data, one of the central aims in any analysis of political culture – namely the empirical scrutiny of political culture's influence on the stability and performance of political systems – is impossible to achieve." Critics also question the very validity of political culture (and in particular, legitimacy) as a concept which offers a significant explanation for democratic stability and change. Welch (1993: 75f.) among others, believes that there are three principle constraints on comparative approaches within behavioralist political culture research. The first is the "problem of complexity": there are, he argues, too many potentially relevant variables and possible correlations between them to reduce them to a single explanatory variable. Secondly, he identifies a "problem of salience": politics and its objects are given different priority in different cultures. Finally, there is the "problem of indexicality": the answers to certain survey questions must be interpreted according to their particular cultural context. This, so the counterargument runs, is an inevitable return to interpretative methods which are hard to reconcile with the behavioristic concept of political culture research based on survey data.

Thus there are also doubts about the validity of using variables of political culture to explain concrete advances in Eastern European consolidation (see von Beyme, 1994a: 364ff.; Kaase, 1994a: 266ff.). This may in part be due to the fact that studies of political culture usually adopt a sociological approach to explain attitudes on the individual level. The impact of attitudes such as legitimacy or trust in institutions on the progress of democratization is then often either not discussed or assumed to be self-explanatory. Studies on Eastern Europe often focus on finding explanations for legitimacy and the support of political and economic reforms, especially whether or not there is a strong correlation between (the evaluation of) economic progress and the development of political support. At present, however, a true compilation of knowledge on the subject is only in its early stages, largely because of a lack of elaborated theories to back up the concepts.

The unfortunate consequence is that questions and answers – especially those pertinent to the issue of democratic legitimacy – cannot be compared. Morlino and Montero's verdict on legitimacy research in general applies equally well to the case of East (Central) Europe: There is a "remarkable gap between the relatively high level of theoretical and conceptual development, on the one hand, and, on the other, the weakness of the many empirical indicators that have been used to date" (1995: 233). Studies on Eastern Europe often ignore fundamental differences or single out a particular dimension of support as the only significant influence on the stability or consolidation of democracy. In doing so, they neglect other forms of support and their possible compensating or reinforcing effects. Rose and Mishler (1994: 168), for instance, take a "realist approach", in which a decisive factor is "whether or not people will support the current regime *as it is, here and now, an indivisible whole.*" The demand to know "how the government works" (cf. also Tóka, 1995: 359) at first appears to refer to the present government, but they subsequently ask for evaluations of the former regime, the current one, and the one expected to be in power in five years' time. The question probably also relates to the performance and output of a system and, therefore, to specific support in Easton's sense of the term. A negative assessment of the efficacy of government should, however, not be seen as an immediate threat to democratic stability or consolidation, since it may be based on a conviction that the present regime is doing a very poor job of complying with democratic criteria. In fact, a positive assessment of regime performance may even have negative consequences for democratic consolidation. Case in point: in a democracy dominated by parties which act undemocratically but nevertheless benefit from public support, authoritarian practices will endanger democratic minimal criteria. Moreover, this view of legitimacy projects an image of citizens as passive subjects who have no choice but to accept the political structures and practices in place as long as the regime even remotely resembles a democracy. Any criticism of the way democracy is developing is implicitly dangerous for the system. This example illustrates the importance of knowing exactly what kind of stabilization is being explained in the first place: Is it the stabilization of current political conditions, of a concrete form of democracy, or merely of democratic miminal criteria?

McIntosh *et al.* (1994) disagree with the above, defending what Rose and Mishler termed an "idealist approach". They ask "how important a multiparty system of government, freedom to criticize the government and a system of justice that treats everyone equally are for a 'society to be called democratic' " (ibid.: 495). In doing so, however, they seem to commit another error: that of blending the evaluative dimension (what is good?) with the cognitive dimension (what is a democracy?).[42]

A comparatively rigorous application of Easton's conceptual dichotomy can be found in Evans and Whitefield (1995b). They separate a "normative commitment to democracy" (measured via approval of "the aim of introducing democracy") from the assessment of the efficacy of democratic practices (gauged by means of a "system-responsiveness index" composed of seven items). Their multiple regression analysis clearly shows that economic variables have very little influence on diffuse support for democracy, and even that depends on corresponding support for the market economy. In contrast, the perception of the responsiveness of a given regime seems to have an impact, albeit moderate, on diffuse support of democracy. This impression is compatible with the assumption that diffuse support of a system does not depend on its output. In each case, the uncoupling of diffuse and specific support, even though it may not be complete, is a sign of progress in democratic consolidation.[43]

In addition to these conceptual deficiencies on the level of legitimacy or political support, research in this field faces a number of other problems. First, there is often a huge time lapse between culling the data and publishing the results, in some cases up to five years (Duch, 1995; McDonough, 1995). During this interval, significant changes can take place in the political situation, but they are rarely incorporated into the interpretation of the data. Another related problem is the above-mentioned relationship of mutual ignorance between survey research and conceptual work on regime change. Duch (1995), for instance, claims that citizens can differentiate between democracy *per se* and incumbents. As evidence, he cites the discrepancy between approval of democratic reform and Gorbachev's popularity in the Soviet Union of 1990. At that time, however, Gorbachev was not a democratic incumbent (he was never democratically elected), nor was the USSR a democracy. Following the elections of 1989, the Congress of Peoples' Deputies was at best semidemocratic. Thus, the support for democracy measured then was not for a real and actual democratic regime. Duch's own data cannot substantiate his claims that people can distinguish incumbents from regime and that they expect accountability of the former. In the absence of democratic legitimation, there were neither "incumbents" nor a democratic regime on which to blame economic chaos.

A final point is that despite the lack of time series data (or, in some cases, the reluctance to use them), attempts are made to predict the trajectory of democratization. Duch (1995), for example, uses semicausal methods to extrapolate future trends in political support on the basis of existing correlations, i.e., between evaluations of democracy and individual economic conditions. Another method, used by Rose and Mishler (1994: 178ff.), is to interpret positive assessment of current political and economic conditions as harbingers of future support for a particular political and economic regime, i.e., democracy and market economy. It follows that "even reactionaries do not plan a return to the *status quo ante*" (ibid.: 282). But the question as to the type of regime anticipated remains unanswered, and this once again leads to a merging of the cognitive (what will be?) and evaluative (how will it be judged?) dimensions. We should add, however, that Rose and Haerpfer (1994b, 19f.) have also proposed another typology that is very useful for consolidation research: it combines evaluation (for or against dissolution of parliament) with expectation (whether the dissolution of parliament is considered possible or impossible).

What degree or which particular constellation of support do studies on legitimacy consider adequate for successful democratic consolidaton? Or, to put it in Reisinger's (1995) terms, how can individual attitudes be aggregated to an explanatory variable on the macro level? McIntosh *et al.* (1994: 487) answer this question with a rule of proportions: "We assume that the larger the proportion of reform enthusiasts to reform sceptics, the greater the probability of successful consolidation of democracy." And since democracy is unthinkable without a market economy, they also count dyed-in-the-wool market enthusiasts among the indirect promoters of consolidation. Rose and Mishler's (1994; cf. Mason, 1995) idea is very similar: they say that there should be a dynamic of "leaders and laggards" rather than a polarization between friends and enemies of reform or a rift between elites and the masses. Arguments as general as these are, however, rather unconvincing. What should this proportion be? How high must the degree of legitimacy be (cf. O'Donnell, 1996b: 165f.)? How long can laggards drag their feet before polarization becomes inevitable?

We see an urgent need for empirical research to become more conceptually precise and standardized (What kinds and levels support exist? How should democratic stability be interpreted? Which stages of regime change must be studied?). Our most important conclusion, however, is that research on such attitudes will never advance beyond vague suppositions until we take structural, institutional and behavioral context variables into consideration in trying to determine the extent to which and especially how and through which mechanisms attitudes impact political decision making. Explanations of regime change or any of its aspects fail not only because of the unavailability of time series, but also because of the unwarranted assumption that data on attitudes can function out of context as explanatory factors in the abstract. Our first step should be a theoretical analysis of the likely consequences of a withdrawal of various types of support. Since an erosion of support on the attitudinal level has, in and of itself, no effect whatsoever, we examine the real consequences; namely the political actions and reactions it engenders and their political impact. We therefore need to ask the following questions:

1. When support is withdrawn from a particular political object, can we expect inimical behavior directed at this object? Examples might include floating voters, abstention from voting, political protest, and violence.

2. How are actors on the level of parties, organized interests and political elites likely to react to the withdrawal of support? A few possibilities are changes in party programs, radicalization, antidemocratic mobilization, separatist movements, and calls for violence.

3. Under which micro- or macropolitical conditions are the behaviors in questions 1 and 2 most likely? Fractionalization, polarization of parties, weak party affiliations, traditional mood of protest, strong extremist parties, and semipresidentialism are among the possible conditions.

4. What specific political, structural or institutional conditions are likely to have negative consequences for democracy? In particular, we should ask whether or not the object of support in question really complies (formally or behaviorally) with the minimal criteria of democracy.

An analysis of this kind – one which attempts to identify the possible impact of political support under specific political and structural circumstances – would pursue a line of reasoning more or less the direct reverse of that used by Weil (1994: 67f.). He showed that legitimacy is an indispensible, intervening variable in relations between "oppositional structures" ("an umbrella term for party systems and government coalition structures") and "democratic outcome" ("successful creation, maintenance, or survival of a democratic regime"): "A theory of democratic outcomes should account for the interaction of social actors and the combined effects of legitimation and oppositional structure (or, more broadly, political culture and political structure." (ibid.: 71).

A theoretical analysis of these correlations begins by asking under what circumstances political cultures and attitudes are most likely to induce actions – which are of course ultimately decisive[44] – and through which mechanisms they influence macropolitical outcomes. As Reisinger (1995) has noted, there is a lack of precisely such "convincing arguments from political culture theorists about the conceptual links between orientations and behavior, first, and subsequently between individuals and the larger political system." In analyses of this kind, we have to refer to survey data on the forms of participation among citizens and their disposition towards it. This data will allow us to estimate both the probability of (non) support making itself felt in political action and the ways in which this is likely to happen.

2.3.3. Elite and Mass Levels of Consolidation

Transitology has long focused on elites, and basic theoretical assumptions about the uniquely decisive role of elites were also introduced into consolidation research. The definition of consolidation proposed by Burton, Gunther and Higley (1992a) is characteristic of this fixation on elites in that it contains only a single reference to the masses: elections. According to this school of thought, consolidation occurs when there is either a sudden "elite settlement" (Burton and Higley, 1987) or an "elite convergence" (Burton, Gunther and Higley, 1992a) which turns disagreement over basic political rules and structural disintegration into consensus and "structural unity".[45] Interestingly enough, in elite settlements, there is hardly any distinction between transition and consolidation. Once the longsmoldering strife has been resolved through an inclusive pact, all subsequent conflict over the stabilization of democracy becomes incidental.[46] If consolidation does not take place, then it was never an elite settlement at all but does confirm the theory that original consensus is essential. Elite convergence, in contrast, comes closer to separating transition (first agreement) from consolidation (inclusion of all forces in the democratic process), although relative autonomy from the pressure of the masses remains an indispensable requirement for consolidation (cf. also Higley and Pakulsky, 1992; 1994). Consolidation thus becomes an elitist enterprise, one in which the masses had better not try to participate.

The Round Tables of Poland and Hungary have been identified as elite settlements (Higley and Pakulsky, 1992: 113f.), but this now seems inappropriate given the degree of constant tension among the elites. This was evident in Hungary, where the conservative government and the opposition were at odds before the elections of 1994 (Ágh, 1996c); or in Poland, where the presidential elections of 1995 were a high point of renewed extreme polarization between left and right (Osiatynski, 1995). In Slovakia, Prime Minister Meciar and President Kovac were engaged in personal conflict (Zifcak, 1995), and even in the Czech Republic, the (comparatively moderate) rivalry between Chancellor Klaus and Parliamentary President Zeman is ample evidence that elite settlement may have been a misconception. There has been speculation about a new form of direct elite transformation in the context of Eastern Europe, whereby "new elites interact cooperatively with elite survivors of the old regimes in order to avoid economic collapse, civil strife, and other calamities", (...) "recriminations for earlier failures and misdeeds are downplayed, and the basic condition of elite structural unity continues" (Burton, Gunther and Higley, 1992b: 345). These predictions have unfortunately proven to be premature: cooperation has not been smooth anywhere.

However useful the theory of Burton and others may be as a typology of possible transformations on the elite level and within a process of consolidation, it does not provide an explanation of consolidation as such and neglects three of its crucial aspects. The first of these is consolidation on the level of the masses: "We see little evidence to support classical elitist notions that the characteristics of mass populations constitute the major barrier to stable democracy" (Burton, Gunther and Higley, 1992b: 343). As previously stated, the legitimacy of democracy or its absence can be decisive. Even if elites are united consensually and structurally, this does not necessarily lead to consolidation: "A sizeable segment of a population that is alienated from a regime may be mobilized at some point in the future, given the right circumstances, elite stimuli, or organizational opportunities." (Gunther, Puhle and Diamandouros, 1995: 17). This excludes the possibility of a consolidation that compensates for a lack of elite consolidation by drawing support from a population broadly committed to democracy. But precisely this factor is repeatedly emphasized in the context of East-Central Europe, where the prevalence of democratic legitimacy among the population has tended to curb the spread of elite-stimulated populism (Ágh, 1996c: 53).

Second, this approach ignores the level of institutions: "We are interested in how national elites sometimes transcend their disunity through settlements and convergences, and we regard the specific institutional arrangements that follow these events as secondary matters." (Burton, Gunther and Higley, 1992a: 32). Such unity is rarely achieved in a single effort, though; it happens in many stages, and the institutions initially created can and will affect subsequent developments.

Third, the image of lofty elites advancing consolidation in virtual isolation from cultural, societal or economic forces is highly questionable. Thus formulated, the image carries to extremes a tendency Diamond (1993a: 1-11; cf. Mainwaring, 1992: 308-312) criticized as inherent in all transition and consolidation research: that of isolating elites from political and cultural developments. Transition theory has long insisted on the necessity of behavioral adaptation among elites, i.e., willingness to tolerate, negotiate and compromise, as well as moderation, reconciliation and, above all, acceptance of rules. To date, however, efforts to search for possible causes of such adaptation and to establish its relatedness with changes in the political-cultural context have been halfhearted. Changes in elite behavior which facilitate transition may, for instance, feed on a lengthy and comprehensive process of sociocultural transformation, as seems to have been the case in Spain (Desfor Edles, 1995). Alternatively, the opposition might choose to rely on an intellectual counter-ideology which does not induce any comprehensive change in the behavior and political culture of elites. A prime example of this is Eastern Europe's cherished concept of civil society[47], in which members of the opposition and dissidents emphasized the contrast between "evil politics" (represented by the Communist regime) and "good society". In doing so, they often replace politics with a mythicized social sphere. The counterelites' moral stance against the Communists seemed to eliminate any chance of compromise. Somewhat paradoxically, the transitions negotiated in Poland and Hungary represented a move away from the unwillingness to compromise enshrined in Eastern European civil society concepts, and strategic considerations eventually led to agreements with the Communist regime. Yet in the course of consolidation, traces of this concept resurface among political elites. They are the "politicians of morals" (Ágh, 1996c: 53) who claim to be in exclusive possession of the political truth and prove incapable of compromising, especially when representatives of postcommunist parties are involved. Transitions based on pacts or elite settlements, therefore, do not exclude the need for democratic change in elite behavior and political culture.

In conclusion, politically active elites must not only change their behavior, but also thoroughly democratize their political culture. Broad instrumental acceptance of democratic procedures can support a democracy during phases of political harmony, but not in times of crisis. For the overwhelming majority of the population, in contrast, several factors provide a sufficient basis for democratic consolidation. They are: diffuse legitimacy, the absence of alternatives, confidence in the democracy's ability to survive, and the refusal to support or participate in political practices perceived as semiloyal or disloyal.

2.3.4. Consolidation of Democracy or its "Partial Regimes"

In this final part of our introduction, we turn to Schmitter's (1988; 1992; 1995) concept of consolidation, in which he says that a democracy should be "disaggregated" and seen as an ensemble of "partial regimes" (cf. Schneider, 1995). It is thus not democracy as a whole that is consolidated, but its components, including:

1. The electoral regime, which connects voters with the legislature via parties.
2. The "representational regime", which links potential social groups and organized interests with parties, or more precisely, parties represented in the legislature.
3. The "pressure regime", which connects social groups and associations with the legislature.
4. The "concertation regime", which connects organized interests or the population concerned with state or parastate institutions.
5. The "clientelist regime that may or may not link specific established localities via political parties to specific state agencies" (Schmitter, 1988: 57).

Constitutions can only shape these relationships to a limited extent. Constitutions are an "effort to establish a single, overarching set of 'metarules' that would render partial regimes coherent by assigning specific tasks to each and enforcing some hierarchical relation among them" (Schmitter, 1992: 47). This depends to a great degree in informal practices or at least practices that cannot be controlled by government institutions. Each partial regime has its own norms and decision-making rules, although they all come under the heading of democracy. By concentrating on the process of "regime structuration", which determines the relations between various political institutions, Schmitter ultimately shifts the focus of analysis away from the question of whether or not a democracy is being consolidated and focuses instead on what type of democracy is about to emerge.

> *[T]he challenging question facing political scientists becomes not whether autocracy will be succeeded by democracy but by what type of democracy?* It could be argued that in the contemporary period (or at least since April 25, 1974 when the Portuguese "Revolution of the Carnations" launched the current wave), most polities are condemned to be democratic. (Schmitter, 1992: 429; italics original).

The problem is that Schmitter does not define the relationship between his view of the consolidation of partial regimes and his definitions of the consolidation of democracy *per se*. He tries to explain this, especially with regard to partial regimes involving organized interests, as follows:

> [M]y hunch is that such class, sectoral, and professional associations will *not* be a major factor in determining whether democracy as a general mode of domination will succeed authoritarian rule and persist in the near future; rather, their (delayed) impact will be significant in determining what *type* of democracy will eventually be consolidated. [...] Another way of putting this is that the *quality of democracy*, rather than its quantity and duration, will vary with the emergent properties of associability. (Schmitter, 1992: 433).

But if organized interests are to participate in the shaping of the type of democracy to be consolidated, then both they and the partial regimes to which they belong must be consolidated prior to the end of consolidation. We might thus be tempted to conclude that the consolidation of democracy is the sum of the consolidations of its partial regimes. But even if democracy is the paramount system of reference in regime changes, it is still imperative to ask questions about the stabilization of basic principles of democracy *per se* and not just about the type of democracy emerging. Schmitter's reference to a system of organized interests which influence the quality of democracy may already provide some answers: he suggests a separation between consolidation (as defined by the minimal criteria of a democratic regime) and the deepening and broadening of democracy. The latter includes the emergence and consolidation of all partial regimes that are not part of the minimal concept of democracy. In any case, it is essential that the organization of interests – as important components of several partial regimes – be accepted. There must also be acceptance of their access to and participation in procedures of political decision making. Thus we conclude that in order for democratic consolidation to be achieved, the emergence of partial regimes – in Schmitter's sense – and their main actors must have *begun, but not necessarily been completed.*

The electoral regime presents a possible exception, since it is part of the procedural minimum of democracy. Much attention has therefore been paid to parties as the main participants (in addition, of course, to the electorate) in the electoral regime (see Pridham, 1990a and b). Research has focused on East-Central European parties, and their main arenas, the parliaments.[48] Is it then possible to suggest that the consolidation of a party system is not significant for overall consolidation? Our preliminary response must be: certainly not, since parties are at the center of the democratic process and fulfill a number of vital functions, not the least of which is providing a link between citizens and government institutions.

Starting with the assumption "that the varied and wider systemic tasks of democratic consolidation are much more attuned to the role of parties than to other types of actor" (Pridham and Lewis, 1996b: 8), Pridham (1990b: 19-26) has defined five tasks of parties during consolidation:

1. Their behavior and attitude must contribute to the elimination of transitional insecurities.
2. They must establish relations with the state.
3. They must fulfill a visible and regular role in the political process and thereby substantiate constitutional rules.

4. They establish relations with society and its organizations and thereby contribute to the political socialization of citizens.
5. They reinforce the legitimacy of democracy.

Which of these items are then essential for consolidation? Even though they partially overlap, items 1, 2 and 5 certainly belong in this category, but caution is called for in dealing with items 2 and 4. This is easiest to demonstrate in the context of establishing relations with society. As Pridham (ibid.: 38) himself concedes, unstable relations between parties and society are not necessarily an obstacle to consolidation. This also holds true for East-Central Europe: mass parties (Duverger) with huge membership roles of extremely loyal voters (e.g., the Polish Peasant Party or some postcommunist parties) are the exception, while catch-all parties (Kirchheimer) with their concentration on electoral competition, loose ties to voters and focus on leaders, are becoming the rule even though they still lack the necessary professional organizational structures (Lewis and Gortat, 1995). We should not be too hasty in insisting that young democracies adopt a rigid model of parties which relies on specific structural traits (i.e., strong basis of membership, party organization, ties with organized interests, etc.). Theoretically, overly stable relations between parties and voters can even impede consolidation if they go hand in hand with inefficient or unstable governments.

If consolidation is all about stabilizing behavior and attitudes compatible with minimal democratic criteria, it is nevertheless legitimate to ask what kind of party-state and party-society-state relations are most suited to this task. This question has often been answered rashly with a simple transfer of Western party models. Kitschelt (1995) is one of the few researchers to offer theoretically substantiated analyses. With reference to party-voter relations, he maintains that programmatic parties are most likely to contribute to democratic consolidation, while charismatic or clientelistic parties will hinder rather than support it.

> Although programmatic parties are harder to build than charismatic or clientelistic parties, they are more likely to reinforce the consolidation and stability of democratic regimes than the two alternative modes of party-voter linkage. Programmatic party competition provides a rational motivation for citizens' participation in elections and thus a rational justification of the democratic rules of the game. Charismatic and clientilistic parties have a tendency to make

> democratic competition look irrelevant or irrational from the perspective of deliberating voters (ibid.: 1995a: 450).

Morlino (1995) argues that in some cases, a stable party system may be the decisive factor in the consolidation of democracy:

> I contend that the stabilization of electoral behavior, the establishment of the party system, and the stabilization of the political class can play an important role in the consolidation of a democratic regime. More specifically, I contend that if the legitimation process has not gone far enough to consolidate a regime, stabilization of the party system may be indispensable for successful completion of the consolidation process. This is what unfolded in Italy, where the legitimation process had (fifteen years after the installation of democracy) succeeded in producing only a limited or exclusive legitimacy, but where party dominance was characteristic of relationships with interest groups (ibid.: 373f.).

The reverse is also conceivable: that parties do not form strong organizational links with society in general and civil society in particular, but that the sweeping expansion of legitimacy and behavior compatible with democracy nevertheless ensure democratic consolidation. In this case, which corresponds to that of Spain, Morlino regards party elites as the decisive actors, since they are able to improve the legitimacy of democracy despite weak intermediary structures. Strong party organization and a high degree of legitimacy, he argues, are an ideal scenario, whereas deficient political integration of society through parties combined with poor legitimacy bode ill for consolidation. "Under these circumstances, the regime is potentially unstable and is likely to survive only in an international context highly favorable to democracy." (1995: 362). In sum, there are four possible combinations, which Morlino (ibid.: 359-362) terms "state consolidation" (strong parties, high level of legitimacy), "elite consolidation" (weak parties, high level of legitimacy), "party consolidation" (strong parties, low level of legitimacy) and mere "maintenance" (weak parties, low level of legitimacy).[49] If, therefore, strong parties and a surge of legitimacy do not coincide, we are left with only two possible roads towards consolidation:

> [T]he consolidation of a party system is not a necessary condition for the consolidation of democracy. A high level of party-system instability and a low level of organizational development by parties characterized the same period of time when Spanish democracy was being decisively consolidated. However, if the key institutions of a democracy have not secured a sufficient level of legitimacy, a stabilized party system and well-developed party organizations can play a crucial role in consolidating democracy: they can stabilize and structure interactions among actors and groups in society, channeling that behavior into democratic institutionalized arenas with the capacity to contain conflict, and habituating individuals and groups into conformity with democratic rules of the game (Diamandouros, Puhle and Gunther, 1995: 411f.).

If we examine these alternatives more closely and try to establish a connection with our distinction between behavioral and attitudinal dimensions of consolidation, we discover two basically different paths towards consolidation. One possibility is that despite only rudimentary party structures, consolidation relies on the broad legitimacy of democracy, which in turn promotes democratic behavior. In contrast, consolidation may also come about (albeit somewhat belatedly) because strong party structures guarantee that the political process will be shaped according to democratic principles. Only such behavior as complies with democratic requirements will be accepted, and semiloyal or disloyal behavior will be neutralized or marginalized. Even though the initial legitimacy of the regime may be weak, increasing familiarity with the practice of democracy will gradually strengthen it. In some ways, this distinction is analogous to that between elite settlements and elite convergences in Burton *et al*. We should remember, though, that these patterns of consolidation also presuppose a certain disposition on the part of the masses: an elite settlement would be pointless without the peoples' readiness to support the consensus on democratic legitimacy. Similarly, a convergence towards democratic behavior and attitudes can only take place if parties realize that they will not attract additional voters by continuing to pursue semiloyal strategies. That, however, is only possible if democracy enjoys a broad basis of popular support.

In the empirical sections of this book, our goal is to show that on the most general level of support, East-Central European systems of democratic government can draw on a considerable reservoir of democratic legitimacy. For a long time, however, there have been too few reasonably stable parties and too few elites willing and able to build such parties. Opposition leaders who could have used their popularity to create intermediary political institutions – for example Havel or Walesa – preferred to pursue careers as individuals, outside the framework of political associations. "[W]hile in the earlier European transitions strong persons tended to be parliamentary figures, in Eastern Europe they have more often than not tended to hold presidential office. This inevitably places a considerable constraint on the role of parties, especially if such an arrangement becomes permanent" (Pridham, 1995b: 26). Other politicians often neglected to establish a stable basis of political support. "Instead of trying to mobilize people or building strong constituencies and administrative means of achieving reform, new postcommunist political elites preferred parliamentary activities" (Misztal, 1996: 120). This "overparliamentarization" (Ágh, 1994c) is largely an inheritance from posttotalitarian communist regimes which, in contrast to the authoritarian regimes of Southern Europe, did not permit the emergence of even a rudimentarily autonomous political and civil society, nor of a political class equipped with traditional skills such as leading political negotiations, bringing about compromise, keeping in touch with the electorate, etc. (see Linz and Stepan, 1996: 42-50). As a result, there was usually a dire need for stable parties and politicians willing and able to compromise, or even negotiate.

What does this mean for democratic consolidation? In order to answer this question, we must concentrate on the causal relations with the types of behavior and attitudes that are relevant for stabilizing the various components of the democratic minimum. The task of tracing such relations falls to researchers who, armed with the tools of consolidation theory, investigate the role of parties. Although this field of research is still young, Kitschelt's reflections on different types of party and the impact of each on perceptions of the significance of political competition are an auspicious beginning. Often, however, we are presented with little more than an analysis of the symptoms of rudimentary institutionalization in a party system or variable "political space", i.e., high volatility, fractionalization or fission and fusion across the party spectrum, while their impact on democratic consolidation as we understand it is neglected as self-explanatory (cf. Cotta, 1996). What we need is a theoretical and empirical analysis of how and through what mechanisms the characteristics of a party system influence the behavior patterns and attitudes which question or endanger democratic competition, broad popular participation, (horizontally) accountable government, or the set of inalienable basic rights and liberties.

2.4. Summary and Conclusion: Mimimalist Versus Maximalist Conceptions of Consolidation

Our purpose in this theoretical survey has been to outline the concept of democratic consolidation, a key factor in the analysis of emerging democracies. It was also an essential factor in determining the status of political culture research, the central concern of this book, within the field of consolidation research. We have discussed our own concept of consolidation and shown how it compares to the various factors which influence the process of consolidation. We have also mentioned the most important theoretical difficulties and technicalities of consolidation research, as well as the key obstacles to consolidation in East-Central Europe. It has become evident that while the attitudes and expectations of the population are an important part of consolidation, they cannot in themselves explain its successes and failures. This conclusion may come as a disappointment for practitioners of the political culture approach, but we must accept it if we are to avoid jumping to conclusions in our interpretation of attitudinal data.

Our somewhat cursory discussion of the concept of consolidation has revealed that the pertinant literature contains a broad spectrum of models ranging from extremely minimalist concepts to distinctly maximalist ones:

1. Concepts that equate consolidation with an agreement on the implementation of democracy, and thus with the end of transition (Di Palma, 1990a and b; 1991), and those that view consolidation as a process which follows transition and may take up to a generation to be completed (Whitehead, 1989; Merkel, 1996a).

2. Concepts restricted to the level of elites (Burton, Gunther and Higley, 1992a and b; Higley and Pakulski, 1994) versus those which attempt to integrate the mass level.

3. Concepts which emphasize negative consolidation (Linz, 1990; Linz and Stepan, 1996; Valenzuela, 1992; Liebert, 1995) versus those which also explore positive consolidation, i.e., behavior patterns and attitudes supportive of democracy.

4. Concepts which insist on the need to change formal procedural aspects of democracy (Valenzuela, 1992) versus those which focus on processes occurring on the subjective or intersubjective level. In this respect, both Linz and Stepan (1996) and Merkel (1996a) occupy a middle-of-the-road position.

5. Concepts which equate consolidation with changes on the attitudinal level (Diamond, 1994: 1995b) versus others which consider only behavioral adaptations as necessary for the consolidation of democracy (Przeworski, 1991).

6. Concepts which emphasize the attitudinal level but limit themselves to the spread of democratic legitimacy (Diamond, 1994; Linz, 1990; Linz and Stepan, 1996) versus those which also recognize the need to develop a broad-based democratic political culture (Pridham, 1994 and 1995a; Merkel, 1996a; Plasser and Ulram, 1996).

7. Concepts which connect consolidation with the securing of democracy as a principle regime category versus those which view it primarily as a process in which a decision is reached as to the type of democratic regime to be installed.

We have decided on an analytical distinction between transition and consolidation which allows for temporal overlaps. We have defined consolidation as a process of securing the minimal criteria of democracy, both behaviorally and attitudinally. This, we believe, requires adaptations both among elites and on the mass level, but places the heavier burden on elites. In distinguishing between transition and consolidation, we have tried to radicalize the contextual limits of the two processes to reanchor them in a minimal definition of democracy. Transition and consolidation, in our definition, are processes aimed exclusively at the formal implementation of the procedural minimal criteria of democracy and at stabilizing it both attitudinally and behaviorally. Other processes such as the consolidation of partial regimes (which are not part of the minimal core of democracy) or the extension of democratic principles to other political and societal spheres (democratic deepening) may have considerable impact on the consolidation of democracy in the narrower sense, but they are not integral parts of the central process at issue here. A true comparison of democratic regime changes is only possible if we make distinctions among heterogeneous developments. Resisting the temptation to overload the concept of consolidation will enable us to find out exactly what influences the behavioral and attitudinal support of democracy in each particular case. This type of analysis might show, for instance, that in some cases all relevant political actors have changed their behavior, strategies and normative convictions to suit the needs of democracy, even though successful economic reform, the establishment of a stable system of parties and organized interests, federalization, the granting of ethnic or minority rights, democratic deepening, or the emergence and stability of partial regimes have not yet taken place. In other cases, however, certain actors' normative acceptance and behavioral compliance with democratic norms and procedures might depend on one or more of these developments. The problems to be solved and the institutions and structures to be implemented for a full accomplishment of consolidation will thus vary from case to case.

Our attention is therefore drawn to the different images and expectations of democracy that prevail among the elites and citizens of each country. Shedding light on popular conceptions of democracy in East-Central Europe will be the principal contribution of this book's empirical sections. More such work needs to be done, but a reliable assessment of consolidation and the outlook for the stability of emerging democracies is still a remote prospect.

An alternative approach, i.e., one that does not rely on an analytical distinction of the stages of democratic settlement and a procedural minimal definition of democracy, might define consolidation as the period during which all obstacles to the smooth functioning of democracy must be cleared away. Such approaches tend to consider transition rather superficially as the phase that more or less ends once general elections have been held. If we allow for the possibility of transitions being considered complete even though they do not satisfy our minimal criteria, we arrive at the following approximative typology of consolidation concepts, each of which focuses on a different set of tasks faced by new democracies.

1. *Consolidation as the process of eliminating formal and procedural constraints imposed on democracy.* This conceptualization aims primarily at the transition from a diminished subtype of democracy (from a technical point of view) to one that satisfies all the criteria of whatever definition is employed. Minimal criteria may be violated in a variety of ways, e.g., through unfair electoral laws; powers of surveillance or veto granted to the military; prohibition of parties or organizations which have specific political aims but are basically democratic and loyal; deficient democratic legitimation of delegates; areas of politics explicitly removed from the authority of elected governments; limiting the freedom of speech, of assembly, or of the press; limiting the right to organize or any other civil and political liberties; etc.

2. *Consolidation as the elimination, marginalization, neutralization or democratic persuasion of politically relevant actors who could or might stall the democratic process through violence or by other means.* In this view, consolidation becomes a process which involves efforts to prevent the "sudden death" of democracy by means of a *coup d'état* or other undemocratic seizure of power by a particular party. The primary concern here is the political elimination of potentially undemocratic powers of veto, disloyal parties, or other political actors whose political strategy is to cause the collapse of democracy.

3. *Consolidation as habituation to democratic procedures and the stabilization of such political behavior, practices and attitudes as are likely to facilitate the normal functioning of democracy.* This version of consolidation, as we have shown, is conceivable if the emphasis is shifted onto the behavioral or attitudinal level. It may take either a minimalist (legitimacy and rule-bound behavior) or a maximalist form (spread of a comprehensive democratic culture and the behavior associated with it). All versions, however, presuppose the stabilization of politically relevant actions and attitudes which make a "slow death" of democracy unlikely. Slow death may come about, for instance, during

severe political crises, through gradually increasing disrespect for democratic rules and procedures, or as a result of a steady undermining of democratic principles.

4. *Consolidation as the comprehensive process of creating institutions and institutionalizing; that is, developing, stabilizing and anchoring all partial regimes of democracy.* In the most comprehensive version, consolidation is seen as comprising not only the central democratic institutions, but also other democratic processes, structures, organizations and institutions. In this case, the focus of attention shifts from the question of whether democracy and its basic principles are being consolidated to the question of which type of democracy is about to emerge. It is a broad concept that includes all the levels of analysis suggested by Schmitter for processes of democratic consolidation: "group structuration" ("processes whereby political organizations – public or private – acquire identity and autonomy under the new conditions of freedom, competitiveness and accountability"; 1988: 41), "regime structuration" (the development of "networks of power among interdependent or hierarchically ordered institutions"; ibid.: 42) and "hegemonic structuration" ("'rooting' the emergent regime in the everyday practices and norms of society"; ibid.). Consolidation then encompasses the emergence and stabilization of democratic organizations and institutions, of the partial regimes connecting them, and of a democratic political culture and democratic practices beyond the confines of politics.

The problem of determining the point at which consolidation is considered complete, however, becomes even more difficult in the last approach. Democratization is a never-ending process which extends beyond regime change itself; in its most comprehensive version, consolidation can virtually be equated with democratization. Yet the broader the definition of the concept, the more analytically useless it is, since it comprises all the problems related to the durability and development of democracy.

Von Beyme has succinctly expressed the fact that democracy is never complete: "Democracy *is* not but is constantly *becoming*" (1994a: 9). How, then, can we reconcile this insight with the idea of democratic consolidation, which seems to imply some form of permanent settlement or ultimate safe haven (Bunce, 1995b: 125; O'Donnell, 1996a)? Again, we should be wary of viewing consolidation as a linear process which is always uniform and sure to come to a successful conclusion. Liebert recently pointed this out (1995), arguing that one should renounce predominant patterns of thinking in equilibriums. She postulates that consolidation can develop in spurts, ruptures or "cyclical movements from consolidation to reconsolidation" (ibid.: 78).

Implicitly or explicitly, any theory which assumes an automatic consolidation of democracy is based on the supposition that consolidation drastically reduces the chances of the deliberate destruction, collapse or degeneration of democracy. If politics no longer primarily concerns itself with laying down rules and procedures but simply accepts them as given, and if political behavior is adjusted accordingly, then the threat to democracy and the possibility of its being supplanted by another type of regime is indeed greatly reduced. If, on the other hand, politics is a constant process of trial and error in search of new political practices in which rules and procedures are constantly and thoroughly reinterpreted, requalified and eventually remodified, then democracy is less certain to survive. If, further, we assume that consolidation is not necessarily a linear process, we are no longer compelled to conceive of it as a unidimensional process: it comprises changes in the behavior, attitudes and expectations of a great number of political actors. Incipient signs of deconsolidation on one of these levels or among a particular group of actors do not necessarily imply that these tendencies will immediately have a similarly negative influence on another level or among other actors. The aim of future consolidation research should be to reveal interrelations among the three levels and to show how they are influenced by some structural political variables while they influence others. East-Central Europe, especially, presents ideal opportunities for further research, although some theorists argue that transition and consolidation research is not applicable in the context of postcommunist states (cf. Bunce, 1995a, b, c). The widespread use of concepts such as ambivalence, insecurity, unstructuredness, or "liminality" (cf. Misztal, 1996: 105f.) in descriptions of specifically postcommunist political conditions testify to the fact that seven years after the revolutions of 1989, people's actions, attitudes and expectations were still not sufficiently embedded in the rules of the democracies established then.

Formal basic principles of democracy must be given concrete shape and stabilized by fostering political behavior and attitudes compatible with them. Like any other institutional arrangement, democracy depends on the continuous reproduction of its parts. It is, in other words, not a set of rules and concomitant behavior patterns that is established once and for all. In a democracy, normative expectations and, therefore, behavior, are subject to change. This is a potential source of continuous democratization even after democratic regime change has been achieved, but it could also cause a democracy to degenerate or even disintegrate. In the final analysis, the consolidation of a political regime can only increase the probability of its survival, but it can never entirely eliminate the possibility of its downfall or collapse. Our theory of consolidation could of course prove false if a democracy which could be called consolidated by the standards of this theory were to suddenly collapse (for reasons other than unalterable external force) or suffer a degeneration which few or none of the political actors are capable of preventing. In other words, disproving the consolidation theory would necessarily mean refuting the hypothesis that it takes either an external force which is *a priori* impossible to avert (i.e., annexion) or a long and controversial process of deconsolidation to destroy a consolidated democratic regime.

Notes

1. On transition and consolidation research in general, see Bermeo (1990), Bos (1994), Huffman and Gautier (1993), Linz (1990), Mainwaring (1992), Schmidt (1995: 309-330) and Shin (1994). On its applicability to East-Central Europe, see Waldrauch (1996a, b), where some theoretical light is shed on the dispute between Schmitter and Karl (1994; cf. also Karl and Schmitter, 1995) on the one hand, and Bunce (1995a, b, c) on the other.

2. For a survey of definitions of regime, see Munck (1995, 1996).

3. In the latest version of his concept, Munck (1996) has replaced the "formal" with a "procedural" dimension in order to include informal rules which, he says, have a strong bearing on the character of a regime. But informal rules do not have a life of their own. They are contingent on the performance of political actors and cannot be laid down the same way formal rules are. Rather, they develop from and parallel to the practices of political actors. In regimes which rely primarily on informal rules – and such regimes are unlikely to be democratic – any distinction between the two dimensions therefore collapses. This coincides with the fact that lines dividing regime, government and state in nondemocratic regimes are at best blurred (Lawson, 1993). We try to show instead that democracies rely on the formal stipulation of rules and use this particular feature to mark the watershed between transition and consolidation. In the context of regime changes, it seems appropriate to retain the distinction between the formal and informal dimension of a regime, even if informal rules dominated the regime left behind by transition.

4. In the following, our term "society" will comprise political and civil society. Civil society may be defined as "the *realm of organized social life that is voluntary, self-generating, (largely) self-supporting, autonomous from the state, and bound by a legal order or set of shared rules*" (Diamond, 1994: 5; author's italics). Political society designates the sphere of political parties.

5. Some may be object that non-democratic methods of stabilization subsumed under item 3) are, as the name implies, transient phenomena of settlement not inherently part of such regimes, or that democratic, procedural legitimation ought to be included under 2). But since a regime without any stabilization measures is clearly unthinkable, and since participation exclusively conceived of as the wielding of influence ignores its stabilizing function and effect, it seems reasonable to consider stabilization as an inherent element of any regimes.

6. Linz and Stepan's regime typology (totalitarian, post-totalitarian, authoritarian, sultanist and democratic) can be reconstructed on the basis of these four dimensions of regime. See Waldrauch (1996a).

7. For reasons of space, we cannot quote the usually lengthy definitions here. See Waldrauch (1996a) for a summary of the most influential definitions and conceptions of transition and consolidation.

8. For examples, see Mainwaring (1992: 297) or Diamond, Linz and Lipset (1995: 6). Collier and Levitsky (1995) and Dawisha and Parrott (1997) provide a survey of definitions used in comparative research.

9. On the autonomy of the economy and judiciary, see Linz and Stepan (1996: 7-15); on the economy in democracies, see also Dahl (1992); on the unavoidability of the rule of law and constitutionalism in liberal democracies from the perspective of constitutional law, see Kommers and Thompson (1995). On institutional autonomy as a general prerequisite of democratic consolidation, see Rüb (1996).

10. This stipulation is also reflected in the way various authors identify the end of transition: Linz (1990: 157) lists the first democratic elections, the convention of the first parliament, the inauguration of the first elected president and the existence of a democratic constitution. O'Donnell (1992: 18) says it is the existence of democratic government. Schmitter (1988: 25) equates the stabilization of party and organized interest membership with the end of transition. But as Morlino (1995) has shown in the case of Spain, a stabilized party system is not even necessary to accomplish consolidation. Schmitter has not reaffirmed his view since then, presumably on account of the radically different context in Eastern Europe. Pridham (1994: 22) includes the first few years following the ratification of a constitution in the transition stage but gives no intelligible conceptual or theoretical reasons for doing so.

11. O'Donnell (1996) recently denounced the concept of consolidation. He criticizes not only arguments borrowed from other critics (When is consolidation over? How does the image of democracy as a process square with the stability implicit in consolidation? How many and what kinds of actors must consider democracy as legitimate? etc.), but also and above all the proposal that consolidation will lead to a "close fit between formal rules

and actual behavior" (ibid.: 41). Our conceptualization also assumes this, but with a reminder that we are merely assuming that the actors concerned will comply with the minimal criteria of democracy. If there is no such concurrence, we cannot speak of a democratic regime, since the formal basic rules do not actually guide the political process. In refusing to acknowledge the Dominican Republic, Haiti and Mexico as democracies because elections there were held but manipulated (and thus did not conform to democratic practices), O'Donnell seems to agree with us, at least on this point.

12. As a result, actor-theoretical models of the choice and stability of institutions during processes of regime change use the following explanatory variables. *For the original choice of institutions*: a) mutual perception of the positions and relations of power by the actors involved in transition, and b) expectations regarding power relations after founding elections. *For stability of institutions after transition*: a) degree to which original expectations and actual results of founding elections match, b) degree of stability and inclusiveness of the set of actors involved in the original design and establishment of institutions, and c) perception of the functioning of such institutions, i.e., of their efficacy, inclusiveness and correspondence to what decisive political actors consider adequately constituted political institutions. On this, see Colomer (1995); Geddes (1995); Lijphart (1992); Munck (1994b); Kasapovic and Nohlen (1996); Przeworski (1991: 66-88); and Rüb (1996).

13. Our terms "extending" and "deepening" only partially concur with what Diamond (1995b) has called "democratic deepening". His concept is contained in our definition of consolidation as the stabilization and deepening of behavior and practices which support the minimal criteria of democracy. Since Diamond defines consolidation only from an attitudinal perspective, he can then proceed to denote the behavioral component of consolidation as "democratic deepening".

14. The exception here is Di Palma (1990a and b), for whom consolidation represents, by definition, the final stage of transition.

15. Interestingly, very few of those who apply the concepts of transition and consolidation exclusively in a postcommunist context seem to reflect on them. This is true in particular of transition, which is mostly used as a cardinal concept of all political change. For instance, Ágh (1994a; 1995a, b) sees transition as continuing to the present day and places consolidation somewhere in the distant future. We will later show that this usage does not correspond to that established in Western regime change research.

16. For the most recent institutions-theoretical approaches to consolidation, see, for instance, Liebert (1995); and Merkel, Sandschneider and Segert (1996a). Di Palma (1990a, b) and Valenzuela (1992) both explicitly relegate institutionalization to the period after consolidation.

17. Definitions of the concept of institution refer, among other things, to rules, routinized behavior, procedures, norms, practices, organizational standards, patterns of interaction, normative constraints, systematic encouragement, conventions, habits, expectation, and durable patterns of social

relations: cf. Dowding (1994); Goodin (1995); Kato (1996); Koelble (1995); Hall and Taylor (1996); March and Olson (1989); Thelen and Steinmo (1992). Each definition places its own characteristic emphasis: it may single out the *origin* of institutions (and how they lend permanence to patterns of action), their *function* or impact (how they impose social norms, structure actions, constrain, and solve problems), their manifestation (forms of organization, rules, patterns of interaction, durability) or their societal status (collective and undergirded by norms).

18. This distinction relies on models of institution building as described by Schedler (1995): 1) evolution resulting from decentralized actions and decisions without negotiations and within loose networks of many actors, 2) concerted and cooperative negotiations involving communities with a discernible center and, therefore a restricted number of delegates, and 3) centralized engineering or design by small authorities which create institutional rules for others. In the final analysis, we are dealing with two opposites: evolution without direction and design without participation. Cooperative negotiations provide a kind of neutral ground between the two.

19. In the following, we will discuss the most frequently mentioned problems from the vantage point of their general significance for democratic consolidation. The scope of the present study does not allow us to elaborate on all the possible variations and combinations of problems which provide the context for consolidation.

20. Valenzuela adds to this the requirement of neutralizing actors who do not recognize elections as the only path to power. As is readily apparent, this belongs to the behavioral and/or attitudinal dimension of regime change – and therefore, to consolidation.

21. On the significance of these principles of constitutionalism in liberal democracies, see Elster and Slagstad (1988); Hesse and Johnson (1995); and *Political Studies*, Special Issue on 'Constitutionalism in Transformation: European and Constitutional Perspectives'. On the implementation of constitutional principles in postcommunist states, see Preuss (1995); and Pogany (1996).

22. In this context, the standard of organization and general institutionalization of central government institutions must also be considered: internal rules must be decided upon, administrative hierarchies put in place, infrastructural foundations laid, etc. Only such provisions will ensure the concrete implementation of the rules and procedures that constitute the heart of democracy.

23. On the reform of the bureaucracy and the state, as well as on the roles played by both in this process, see, among others, Hesse (1993) and Misztal (1996); on the issue of retroactive justice and lustration, see Holmes (1994), Osiatynski (1994) and *East European Constitutional Review*, no. 2/1992.

24. In its most extreme version, this approach assumes a "general incompatibility" between economic and political reform. Offe (1994a) and Przeworski (1991) are prominent among its advocates. Cf. also Przeworski *et al.* (1996), where the author questions the concept of consolidation and isolates economic development as decisive for the survival of democracy.

On the interrelationship of economic and political reform, cf. also *Journal of Democracy*, Special Issue no. 4, 1994, 'Economic Reform and Democracy'.

25. It is impossible to deal here in any detail with complicated questions of citizenship such as to whom it should be granted and, above all, who should make the decision. This is a particularly urgent issue in the Baltic states (Chinn and Truex, 1996), but many East (Central) European states also face similar problems regarding the granting of citizenship. The circumstances under which a minority problem is either a part of consolidation or of formal democracy as such cannot be discussed here. On the relationship between ethnic conflict and democracy, see Diamond and Plattner (1994).

26. Because his "deepening" concept is closely related to that of consolidation, however, Diamond in essence brings democratic practices and types of behavior in through the back door.

27. This is what Linz's and Stepan's (1996: 5f.) definition of consolidation essentially amounts to. They also discuss an "attitudinal dimension" (support of democratic institutions) and a "constitutional dimension" (subjection to, familiarization with, and conflict resolution within the limits of democratic rules and procedures). The latter dimension is in some ways the weakest point in the concept of Linz and Stepan, because it suggests constitutionally established rules, while mainly describing the behavioral dimension in its positive aspect of strengthening political rules. At the same time, the authors' "behavioral dimension" denotes the negative aspect of checking and circumscribing certain forms of political behavior.

28. His criteria of disloyalty are: refusal to forego violence; politics of "'knocking at the barracks' for armed forces support" (ibid.: 30); refusal to acknowledge the legitimacy of elected parties declaring their loyalty; readiness to restrict opposition rights; wholesale rejection of the political system; systematic defamation of politicians and parties; cooperation with other disloyal groups; and the misrepresentation of political adversaries as foreign agents (cf. also Morlino, 1995: 362-370).

29. Among characteristic features of semiloyal groups, Linz (ibid.) mentions: negotiation with groups clearly perceived as disloyal; trivializing, excusing or justifying patently disloyal action; partiality in the dispensing of justice where disloyal actors are concerned; or stronger leanings toward disloyal groups on one's own side of the political spectrum than toward loyal groups on the opposite side.

30. Both political behavior which generally aims at fostering loyalty and other behavior of a more technical or instrumental character must of course be stabilized. The necessity of routinizing and professionalizing activities such as formulating laws, establishing parliamentary procedures, managing election campaigns, public and media relations, etc. should be pointed out here.

31. Pasquino (1995) has argued that in contrast to transition, which calls for an open and consultative mode of politics, consolidation is likely to be speeded up if the executive takes a more confrontational and effective stance toward the legislative.

32. See Malova (1996) and the most recent "Constitutional Updates" in *East European Constitutional Review*.

33. See, for instance, *Journal of Communist Studies & Transition Politics*, Special Issue 'Postcommunism and the Media in Eastern Europe', no. 4/1996, as well as East European Constitutional Review, 'Media Freedoms in Eastern Europe', no. 3/1993.

34. For a typology of process models which link culture and structure, see Brint (1994: 30-34).

35. Nelson (1995) has nevertheless tried to show that the explanation for regime changes in Eastern Europe is to be found in the move in political culture towards increasing demand for participation. But other empirical sources (some compiled by the same author; see Mason, Nelson and Szklarski, 1991) from before and after transition contradict this assertion.

36. This is apparently derived from Rustow's repeatedly invoked rule, according to which democratization cannot progress without secure national borders.

37. On the related question of whether a civic culture leads to the stability of democracy or is *per se* equivalent to it, see Welch (1993: 24f): "Suppose that attitudes hostile to democracy were widespread – would this be seen as *leading* to instability, or would it be seen *as* instability?"

38. For O'Donnell (1995: 26), "[t]his mood, less enamored of democracy than fearful of authoritarianism, is probably the most valuable asset that democratic leaders have."

39. "The higher the prestige of foreign liberal democracies, the more likely actors in non-democracies are to adopt liberal democratic norms. These 'demonstration' effects can counteract lags after a transition to democracy: indeed, they can produce 'acceleration' effects. Demonstration effects can provide a functional equivalent in new democracies to the reservoir of legitimation that older democracies possess." (Weil, 1994: 88; cf. also Linz and Stepan, 1996: 74-76). On sources of legitimacy and political culture in general, see Diamond, 1993b.

40. Compare O'Donnell' s definition of polyarchy (1993: 35f.).

41. Brint (1994: 37, n. 9) argues, in this context, for a "reanalysis of the cynicism and disengagement" of citizens. "It may be that the large parts of the public are not so much underequipped for public involvement as too much aware of the disconnection between the spectacles of persuasion and the actual actions of politicians. A public that can see itself being deceived – and for the wrong reasons – has every right to reciprocate with high levels of cynicism, disengagement, and distrust."

42. Two further examples may help to illustrate this often-encountered but dangerous confusion of attitudinal objects and types of attitudes: McDonough (1995) does not separate different objects of support. He uses the concepts of regime and government "interchangeably to avoid monotony, not to imply a rigorous distinction between popularity and regime legitimacy." (ibid.: 656, n. 9). Although he is aware that it is possible to

distinguish between them, he does not allow this to influence his interpretation of data. Zagorski (1994) completely avoids distinguishing between support for economic reforms and support for political reforms simply by combining five items to form a scale which he says can measure the "general acceptance of systematic changes" (ibid.: 364).

43. Morlino and Montero (1995) confirm the hypothesis of a weak interdependence of legitimacy and perceived efficacy or responsiveness for the case of Southern Europe. On the stability of legitimacy in Spain despite grim economic prospects, see Linz and Stepan (1989).

44. The attitudinal dimension has been integrated into the concept of democratic consolidation for no other reason than that attitudes are probably the most direct incitement to action. Attitudes are never politically effective unless they are translated into action, either one's own or someone else's.

45. "Structural integration involves the relative inclusiveness of formal and informal networks of communication and influence among elite persons, groups and factions" (Burton, Gunther and Higley, 1992a: 10).

46. This comes very close to Di Palma's (1990a and b) concept of consolidation.

47. On the concept of civil society in Eastern Europe, see, among others, Arato and Cohen (1992); Bernhard (1993); von Beyme (1994a: 100-123); Havel, Klaus and Pithart (1996); Lewis (1992); Rau (1991); Smolar (1996). On relations between the concepts of civil society and democratic consolidation, see Diamond (1994).

48. On Eastern European party systems, see, among others, *Party Politics*, Special Issue no. 4, 1995; Berglund and Dellenbrant (1994); von Beyme (1994: 278-327); Cotta (1994); Lewis, Lomax and Wightman (1994); Pridham and Lewis (1996a); Wightman (1995). On parliaments in Eastern Europe, see Ágh (1994a); Ágh and Kurtán (1995); Olsen and Norton (1996); Remington (1994); and *East European Constitutional Review*, no. 2/1995.

49. The terms "state" and "elite" consolidation seem particularly inauspicious. Renaming the latter could help us not lose sight of the possibility that the population may stimulate increasing legitimation of democracy.

3

Consolidation and Comparative Political Culture Research: Some Methodological Considerations

3.1. Concepts and Research Designs

Democratic consolidation in postcommunist societies has brought about a spectacular renaissance in comparative political culture research. One of its pioneers, Gabriel A. Almond, has already identified a "return to political culture" (1994). Larry Diamond also emphasizes, albeit cautiously, the central importance of civil society as a factor in democratic consolidation: "Although many contemporary theorists are strangely determined to avoid the term, I believe that these elements of the consolidation process encompass a shift in *political culture*" (Diamond, 1996: 33). Robert Dahl proves more willing to accept the significance of cultural factors when he points out "the *crucial* place of democratic beliefs and democratic culture" (1995: 10) for the prospects of consolidation in postauthoritarian or postcommunist societies. For years, debate on theory and methodology has been all but gridlocked, and scholars have been engaged in highly abstract disputes over the analytical relevance of the concept of "political culture" in explaining political change. Now there is fierce competition among international research networks for access to the latest data on political orientations and trends in the political culture of postcommunist societies.[1] The time lapse between gathering data and publishing research results is growing ever shorter, and the race to keep up with the dynamics of political change in Eastern Europe has increased both the rivalry between scholars and the danger of superficial or speculative interpretation. The lack of time series data and the conceptual and methodological weaknesses of survey research inevitably result in contradictory assessments and overinterpretation of fluctuating but suggestive data (Plasser and Ulram, 1996). Research on East European political culture is currently still a long way from establishing a theory which allows it to differentiate among the political cultures of these countries (von Beyme, 1994a: 349). The most common and often-justified criticisms of current practices in political culture research include:

1. Criticism of a *safari approach* to data gathering (Kaase, 1994). Including as many countries and cases as possible in an analysis creates a problematic distance between the researcher and the research object. It can also result in sterile research designs as well as schematic and inadequately contextualized interpretation.

2. Criticism of *numbering and ranking*. Insufficient linguistic competence, unfamiliarity with local cultures, and a poor understanding of current processes and developments in the countries under scrutiny produce flatly descriptive or illustrative interpretations. The core and key question in political culture research is how individual attitudes on the micro level can be condensed into parameters of political culture on the macro level. The search for answers usually involves applying the rule of aggregation that Gabriel A. Almond and Sidney Verba (1989a, b) provided in their classic approach: the political culture of a country consists of the distribution of its citizens' individual attitudes (Gabriel, 1994: 97). As Müller (1993), however, pointedly observed, this rule is as appealing as it is unrealistic for studies that plan to use the concept of political culture as an explanatory variable in attitudes toward political systems. Almond and Powell also recently emphasized the *interpretive function* of political culture, which is understood as medium that gives shape and meaning to the inputs and outputs of a political system. "Politics emerge from structures and processes and are interpreted through the lens of political culture, as are society's responses" (Reisinger, 1995: 346). In this interpretation, political culture is not merely the specific distribution of political attitudes, orientations, values and abilities; rather it is the cultural "encoding" of a political system (Rohe, 1994). "As people's attitudes affect what they will do, a nation's

political culture affects the conduct of its citizens and leaders throughout the political system" (Almond, Powell and Mundt, 1993: 55).

3. A third and more fundamental type of criticism questions the usefulness of mass survey data for the analysis of political orientations. Survey data and their standardized questionnaires, so the argument goes, can at best reflect fleeting *ad hoc* opinions and moods. These critics argue in favor of qualitative research methods that are more sensitive to the political culture of daily life than standardized survey instruments and quantitative tools (Rieder, 1994; Kreuzer, 1996).

Despite the massive and largely justified criticism discussed in our introduction, survey data are indispensable for analyzing change in political culture. Comparative political culture research requires representative survey data, internationally standardized questionnaires, and the densest possible time series. "In times of rapid socio-political change – as is typical for the situation in Central and Eastern Europe – it is particularly desirable to obtain longitudinal data, be it on a cross-sectional basis or as panel data, the latter of course enabling one, also, to study processes and not only aggregate change" (Kaase, 1994b: 81). The prerequisite for professionalization of data gathering and analysis techniques in international comparative research is finding solutions for a number of theoretical and methodological problems:

1. Comparative political culture research on Eastern Europe is confronted with questions that it cannot answer using its current tools of analysis. These primarily concern aspects of the progress of the new democracies toward democratic consolidation, their stability, and their resilience (Gabriel, 1996; Dawisha, 1997). If we take consolidation to be a "process by which democracy becomes so broadly and profoundly legitimate among its citizens that it is very unlikely to break down" (Diamond, 1994: 15), then the present data only allow for speculative assessments. At the present time, it is not possible to determine whether or not reform countries have crossed the magic threshold of consolidation and evolved from "insecure" to "secure" democracies. All that political culture research can do, for now, is to advance cautious propositions concerning the

spread of democratic orientation and values (Linz and Stepan, 1996a). Questions as to the ability of new "rules of the game" to survive a state of crisis and the extent to which citizens would resist populist appeals and the lure of authoritarian solutions can only be answered tentatively from today's point of view (Huntington, 1996).

2. This leads us to a central problem in comparative political culture research: the difficulty of establishing criteria for measuring the degree and intensity of the democratic attitudes prevalent among citizens. Is there, for instance, any point in comparing the latest data on postcommunist countries with empirical findings on the redemocratization stages of post-authoritarian democracies like Austria, Germany or Italy? Apart from the fact that the available data are far from satisfactory, the contexts of these two waves of democratization are so fundamentally different that trend patterns of the 1950s cannot serve as a basis of direct comparison for current trends in Eastern Europe. The same applies to the wave of democratization in Southern Europe in the 1970s (Montero and Torcal, 1990; Morlino and Montero, 1995) and the democratic transitions in Latin America (Linz, Stepan and Gunther, 1995; Lagos, 1997). The historical uniqueness of simultaneous political and economic transformations precludes the *linear* transfer of trends observed at other times and under very different circumstances (Linz and Stepan, 1996; Dawisha and Parrott, 1997).

3. Comparative political culture research on Eastern Europe suffers from a *tabula rasa* problem: the first data suitable for comparison were collected in 1990. Empirical data on patterns of political culture prior to regime change are hard to find, and because the questions used usually had a heavy pro-regime bias, they provide, at best, vague insight into everyday political culture under communist rule (Nelson, 1995). The conspicuous country-specific variations in central political values and orientations make it necessary to examine the differences in the formative political socialization under different regimes (Meyer, 1993; Wolff-Poweska, 1993). In other words, we need to know the extent to which the political experience, values and images of society inherited from the past shape present attitudes toward actors and institutions within the democratic system. Of

course, retrospective questions about past political experiences in present surveys are no substitute for data on the political culture of the 1970s and 1980s. "Thus, one important element of political culture studies, the longitudinal analysis of the distribution of political, cultural and social orientations, and its *change* over time through *variations* in socialization structures and practices, through events and other factors, cannot easily be brought to bear on the analysis of transitions in Central and Eastern Europe" (Kaase, 1994a: 82).

4. This *tabula rasa* problem is evident in areas other than the scarcity of comparative measurements of the political culture under communist regimes. The absence of dense and comparable time series also presents an obstacle to current research (Bartolini, 1993). "Mature research on political culture will require longer periods of observation, and the results of currently available data will have to undergo further statistical analyses before methodologically sound levels of civic culture, political action or postmaterialism research can be achieved" (von Beyme, 1994a: 332). The limited resources and tight research budgets available cannot cover the high costs of continuous and comparative trend research. With the gradual "normalization" of politics in reform countries, there is less willingness to fund complex research projects. For political culture research, this means that available resources must be used as efficiently as possible and that the various international research groups should work in much closer cooperation, as they did on Western Europe's successful "Beliefs in Government" project (Kaase and Newton, 1995).

5. In most of its analyses, political culture research uses the classic concepts of Almond and Verba's model, which differentiates among three kinds of orientations: input, output, and system (Almond and Verba, 1989a, b). Although Almond and Verba introduced the concept of civic culture as a critical standard in the description and evaluation of Western democracies, they did not precisely define it. Even after decades of political stability, economic growth and social affluence, none of the European Union's core member states – with the exception of Denmark – fulfills the criteria of civic culture (Gabriel, 1994b: 127). This naturally raises the question of whether "classic" no-

tions of political culture research can reasonably be applied to the new democracies of East-Central Europe (Gabriel, 1996: 240). Typological concepts such as "subject culture" or "civic culture", state-oriented versus civic-minded culture, or action-stimulating versus action-programming cultures are of limited use even in strong traditional democracies (Rohe, 1994). It seems, at least for now, all the more inappropriate to apply such typological imagery to the new East European democracies (Miller, Reisinger and Hesli, 1993; 1996).

6. A central problem in comparative political research is the theoretical status of culturalist factors in explanations of political system change. Is political culture a dependent, an independent, a residual or an intervening variable (Lane, 1992; Gabriel, 1994a; Barnes, 1994)? Is it a cause or effect of macropolitical changes (Diamond, 1994; Gibson, 1995; Muller and Seligson, 1994)? In his critical survey of theoretical and methodological problem areas in political culture research, Reisinger (1995) identified seven cardinal challenges to be met, ideally, as part of the research process:

> The challenges are to *define* the term, to *disentangle* subcultures from a society's overall political culture, to *integrate* the many individual-level orientations of which the concept is composed, to *create* a societal-level variable from individual-level components, to *develop* techniques of measuring the resulting concept, to *derive* hypotheses about individual political behavior from the subjective orientations under study and to *theorize* how political culture interacts with insti-tutions and other attributes of a polity to produce political outcomes (Reisinger, 1995: 347).

Not surprisingly, these tasks have so far been only rudimentarily and selectively accomplished. There is no doubt that causal vectors connecting culture and structure point in both directions (Almond, 1987: 29), but this in itself does not answer questions relating to the complex interplay between structure and culture. In their concluding summary of the "Beliefs in Government" project, Kaase and Newton (1995) develop a *reciprocal* causality model of political change, a modified form of which can be used for analyses of political-cultural change in new postcommunist democracies.

> Theories of change usually assume one or both of two things: first, structural and institutional shifts at the macro level somehow *trickle down* through the mass media and different organizations and social groups to individual citizens. Secondly, changes at the mass level *bubble up* through group and institutional channels of communication to the elite level. Such a multi-level process of reciprocal cause-and-effect can be used as a heuristic device to try to understand the process by which micro and macro factors interact (ibid.: 6).

7. If political culture research is to counter the criticism that it is no more than a nonspecific category in research on political attitudes (Reisinger, 1995; Dalton, 1996; Eckstein, 1996; Edvardsen, 1997), it must refine both its theoretical framework and its instruments in order to arrive at more precise research design (Berg-Schlosser, 1994; Gabriel, 1994a and b; Müller, 1993; Plasser and Ulram, 1996). Influenced by David Easton's model of systems, Gabriel Almond revised and modified the classic twelve-field matrix of his pioneering study, *Civic Culture* (Niedermayer and Westle, 1995: 134f.). He replaced orientations – toward the political system as a whole, the system performance (output), the structures of motivational formation (input) and the self as object – with a division into three parts: system culture, process culture and policy culture. *System culture*, in Almond's definition, comprises what members of a political system know, think and feel about political authorities, incumbents, the regime (i.e., the institutionalized structure) and the nation. *Process culture* includes what members of a political system know, think and feel about other political actors, including other groups such as parties, organized interests and certain political elites. *Policy culture*, finally, denotes all knowledge, evaluations and feelings of members of a political system regarding its output; that is, its domestic and foreign policy (Almond, 1987: 37). Combining the three central attitudinal objects with three modalities or dimensions of political attitudes results in a nine-field matrix that provides a systemic grid for empirical research designs and their operationalization.

Figure 1: Matrix of political culture research according to Gabriel Almond

Dimensions of political orientation	Objects of political orientation		
	System culture	Process culture	Policy culture
	Indicators	Indicators	Indicators
Cognitive	Concept of democracy (cognitive meaning)	Political efficacy, political involvement	Assessment of economic development
Affective	Diffuse legitimacy	Identification with parties, trust in collective actors	Identification with the economic order
Evaluative	Satisfaction with the functioning of democracy	Evaluation of political elites or of political competition	Assessment of subjective costs or benefits of economic transformation

Source: Figure based on Almond (1987; 1989) and supplemented with exemplary indicators.

8. Comparative political culture research in postcommunist democracies is plagued by a scarcity of data to feed its research matrices. There are serious shortages of transnational replication studies, comparable time series, and data from panel studies. Comparative transition and consolidation research, which originally focused on so-called Third World countries and Southern European nations undergoing system change, has now established itself as a subdiscipline of political science (Diamond and Plattner, 1993; Huntington, 1991; Linz and Stepan, 1996; Merkel, 1994, 1996a, 1997; Sandschneider, 1995; Dawisha, 1997). Yet comparative empirical studies of the system transformation and ensuing stages of consolidation of several countries are still few and far between. The most important of them available in print are:

   - The annual 'Central and Eastern Eurobarometer' (1990-1997), now covering 20 Eastern European and CIS states.

   - The 'Times Mirror' study of 1991, carried out in eight Eastern European countries.

   - The 'USIA Surveys' conducted in Eastern European reform nations (McIntosh, Abele and McIver, 1992; McIntosh *et al.*, 1994 and 1996).

   - Comparative surveys of the Central European University Foundation (1990-1994) conducted in four countries (Tóka, 1995).

   - The World Value Surveys (1990-91 and 1996-97) covering 43 societies (Inglehart, 1997).

   - The annual 'New Democracies Barometer' (1991-1996) by the British-Austrian research team of Rose and Haerpfer (1991; 1992; 1993; 1994a, b; 1996), which covers ten Eastern European nations.

   - The project 'Politischer Kulturwandel' (1990-1997) headed by the Austrian research team of Plasser and Ulram (1992a, b; 1993a, b; 1994a, b; 1996; 1997) and launched in four reform countries of East-Central Europe; it also includes studies on the political culture of Russia, Slovenia and the former GDR.

The first two projects are, geographically speaking, broadly conceived, but not always methodologically and conceptually adequate (von Beyme, 1994a, b; Kaase, 1994a, b). 'Central and Eastern Eurobarometer' concentrates on subjective indicators of economic development and on the Eastern European attitudes which are relevant for the European Union, but very few indicators touch on core questions of political culture research. The 'New Democracies Barometer' also focuses primarily on economic factors and aspects of economic policy. Although they present only a few indicators on political orientations, the data do allow for insights into citizens' basic perceptions of system change. In addition, there are numerous national studies, some of which use remarkably sophisticated methodology and include attempts to empirically trace developments in their respective countries. However, most current empirical research – with the exception of some of the comparative studies on East-Central Europe named above – seems to have one feature in common: the variables used are difficult if not impossible to compare with those of other international comparison studies in the field.

3.2. Research Experience: The Project 'Politischer Kulturwandel in Ost-Mitteleuropa' (1990-1997)

Between 1990 and 1991, the Austrian "Fonds zur Förderung wissenschaftlicher Forschung" financed a broad-based comparative research project to deal with attitudes and opinions on politics and democracy in the new democracies of East-Central Europe.[2] Within the framework of the project, we were able to conduct representative, comparative surveys in the former Czechoslovakia, Hungary and Poland; we then attempted a first empirical measurement of central political-cultural attitudes and value orientations. The results of this international comparative project, which was carried out in close cooperation with political scientists from all the countries concerned, have since been made available in several publications and are widely accepted as reliable sources of data and reference.[3]

However, empirical democratization research based on opinion polls should not content itself with snapshot-like information. Its aim should be to follow and understand the dynamics of change in political culture, and to do that, it needs time series.

In 1992, with the help of Vienna's Fessel+GfK Institute and its partner institutes in Prague, Bratislava, Budapest and Warsaw, we carried out a second survey using selected questions from the comparative survey questionnaire of 1991. Fessel+GfK Austria also supported the gathering of selected comparative data in the Czech and Slovak Republics in 1993. The following year, friendly cooperation with the research team of Rose and Haerpfer made it possible for us to replicate central attitudinal variables in the Czech and Slovak Republics, Hungary and Poland within the framework of the 'New Democracies Barometer'. In 1995, the Austrian Ministry of Science funded a more comprehensive replication of the 1991 study in the same four countries.[4] And finally, in 1997, Fessel+GfK provided the funding that enabled us to continue our representative trend surveys in the four reform countries. The objectives of 'Politischer Kulturwandel in Ost-Mitteleuropa' (1990-1997) were, among others, the following:

1. To update existing time series on the dynamics of political culture in processes of democratic consolidation.

2. To specify in detail and update questionnaires used in the 1991 study. The first step of the project was initially meant to be a "ground zero" measurement of the first phase of democratization. In the meanwhile, however, the "inner transition" of reform countries had advanced considerably, and citizens had much more knowledge of and everyday experience with the central institutions and representatives of democratic systems. As a result, we could ask more specific questions; in particular, we were able to probe the issue of trust in and willingness to identify with central institutions and actors of the political system in greater detail and with more analytical clarity.

3. To increase comparability with existing comparative studies. During the project's first stage, we focused on ensuring the compatibility of our data with data on political culture in Austrian or German studies. Since then, independent traditions of empirical political science have evolved, though to varying

degrees, in the reform countries. The goal of the second phase was to maintain full compatibility with existing country-specific time series data without sacrificing comparability with international studies.

4. To include Slovenia in the empirical framework. Earlier stages of the project were restricted to four countries (Czech Republic, Slovak Republic, Hungary and Poland); Slovenia was included for the first time in 1995.

5. To increase the use of multivariate techniques of data analysis. For some specific indicators, we now have comparable time series which – updated and with some country-specific variations – cover the first period of democratic consolidation (1990-97). In using multivariate techniques of analysis, we hoped to do two things: discover deep structures and latent patterns in the data, and reduce dynamic changes in central political-cultural attitudes to model-type "critical" factors of influence.

6. To intensify and institutionalize cooperation with empirically oriented political science research teams in reform countries. As early as 1991, during the initial stage of our project, we sought and found intense cooperation with local research teams whose work in preparing and carrying out surveys, as well as in interpreting and publishing data and results, was invaluable. This process of a mutual exchange of ideas and data is ongoing;[5] its aim is to establish and maintain contacts with other researchers in the field, especially those in the reform countries. An extended and updated trend study (replication of the comparative political culture study of 1991) therefore fulfills four purposes. First, it constitutes a further contribution towards the empirical analysis of changes in the political culture of new East-Central European democracies. It also ensures the continuity of comparative studies begun in 1991 and allows for country-specific trend analyses by establishing time series. Finally, it allows for empirical insights into the "beliefs in democracy" of postcommunist societies.[6]

As a result, we have now dense time series (1990-1997) for central indicators of democratic orientations and legitimacy beliefs as well as for assessments of political and economic conditions and performance.

The following empirically-oriented sections are primarily based on six modules of the larger project 'Politischer Kulturwandel in Ost-Mitteleuropa' (cf. figure 2). These modules focus on the analysis of *trends* in democratic orientations and of selected indicators of political culture over the time period studied.[7] In the first part, we deal with conceptions of politics and democracy, potential political support, and trust in the political institutions of postcommunist societies. In the second part, we examine the extent of respondents' political involvement, their awareness of political efficacy, and the relationships between parties and voters. We look at patterns in party preferences, profile voter coalitions, and analyse the conflict potential of sociopolitical cleavages in the four societies from a political-cultural perspective. In the third part, we turn to citizens' attitudes toward economic transformation and their expectations of regime change. We also relate socioeconomic factors to orientations of political culture.

Figure 2: Data sources of 'Politischer Kulturwandel in Ostmitteleuropa' (Changes in East Central European Political Culture) 1990-1997

Year	Project	Field Work	Sample size	Sample size	Sample size	Sample size
			CZ	SK	H	PL
1990	Regime Change in the ČSFR	October - November	N = 670	N = 330	-	-
1991	Conceptions of Democracy and Parliament in East Central Europe	May - August	N = 1.350	N = 650	N = 2.000	N = 2.000
1992	Political Culture in the New Democracies of East Central Europe	November - December	N = 670	N = 330	N = 1.000	N = 1.000
1993	Political Culture in the Czech and Slovak Republics	February - March	N = 670	N = 330	-	-
1994	Political Culture and New Democracies Barometer	January - February	N = 1.000	N = 500	N = 1.000	N = 1.000
1995	Political Culture and Conceptions of Democracy in East Central Europe in Trend Comparison	November - December	N = 1.000	N = 1.000	N = 1.000	N = 1.000
1997	Changes in East Central European Political Culture	January - April	N = 1.000	N = 1.000	N = 1.000	N = 1.000

Methodology: face-to-face interviews, random sampling (voter registration rolls), socio-structural weighting of factors, figures rounded off. For further technical details, see list of empirical sources.

Notes

1. For empirical introductions to the dynamics of change in postcommunist political culture, see Dawisha and Parrott (1997); Gerlich, Plasser and Ulram (1992); Kaase (1994a, b); Linz and Stepan (1996b: 235-457); Plasser and Ulram (1993); Plasser and Pribersky (1996); Rose (1997); Tismaneanu (1995). On the dynamics of political culture in East Germany, see Gabriel (1996).

2. The project's full title is 'Politische Kultur, Parlaments- und Demokratieverständnis in Österreich, Ungarn und der CSFR'. It was submitted by Peter Gerlich headed by Fritz Plasser and Peter A. Ulram. Additional funds came from Austria's Ministry of Science and Research.

3. To date, two extensive collections of essays are available in book form: Peter Gerlich, Fritz Plasser and Peter A. Ulram (ed.), *Regimewechsel. Demokratisierung und politische Kultur in Ostmitteleuropa*, Böhlau Verlag, Vienna *et al.*, 1992; and Fritz Plasser and Peter A. Ulram (ed.), *Transformation oder Stagnation? Aktuelle politische Trends in Osteuropa*, Signum, Vienna 1993. Parts of the project have been presented for discussion in many contributions in books, journals, and papers at international conferences (e.g., WAPOR 1993, 1997; IPSA 1994). An updated presentation of research results (1990-1994) in English may be found in Plasser and Ulram (1996). See also Plasser, Ulram and Waldrauch (1997).

4. Full project title: 'Politischer Kulturwandel und Demokratieverständnis in der Tschechischen Republik, der Slowakischen Republik, Ungarn, Slowenien und Polen im Trendvergleich', submitted by Fritz Plasser and financed by the Austrian Ministry of Arts and Sciences.

5. Thus Austria's Political Science Association instigated an institutionalized series of specialist conferences and project workshops with Central European academics. The proceedings of the Viennese meeting in Autumn 1994 are available in English. See Plasser and Pribersky (1996).

6. For further technical or methodological information, see list of empirical sources.

7. We are working on condensed multivariate analyses to be published at a later date.

4

Attitudes towards the Political System: Conceptions of Democracy and Images of Politics

According to Almond (1987; 1989b), each political system comprises a system culture, a process culture and a policy culture. Attitudes towards the political system constitute the core of the system culture, which Almond says is composed of the knowledge and evaluations of, as well as feelings towards, political authorities and incumbents, the regime – i.e., the institutional structure – and the nation (Almond, 1987: 37). We can draw on dense time series and trend data on regime satisfaction in Western democracies ('Eurobarometer. Trends 1974-1994, 1995') and surveys of satisfaction with the development of democracy in several East-Central European countries since 1990 (carried out as part of 'Central and Eastern Eurobarometer' studies). There is, however, surprisingly little comparable data on *cognitive* conceptions of democracy. In other words, we lack information on subjective interpretations of what democracy means. Presupposing the existence of a single, largely identical conception of democracy which varies only in nuance from one case to another presents a problem even in the context of Western Europe. In post-communist societies, one cannot yet assume the existence of consistent intercultural patterns of understanding. An empirical clarification of the cognitive core of democracy's meanings is a precondition for understanding feelings and assessments related to the political regime. Data gathered as part of the 'Politischer Kulturwandel in Ost-Mitteleuropa' (PKOM) project provide a tentative avenue of approach to the (cognitive) conceptions of democracy prevalent among citizens of the new democracies. Through the use of open questions, we were able to ascertain the core meanings of the concept of democracy. As a result, it was possible to test four hotly debated hypotheses regarding conceptions of democracy in postcommunist societies:

1. The assumption that conceptions of democracy are *instrumental-economic,* i.e., that citizens of postcommunist societies primarily associate democracy with more material wealth and consumerism. "Despite their support for liberal democratic values, these publics define democracy predominantly in economic rather than political terms" (McIntosh and McIver, 1992: 381).

2. The assumption of *liberal and individualist* conceptions of democracy, according to which citizens of postcommunist societies primarily associate democracy with civil liberties and opportunities for improvement.

3. The assumption that citizens of postcommunist societies are *socially oriented* in their understanding of democracy, i.e., that they chiefly associate it with equal opportunities and social justice.

4. The assumption of *postsocialist* conceptions of democracy, in which there is a latent predominance of the central values of the goal culture of a "socialist democracy" (Westle, 1994: 587; Fuchs, 1997).

These data indicate distinct country-specific and culture-specific emphases in the conceptions of democracy, with variations both among postcommunist societies and in contrast to Austria or Spain (see Table 1).

Even though individual liberties are the most salient core aspect of democracy in all of the six countries for which comparable data exist, there are considerable discrepancies in the different societies' interpretation of them. In the Czech and Slovak Republics, democracy means first and foremost freedom, rule of law and opportunities for political participation. In Hungary and Poland, on the other hand, the central value of freedom is overshadowed by an understanding of democracy based on social justice and social fairness, especially among the elderly. To what extent this is a result of socialization under the "old" regime or a reaction to the uncertainty of social and economic transformation cannot be deter-

Table 1: Central cognitive meanings of democracy (1995)

What do you think "democracy" is? What does democracy mean to you?						
Percentage of those who view "democracy" as (first answer)	CZ	SK	H	PL	SP	A
Freedom	58	59	31	38	57	34
Rule of law	12	11	15	16	4	8
Participation	10	10	15	7	14	31
Democracy with social values	3	4	14	16	11	1
Values	4	3	3	2	4	4
Parties, elections	3	4	6	9	6	10
Feelings, moods	2	2	4	0	2	6
Other	2	1	1	1	2	6
No response	6	4	10	11	1	1

Source: 'Politischer Kulturwandel' (1990-1995); Fessel+GfK, 'Repräsentativumfrage in Österreich' (1994); Spanish data in Montero and Torcal (1990).

mined on the basis of the present data. This emphasis on social values in conceptions of democracy was also evident among Spanish citizens during the 1980s, where one out of ten respondents associated democracy primarily with social welfare and social responsibility. In Austria, cognitive conceptions of democracy also have specific traits: Austrians rank the opportunity to participate and have a voice in government only slightly ahead of freedom. Whatever the differences, a comparison of these six countries reveals two important common features:

1. For citizens, the concept of democracy has definitive core meanings which correspond to key characteristics of the democratic regime type.

2. Country-specific variations notwithstanding, individual freedom and self-realization predominate in the political semantics of democracy. In all the countries surveyed, personal freedom is the core concept in definitions of democracy.

Conceptions of democracy are, of course, subject to change. They reflect not only established norms, but also current preferences and expectations. In one country, Hungary, four surveys conducted over a period of seven years (Simon, 1994) reveal shifting emphases in conceptions of democracy.

Table 2: Conceptions of democracy in Hungary (1989-1995)

Percentage of those who view democracy as	1989	1990	1993	1995	PPD
Freedom	31	28	35	35	+4
Rule of law	23	15	10	17	-6
Participation	2	6	8	16	+14
Democracy with social values	32	32	26	15	-17
Values	4	4	7	4	+-0
Parties, elections	1	4	6	6	+5
Feelings, moods	3	6	7	4	+1
Other/No response	3	4	2	3	+-0

Source: Data for 1989-1993 in Simon (1994); 1995 data in 'Politischer Kulturwandel' (1990-1995).
Note: These percentages reflect respondents' answers which fit any of the above categories, hence the divergences from Table 1.
PPD = percentage point difference, 1989-1995.

Freedom continued to be the central association in interpretations of democracy throughout the period studied, whereas other, more socially-oriented connotations clearly lost their relevance. In 1989, 32 percent of Hungarian respondents associated democracy primarily with values of social justice, while only 15 percent did so in 1995. The importance of participatory elements dropped by 13 percent between 1989 and 1993 but rose again in the three years which followed. In 1995, 17 percent of Hungarian respondents associated democracy primarily with the right to participate in the political process and have a voice in decision making. Other aspects such as the rule of law (plus 14 percent) and parties and elections (plus 5 percent), gained in importance as defining features of democracy. These changes in Hungarian conceptions of democracy could be described as a shift from *idealistic* to *realistic* conceptions, which are normally characterized by an increasing emphasis on institutional and rule of law aspects at the expense of sociopolitical opportunities and expectations. Realistic conceptions are also accompanied by a higher incidence of negative associations with and criticism of democratic practices. "Summing it up we can say that compared to 1989, in 1993 besides the description of the 'desired' democracy, the criticism of the 'existing' democracy could be heard more and more from the interpretation of democracy" (Simon, 1994: 6).

Two representative surveys sponsored by the National Endowment for Democracy and conducted in the Czech Republic and Slovakia in 1994 give additional insight into conceptions of democracy prevalent among the citizens of both countries. Closed questions encouraged respondents to specify the meaning of various components of a democratic system. Data from the Czech Republic are by and large identical with those compiled on the basis of PKOM's open questions: personal freedom and fair laws are more important than guaranteed economic security in Czech conceptions of democracy. Slovaks, on the contrary, saw securing the basic material needs of the population as by far the most important task of "democracy" in 1994. The economic hardship, existential fears and longing for security which surface in times of profound economic crises brought about by adaptation and transformation influence conceptions of democracy. The questions asked, however, deliberately targeted the performance of democratic regimes.[1]

Liberal democracy is not based solely on a set of formal (e.g., institutional, legal, or procedural) prerequisites (Diamond, 1996); it also implies particular forms of political practice. These include disagreement among and within political parties, organized interests and social groups; conflict, consensus and compromise; and pushing through decisions in the face of open resistance. Thus the democratic process[2] and its practices in many ways contradict popular idealizations[3] of democracy – which a desire for harmony has often raised to unrealistic heights – and become a source of political dissatisfaction. At the same time, experiencing the difficulties, contradictions and hard daily realities of politics can also reinforce prejudices. This in turn may result, for instance, in the familiar image of politics as a "dirty business".

For the majority of East-Central Europeans, "politics" has few positive connotations. Only one fourth of Polish, Hungarian and Slovak citizens associate it with feelings such as interest, participation, or even passion and enthusiasm. In the Czech Republic, the percentage of positive associations is now higher. The gloomy views of politics so evident during the first few years of transition have only recently been replaced by more positive outlooks which are nevertheless more critical than they were in 1991. Predominantly negative views characterize the image of politics in Hungary and Slovakia, where roughly half of all citizens express distrust, anger or dis-

Table 3: Images of politics in comparison

What kind of feelings does politics evoke in you? (First answer in percent)	CZ			SK			H			PL			SLO	A		I
	91	94	95	91	94	95	91	94	95	91	94	95	95	91	96	85
Enthusiasm	3	0	1	1	1	0	1	0	0	1	0	1	0	1	0	1
Passion	1	0	0	1	0	1	2	1	1	2	1	1	1	1	2	2
Participation	13	11	13	5	12	5	2	3	2	2	1	1	26	14	8	4
Interest	41	21	30	24	25	20	26	20	21	17	15	20	5	21	20	19
All positive associations	**58**	**32**	**44**	**31**	**38**	**26**	**31**	**24**	**24**	**22**	**17**	**23**	**32**	**37**	**30**	**26**
Indifference	8	17	20	12	20	19	25	21	21	26	31	28	9	17	13	21
Boredom	3	5	6	4	6	6	8	8	8	7	11	12	10	4	3	12
All distant associations	**11**	**22**	**26**	**16**	**26**	**25**	**33**	**29**	**29**	**33**	**42**	**40**	**19**	**21**	**26**	**33**
Distrust	24	34	22	36	28	33	17	20	26	20	16	19	29	25	26	14
Anger	8	8	6	13	6	12	16	17	12	11	13	10	9	14	20	17
Revulsion	2	4	2	3	2	5	4	7	8	12	11	8	5	4	4	10
All negative associations	**34**	**46**	**30**	**52**	**36**	**50**	**37**	**44**	**46**	**43**	**40**	**37**	**43**	**43**	**50**	**41**

Source: 'Politischer Kulturwandel' (1990-1995); 'Politischer Kulturwandel in Österreich' (1996); Morlino and Montero (1995).
* Discrepancy between percentage given and 100% = no answer.

gust. Poles tend to follow the political process in their country from a distance, and in Slovenia, extremely negative and critical views exist alongside distinctly positive ("participation") sentiments. In the Czech Republic and, to some degree, in Poland, where negative associations have been slowly fading, there are signs of an incipient process of "critical normalization": even though many hopes have not been fulfilled, there is less and less negative reaction to daily - politics. Conversely, Hungarians' opinions of their country's politics are increasingly colored by negative emotions, and in Slovakia, a similar trend was reversed only temporarily.

But even in firmly established democracies, there are considerable differences in the (emotional) image of politics. Whereas negative associations are found only among minorities in Switzerland's traditional democracy (Longchamp, 1993)[4], they are much more prevalent in Italy and Austria. Both countries are characterized by a high degree of disappointment in parties and politicians and by severe doubts about the responsiveness and the (not merely moral) qualifications of the political class (Ulram, 1990). Although this does not seem to undermine the fundamental democratic consensus, it does prepare the ground for radical populism in politics.

Notes

1. From the code book of two representative surveys sponsored by the National Endowment for Democracy and conducted in the Czech Republic (N= 2300) and Slovakia (N= 2300): Question wording (supported): People have different ideas about what democracy means. Which of the following (card shown) do you consider most important for democracy?

2. This applies in particular to periods of change in economic or political systems. The great majority of both citizens and elites were unfamiliar with everyday democratic processes. New elites, often recruited from the ranks of former dissidents, had never held administrative or political positions. The new Czech and Slovak politicians therefore had virtually no political experience, while their Polish colleagues' experience was limited to their activities in which the outlawed opposition.

3. Such as the notion of "unpolitical politics", which is especially widespread in the Czech Republic but also exists elsewhere (cf. Brokl and Mansfeldová, 1992).

4. Swiss data cannot be directly compared to those culled in East-Central Europe because the choice of possible answers offered was different. When identical categories are used, as was the case in surveys conducted in Austria and Switzerland in 1989 and 1991, the results confirm the above interpretation. Unlike Mannheimer and Sani (1987), we consider "distrust" a negative sentiment.

5

Attitudes towards the Political Regime: Satisfaction with Democracy

Peoples' attitudes and their many ways of relating to the political regime are widely recognized as central to political culture. Whether or not citizens consider the political system effective and legitimate directly affects the stability of any democracy (Gabriel, 1994a: 103f.; 1994b, 31f.). One of the indicators most frequently used in assessing people's trust in politics is therefore 'satisfaction with democracy.' This does not, however, tell us the degree of empirically measured satisfaction necessary for a democracy to be considered sufficiently consolidated to survive sustained periods of poor government performance, economic crises or structural deficiencies without endangering its legitimacy (Beetham, 1994; Westle, 1989). "There is no objective criterion by which to determine how widespread satisfaction must be before we can talk of a stable democracy. However it is implausible to assume that a democracy is in jeopardy if a majority of citizens are content with the political system" (Fuchs, Guidorossi and Svensson, 1995: 342). The operationalization of "satisfaction with democracy" poses even more methodological problems. Empirical research has yet to devise a conceptual tool that allows us to draw a sharp distinction between diffuse and specific system support, or between support for political actors and support for overall system performance (see Westle, 1989: 165f.; Niedermayer and Westle, 1995). "Satisfaction with democracy" is therefore clearly not an optimal indicator: "In measuring a complex attitude, a single indicator can hardly suffice, especially one in which 'satisfaction' presents a vague evaluative dimension" (Gabriel, 1996: 254).

The present data on the development of satisfaction with democracy in postcommunist societies reflect these theoretical and methodological problems. Four core conclusions have emerged from the latest research:

1. The level of satisfaction with democracy in new, postcommunist democracies is markedly lower than in consolidated Western European democracies. In the countries of East-Central Europe, there is a considerable amount of regime criticism and widespread dissatisfaction with the democratic order (Plasser and Ulram, 1992a: 397).

2. The level of dissatisfaction with the development of democracy has, with some country-specific exceptions, not changed much over time. "The worrying situation of a widespread lack of satisfaction with the development of democracy, which was recorded in the previous Eurobarometer survey, seems to have improved a little over the past twelve months, especially in the ten European Agreement countries ... In the CIS countries surveyed, people everywhere (except in Georgia) have an extremely poor view of the way democracy is developing: an overwhelming majority of citizens interviewed expressed their dissatisfaction" ('Central and Eastern Eurobarometer' 1996, 34).

3. Individuals' assessments of living standards and their other, more general views on the transformation process have a direct influence on both satisfaction with the political system and basic attitudes towards democracy and its institutional prerequisites (McIntosh and Abele MacIver, 1992: 388; Plasser and Ulram, 1993a: 66). Tóka and others believe that levels of satisfaction in East-Central European are markedly lower than those in Western Europe primarily because of the more negative evaluation of economic conditions. "In the new democracies, we found a substantial correlation between regime support and popular evaluations of economic conditions, at both the individual and the aggregate level" (Tóka, 1995: 376f.). Similarly, Kaase (1994a, b) interprets time series data of the 'Central and Eastern Eurobarometer' as showing that "the future of democracy in the thinking of the population in Bulgaria, Czechoslovakia, Hungary and Poland was inextricably linked to the way the personal economic well-being and that of the country were developing" (Kaase, 1994b: 108f.).

4. The "satisfaction with democracy" indicator not only varies significantly from country to country but also fluctuates over time within most countries. Economic development factors alone cannot explain these fluctuations; they are more likely related to the endogenous problems and functional deficiencies of the political system functions and the performance of political elites (Plasser and Ulram, 1994a, b; 1996; Mishler and Rose, 1996; Pickel and Pickel, 1996).

In analysing satisfaction with democracy in postcommunist ECE countries (levels, trends over time, and fluctuations), we can draw on two dense data series from comparative research projects:

a) 'Politischer Kulturwandel in Ost-Mitteleuropa' (PKOM) (Plasser and Ulram, 1992a; 1993a; 1994a, b; 1996), which covers the development of satisfaction with democracy in the Czech Republic, Slovak Republic, Hungary and Poland from 1990 to 1997.

b) 'Central and Eastern Eurobarometer' (CEEB), which deals with the evaluation of democracy in the same countries between 1990 and 1997.

Divergent question wordings and response choices do not allow for direct comparisons of these time series, but the trends they reflect can at least be roughly compared and interpreted. PKOM's data series point to trend patterns and developments which are highly specific to each country and do not present a unified picture. Crises of economic adaptation, weak economies, the social costs of transformation, structural and functional deficiencies, political polarization and conflict among elites all account for fluctuating levels of satisfaction in the individual countries. Temporary increases in dissatisfaction in some countries contrast with a general move toward consolidation in others. Discontinuity, rather than linearity, is the key characteristic of the dynamics of system satisfaction in reform countries (see Table 4).

Data on the Czech Republic indicate that levels of regime support there are higher and fluctuate less than in the other countries. Stable and moderate contentment has been characteristic of Czech citizens' attitudes towards their country's new regime. The exception was in 1994, when dissatisfaction with democracy rose due to a temporary economic decline. In 1997, an economic down-

Table 4: Satisfaction with democracy and the political system (1990-1997)

In general, are you satisfied with democracy and the political system in (country) ?						
In Percentage	CZ	SK	H	PL	SLO	A
Satisfied						
1990	14	9				9
1991	4	2	2	5		
1992	4	1	3	·2		
1993/1	6	2				5
1993/2	4	2				
1994	3	3	1	2		
1995	2	2	1	4	3	7
1997	5	2	0	5		5
Somewhat satisfied						
1990	60	55				73
1991	72	56	56	62		
1992	69	68	55	54		
1993/1	73	61				71
1993/2	60	29				
1994	59	70	47	43		
1995	72	43	42	59	63	59
1997	68	51	45	74		66
Not satisfied						
1990	19	28				17
1991	24	41	39	32		
1992	26	29	40	39		
1993/1	20	36				23
1993/2	35	67				
1994	37	27	48	53		
1995	25	55	57	37	28	32
1997	27	47	52	19		29

Source: 'Politischer Kulturwandel' (1990-1997); 'Politischer Kulturwandel in Österreich' (1990-1997).
Note: Discrepancy between percentage given and 100% = no response.

turn combined with instability within the governing coalition caused Czechs' satisfaction with democracy to fall again, though not to the nadir of 1994, the "crisis year". The situation in the Slovak Republic, in contrast, appears much more volatile and unstable. Satisfaction with democracy rose in 1992, the year national independence was attained. The next year, however, marked a phase of disillusionment and worries about the economic consequences of Czechoslovakia's much-vaunted "velvet divorce". In contrast to developments in the Czech Republic, the share of individuals satisfied with Slovak democracy in general and the political system in particular again increased in 1994, only to plummet in the following year to its lowest level since 1990. As 1995 drew to a close, 55 percent of Slovaks were explicitly dissatisfied with the political system, a phenomenon for which domestic political strife, power struggles and elite conflicts were largely responsible. The data for 1997 again indicate a rise in satisfaction with democracy which is linked, in part, to a (relatively) prosperous economy.

Data show that trend patterns in Hungary tend to be stable but negative. In 1997, 39 percent of respondents said they were dissatisfied with democracy and the political system. This figure had risen to 57 percent by 1995 and did not decrease notably in the following years (52 percent in 1997). The Hungarian population is exceptionally critical of the political regime: the high levels of political dissatisfaction and disappointment about the economic burden of the transformation process are both causes for concern. Poland, like Hungary, saw a steady increase in political dissatisfaction among its citizens until 1994. The following year, for the first time, moderate contentment exceeded disillusionment and criticism. Supported by encouraging growth rates of the Polish economy, the upward trend continued: in 1997, 79 percent of Polish respondents declared their satisfaction with democracy and the political system. Thus, general satisfaction with democracy in Poland exceeds levels found in the Czech Republic and in Austria (71 percent in 1997). The present data on satisfaction with democracy in the four countries surveyed indicate four divergent trend patterns. In the Czech Republic and Poland, moderate satisfaction with democracy is the rule, even though trends and levels differ considerably. In Hungary and Slovakia, there was more dissatisfaction than satisfaction (see Figure 3).

These data on trends and levels of satisfaction with democracy in postcommunist societies should not, however, be overdramatized. The methodological problems that still plague the indicator qualify its political meaningfulness, as do comparisons of the data for East-Central Europe with those for a consolidated and highly stable democracy such as Austria. Thus, our data show that in 1995, satisfaction with democracy was higher in the Czech Republic than in Austria.[1] Two years later, satisfaction levels in the Czech Republic and Poland had also risen to nearly the Austrian level of 1995, leaving only Hungary and the Slovak Republic with significantly lower levels than Austria. Again, the data do not allow us to draw convincing conclusions regarding profound legitimacy crises in democratic systems. Careful analysis and cautious interpretation seem advisable whenever we are dealing with isolated, non-contextualized indicators and data series.[2]

Figure 3: Levels and trend patterns of satisfaction with democracy in four countries.

		Level of satisfaction with democracy	
		Moderate satisfaction	Predominant dissatisfaction
Trend	Continuous	CZ	H
	Discontinuous	PL	SK

Source: 'Politischer Kulturwandel' (1990-1997).

The "satisfaction with democracy" indicator is even more strongly geared toward functional aspects of system evaluation. The 'Central and Eastern Eurobarometer' used it to measure satisfaction with the *development* of democracy: percentages of individuals satisfied or dissatisfied with the development of democracy over time are given in the following table. The results of the two surveys show largely comparable trend patterns despite divergent question wording and response choices. In the Czech Republic, satisfaction with democracy was on the increase until 1995 but plummeted again in the following year, and a negative trend was reversed in Poland between 1994 and 1995. The 'Central and Eastern Eurobarometer' indicates a fluctuating trend pattern in Hungary, where the 1995 level of political dissatisfaction exceeded that of any previous year. Current trend patterns in Slovakia contradict the time series in 'Politischer Kulturwandel in Ost-Mitteleuropa'. According to CEEB data, dissatisfaction with the development of democracy was less pronounced in 1995 than in previous years; PKOM data, on the contrary, indicate a sharp increase in political dissatisfaction during the same time period, a development also reflected in the CEEB data of 1996.[3] Finally, political dissatisfaction also rose in Slovenia between 1993 and 1995.

Table 5: Satisfaction with the development or the functioning of democracy (1990-1997): 'Central and Eastern Eurobarometer' and 'Eurobarometer'

Question wording: On the whole, are you very satisfied, fairly satisfied, not very satisfied or not at all satisfied with the way democracy is developing in (your country)?

In Percentage	CZ		SK	H	PL	EU (12)
Very satisfied/fairly satisfied						
1990		30		20	38	56
1991		28		30	27	57
1992	38		23	22	32	49
1993	48		19	20	35	42
1994	44		17	23	23	44
1995	46		27	20	50	47
1996	38		21	21	43	
1997	36		25	30	57	
Not very satisfied						
Not at all satisfied						
1990		65		75	37	40
1991		66		60	50	40
1992	57		74	73	65	47
1993	48		78	74	49	55
1994	53		79	66	63	53
1995	50		67	77	38	51
1996	59		74	72	45	
1997	58		74	64	33	

Source: 'Central and Eastern Eurobarometer' 1/1991-8/1997; data on twelve EU member states (*functioning* of democracy) from *Eurobarometer Trends* (1995: 36) and 'Eurobarometer' 43/1995.

'Eurobarometer' data on EU member states also indicate that while levels of satisfaction with democracy are high in these countries, they fluctuate significantly. Since 1990, satisfaction with democracy in Western Europe has generally decreased despite some country-specific variations. (Küchler, 1992; Fuchs and Klingemann, 1995: 440f.; Inglehart, 1997: 302f.). Many researchers blame this trend on economic and business factors as well as representational deficits, not on a general crisis of legitimacy in Western democracies (Fuchs, Guidorossi and Svensson, 1995; Fuchs and Klingemann, 1995; Kaase and Newton, 1995; Dalton, 1996a). According to 'Eurobarometer 43', only 47 percent of respondents in twelve EU member states were satisfied with the performance of democracy in 1995, compared to an EU average of 56 percent in 1991. In Italy, the share of respondents satisfied with the political *status quo* in 1995 was only 20 percent. Thus, when compared to the barely moderate levels of satisfaction with democracy in Western Europe, the data for the new democracies of East-Central Europe appear less dramatic. In 1995, an average 55 percent of respondents in the ten European Agreement Countries (the Eastern European nations associated with the EU through cooperation treaties) declared their dissatisfaction with the *development* of democracy in their country, while exactly half of EU citizens said they were disappointed with the functioning of democracy. Economic and political contexts in the West are very different from those in the East. Political dissatisfaction in nations with relatively healthy economic and social systems, established rules of political competition and diffuse acceptance of the rule of law cannot be compared to harsh, ever-intensifying regime criticism in countries undergoing exemplary system transformation. Still, we should not place too much significance on Eastern European findings or overinterpret the data. A 1996 ranking of Western and Eastern European countries according to the degree of satisfaction with the development or functioning of democracy revealed a broad range of possible regime attitudes. Levels of democracy were highest in Denmark, followed by Switzerland and the United States, where 71 percent of those asked said they were more or less satisfied with the way democracy was working. Austria ranked sixth behind West Germany. Poles were more satisfied with the development of their democracy than the Portuguese and Spanish were with the functioning of theirs. Italy and Slovakia were tied near the bottom of the scale, and the Russian Republic, where satisfaction with democracy is almost negligible, ranked last (see Table 6).

PKOM data allow for a comparison of segments of the population in which political dissatisfaction and regime criticism are especially widespread. In 1995, in the five countries studied, above-average levels of dissatisfaction were found primarily among the following groups:

- Supporters of opposition parties. The exception was Poland, where discontent was actually stronger among government supporters than among those who sided with the opposition.

- (Former) members and cadres of (former) communist parties. They are distinctly more critical of the democratic regime. Hungary and the Slovak Republic present two notable exceptions, insofar as former communist party members and non-members are equally dissatisfied.

- Workers and industrial laborers. In Hungary and the Czech Republic, the attitudes of civil servants and white collar workers differ significantly from those of blue collar workers, whereas in Poland and the Slovak Republic, there is no perceptible difference between the regime evaluations of these two groups.

- Persons with fundamentally antipluralist attitudes. Respondents who indicate a preference for one-party systems are far more critical of democracy than individuals who believe in pluralism. Again, Slovakia is an exception: the data indicate across-the-board, wholesale dissatisfaction or disillusionment with the current political situation which is only indirectly predetermined by political attitudes and orientations.

- Persons whose general impression of current politics is that of an endless series of failures. With the exception of Poles, people who are thoroughly disgruntled with politics are also inclined to criticize the regime most harshly and/or express the greatest dissatisfaction with it.

- Economic pessimists. In every country except Hungary, pessimists tend to translate their predictions of doom into a relatively pronounced dissatisfaction with democracy and the political system.

- People who feel that democracy has not yet paid off for them. They are clearly more critical than those who believe that their

Table 6: Satisfaction with the functioning or development of democracy in international comparison (1995-1997): 'Eurobarometer' and 'Central and Eastern Eurobarometer'.

Percent of respondents who were very satisfied or fairly satisfied with the functioning (Western Europe, Latin America and U.S.A.) or the development (Eastern Europe) of democracy in their country.	
1. Denmark	83
2. Switzerland	73
3. USA	71
4. Netherlands	69
5. West Germany	68
6. Austria	61
7. Poland	57
8. Belgium	55
9. Sweden	55
10. France	48
11. East Germany	48
12. Britain	48
13. Portugal	42
14. Spain	41
15. Slovenia	40
16. Czech Republic	36
17. Argentinia	34
18. Greek	31
19. Hungary	30
20. Venezuela	30
21. Chile	27
22. Slovak Republic	25
23. Italy	20
24. Brasilia	20
25. GUS-States	18
26. CIS	11
27. Russian Republic	8

Source: Central and Eastern Eurobarometer 7/1997; 8/1998; Eurobarometer 43/1995; Lagos (1997: 133) and 'The National Election Study' (NES) 1996.

expectations have either come true or are about to be fulfilled. Similarly, individuals who have been critical of system change from the very beginning are likely to have the most negative impression of its pace and progress. In 1995, the share of "transformation skeptics" varied from six percent in the Czech Republic to 18 percent in Hungary.

Table 7: Dissatisfaction with democracy by subgroups in five countries compared

Percent of respondents who are dissatisfied with democracy and the political system in general	CZ	SK	H	PL	SLO
Government supporters	9	38	44	48	22
Opposition supporters	38	68	62	32	28
Former Communist Party members	41	52	53	50	30
Non-members	21	55	57	37	30
White collar workers/civil servants	20	58	49	34	30
Blue collar workers	38	60	64	37	30
Those who prefer a one-party system	43	53	71	50	29
Those who prefer a multiparty system	23	55	51	32	28
Those who view current politics as a failure	47	72	68	43	39
Economic pessimists	51	70	62	54	39
Those very disappointed by system change	74	77	76	58	58
Those dissatisfied with their personal economic situation	50	65	68	54	*
Those generally dissatisfied	25	55	57	37	28

Source: 'Politischer Kulturwandel' (1995).

- Persons who are generally dissatisfied with their standard of living. In the Czech Republic, for instance, only 17 percent of respondents who were generally happy with their personal economic situation expressed dissatisfaction with democracy and the political system, whereas 50 percent of those who were economically dissatisfied extended their discontent to include national politics. This correlation between satisfaction or dissatisfaction in the private sphere and the national arena is evident in all four countries studied.

Inglehart (1995) used international comparative data to demon-strate the close correlation between general contentment with life and political satisfaction:

> Life satisfaction, political satisfaction, interpersonal trust, high rates of political discussion, and support for the existing social order all tend to go together: They constitute a syndrome of positive attitudes toward the world in which one lives. What makes this all the more interesting is the fact that this syndrome seems linked with the viability of democratic institutions (ibid.: 41).

Table 8: Correlations between dissatisfaction with life and dissatisfaction with democracy and/or political practices (1995)

In Percentage	Dissatisfied with personal life	Dissatisfied with democracy	Feel that politics often fails	Believe the political order in their country is bad
1. Hungary	58	57	62	45
2. Slovak Republic	47	55	53	48
3. Poland	27	37	57	54
4. Czech Republic	22	25	35	21
5. Austria	6	32	45	19

Source: 'Politischer Kulturwandel' (1995); 'Politischer Kulturwandel in Österreich' (1996).

Empirical evidence also proves the validity of this link in post-communist societies. In Hungary and Slovakia, dissatisfaction with personal circumstances is particularly high, and a predominantly pessimist outlook on life contributes to a marked dissatisfaction with the political process. Conversely, in Poland and the Czech Republic, a predominantly positive evaluation of personal circumstances and chances in life engenders positive attitudes toward the political regime and, to a lesser degree, regime practices.

Data taken from 'Eurobarometer 41' allow for a comparison of personal satisfaction with life in EU member states and new post-communist democracies. The level of satisfaction in the Czech Republic and Poland was only slightly below the EU average. Considering the huge gap between material wealth in the EU nations and in the reform countries, these data cannot be interpreted as a mere reaction to socioeconomic circumstances. They obviously reflect a broader "cultural cluster" not exclusively determined by economic factors. Inglehart (1995) surmises, in this context,

> that those nations characterized by high levels of life satisfaction, interpersonal trust, tolerance, etc., would be likelier to adopt and maintain democratic institutions than those whose publics lacked such attitudes. Conversely, democratic institutions would be more likely to flounder in nations with low levels of life satisfaction, trust, and so on (ibid.)

Notes

1. According to a representative survey conducted by Fessel+GfK in 1997, five percent of Austrian respondents were satisfied, 66 percent more or less satisfied and 29 percent dissatisfied with democracy and the political system.

2. On trends and patterns of satisfaction with democracy in East Germany between 1991 and 1996, see Gabriel (1996).

3. As regards satisfaction with democracy in Slovenia, there are also significant discrepancies between CEE and PKOM data. The explanation might lie in the different methods used to measure and operationalize the indicator 'satisfaction with democracy', or in some contextual factors such as the precise moment and time of conducting the surveys or the sequence of items in questionnaires.

6

Diffuse Support for Democracy

The indicator "satisfaction with democracy" suffers from a blurred distinction between, in the terminology of Easton's seminal model, *diffuse* and *specific* support. Thus, increasing dissatisfaction with a given democracy may well, but need not, imply renunciation of democracy as a normative order. The strong correlation between an individual's evaluation of the current economic situation and his or her level of satisfaction with democracy is reflected in highly volatile trends of opinion, as is the manifest interaction between political dissatisfaction and periods of intense domestic conflict and crisis. Time sequences of the indicator "satisfaction with democracy" show, at least for Western and Southern Europe, "that this indicator of perceived efficacy is sensitive to short term economic and other conditions and is therefore much more volatile than are attitudes of diffuse legitimacy" (Morlino and Montero, 1995: 238).

While the level of satisfaction with democracy informs us about perceived functional deficiencies in any political process, it ignores questions relating to the broader, *diffuse* support for democracy as a form of government. Yet this question is central to empirical research on consolidation: "Attitudinally, a democratic regime is consolidated when a strong majority of public opinion, even in the midst of major economic problems and deep dissatisfaction with incumbents, holds the belief that democratic procedures and institutions are the most appropriate way to govern collective life, and when support for antisystem alternatives is quite small or more or less isolated from prodemocratic forces" (Linz and Stepan, 1996a: 16). Whether or not democratic rules and norms are accepted as "the only game in town" by the majority of the population may be established by applying the following indicators of diffuse legitimacy over a stipulated time period:

1. preference given to democracy over dictatorship
2. preference given to a multi-party system over a single-party system
3. rejection of a dissolution of parliament or any existing party
4. spread of antidemocratic and/or antipluralist orientations.

6.1. Support for Democracy as a Form of Government

Compared to the fluctuating levels of satisfaction with democracy, data on diffuse support for democracy as a form of government primarily indicate stability. In the Czech Republic, the share of respondents who prefer democracy to any dictatorial regime under any circumstances has exceeded 70 percent since 1990, with only slight variations. Worsening economic conditions and the exacerbated political conflicts associated with them caused diffuse support for democracy to fall from 74 percent in 1995 to a mere 66 percent in 1997. In the Slovak Republic, 68 percent of respondents explicitly favor democracy as the best form of government even though, at the same time, 57 percent are dissatisfied with the current realities of the political process. In Hungary, political dissatisfaction has increased steadily during the period examined, but has had no affect on diffuse system support. Thus, 65 percent of Hungarians prefer democracy to any form of dictatorship under any circumstances. In contrast, the dramatic decline of system support which Poland experienced between 1991 and 1992 was directly related to the economic and domestic upheavals taking place at the time. But support has increased since 1994 and has exceeded the 1991 figures continuously since 1995.[1] (see Table 9)

The "hard" core of antidemocratic respondents giving preference to dictatorship over democracy amounts to roughly 13 percent in the Czech Republic. In Hungary, 17 percent expressed antidemocratic preferences in 1997, whereas 18 percent did so in both Poland and Slovakia. There has been very little fluctuation in this segment over the time period surveyed. Pronounced antidemocratic attitudes prevail mainly among (former) members of the Communist party, but also among the unemployed and/or those who are pessimistic about their economic situation and prospects. Between 21 percent (CZ) and 12 percent (H) of interviewees react with indifference or despondency when asked to specify the form of government they

Table 9: Diffuse support for democracy as a form of government (1990-1997)

On this sheet, you will read several opinions on democracy and dictatorship. Which do you agree with?

In percentage	CZ	SK	H	PL
Democracy is preferable to dictatorship under any circumstances.				
1990	72	63		
1991	77	67	69	60
1992	71	68	69	48
1993	72	60		
1994	75	68	73	64
1995	74	66	67	65
1997	66	68	65	65
In some cases, dictatorship may be preferable to democracy.				
1990	8	11		
1991	7	10	9	14
1992	10	11	8	16
1993	9	11		
1994	11	11	8	17
1995	9	12	11	15
1997	13	18	17	18
For people like me, it makes no difference whether we live in a democracy or a dictatorship.				
1990	12	18		
1991	15	22	18	23
1992	18	19	21	30
1993	17	28		
1994	14	19	16	16
1995	16	22	17	17
1997	21	12	14	13

Source: 'Politischer Kulturwandel' (1990-1997).
Note: percent remainder = no response.

most favor. Such indifference is particularly widespread among persons who claim to have been skeptical of system change from the outset, and whose gloomy predictions of its consequences for their lives have apparently been borne out. Compared with relevant data from Western Europe, Southern Europe or the postauthoritarian democracies of Latin America, however, these findings do not confirm the impression of weak support for democracy in the reform countries of East-Central Europe. In contrast to fragile democratic support in the Russian Republic (50 percent) or in Brazil (50 percent), democracy seems by and large to have taken hold attitudinally in the four countries studied here.[2]

Table 10: Diffuse Legitimacy in international comparison

Democracy is preferable to dictatorship under any circumstances				
Affirmative answers in percentage.				
1. Denmark	93	(1989)	92	(1992)
2. Austria	91	(1989)	90	(1996)
3. West Germany	82	(1989)	83	(1992)
4. Spain	68	(1989)	81	(1996)
5. Uruguay	n.a.		80	(1996)
6. Great Britain	77	(1989)	76	(1992)
7. Italy	74	(1989)	73	(1992)
8. Argentina	n.a.		71	(1996)
9. Slovak Republic	63	(1991)	68	(1997)
10. Czech Republic	72	(1990)	66	(1997)
11. Hungary	69	(1991)	65	(1997)
12. Poland	60	(1991)	65	(1997)
13. Venezuela	n.a.		62	(1996)
14. Chile	n.a.		54	(1996)
15. Mexico	n.a.		53	(1996)
16. Russia	n.a.		50	(1994)
17. Brazil	n.a.		50	(1996)

Source: Fuchs, Guidorossi and Svensson (1995: 349); 'Politischer Kulturwandel' (1991-1997); Montero and Torcal (1990: 126); Morlino and Montero (1995: 238); Linz and Stepan (1996b: 222); Plasser, Ulram and Waldrauch (1997); Lagos (1997: 133).

6.2. Support for Pluralist Party Competition

Diffuse support for democracy presupposes the acceptance of a multi-party system, since democracy without pluralist competition and parties would constitute the hybrid "authoritarian or delegative democracy" (Huntington, 1996: 9) prevalent in some Latin American and Asian states. Country-specific variations notwithstanding, a majority of the population in reform nations favor a multi-party system. According to a 1997 poll, 94 percent of respondents in the Czech Republic support pluralist party competition, as compared to only 84 percent in Slovakia. Hungarians and Poles seem to embrace the pluralism of parties with markedly less enthusiasm: in both countries, roughly one fourth of respondents say they would prefer a single-party system to pluralist party competition.

Table 11: Preference for single-party or multi-party system (1991-1997)

Do you think it is better for a country to have only one party, where there is a maximum of unity, or several parties, so that diverse views may be represented?

In percentage	CZ	SK	H	PL
Only one party				
1991	6	14	18	19
1992	8	14	22	31
1993	8	16		
1994	6	20	22	23
1995	6	13	24	24
1997	5	16	24	29
Several parties				
1991	93	84	75	74
1992	90	81	73	61
1993	91	80		
1994	94	77	74	73
1995	95	87	72	73
1997	94	84	72	67
No response				
1991	1	1	7	6
1992	2	5	5	8
1993	1	4		
1994	1	3	5	4
1995	0	0	4	3
1997	1	0	4	4

Source: 'Politischer Kulturwandel' (1991-1997).

In Hungary and Poland, there is a strong correlation between preference for single-party or multi-party systems on the one hand, and education and professional training on the other. Among persons with only a rudimentary education, 35 percent of respondents in these two countries prefer a single-party system. Lack of interest in politics, affiliation or closeness with communist party groupings and pronounced disappointment with the social and economic consequences of the transition in turn increase a weariness *vis-à-vis* pluralist party competition. Periods of exacerbated domestic conflict, power struggles between competing elites or signs of economic downturn similarly trigger scattered resurgences of latent antipluralist attitudes (Plasser and Ulram, 1993a: 49f). Because of its inherent passivity, resignation and lethargy, this potentially antidemocratic force does not pose an immediate threat to consolidating democracies, however receptive to populist appeals it may seem. Juxtaposed with the sparse data on the consolidation periods of other postauthoritarian democracies, the findings on postcommunist democracies appear less dramatic. Thus in the early 1950s, 24 percent of West German respondents favored a single-party system, but within a decade this rate fell to just 11 percent (Weil, 1993: 211). A similar development took place in the consolidation period of Austrian postwar democracy (Plasser and Ulram, 1992a: 46).

6.3. Support for the Parliamentary System

Only in the Czech Republic has support for a parliamentary system grown consistently over the time period under scrutiny. In 1995, 85 percent of Czech citizens resolutely opposed the dissolution of parliament and parliamentary parties. Although one fourth of respondents favored dissolution in 1992, this number had fallen to a mere 15 percent in just three years. Slovak support for parliamentarism, while somewhat less sanguine, has remained stable and close to the 80 percent mark over the entire period. In Hungary, 70 percent of respondents opposed the abolition of parliamentary politics in 1995, while 25 percent favored it. Between 1991 and 1992, Poland saw a dramatic decline in the support for parliamentarism against the backdrop of severe economic and domestic crisis. By 1994, however, democratic consensus in Poland again extended to a stable two thirds of respondents endorsing the parliamentary system – a percentage still markedly lower than in any other of the new democracies compared here. Austrian support for parliamentarism stood at 90 percent in 1991, with only 8 percent of respondents in favor of the dissolution of parliament and political parties.

Table 12: Support for the parliamentary system (1991-1995)

Some people argue that this country could be governed more efficiently if parliament were dissolved and if there were fewer parties. Would you...

In percentage	CZ		SK	H	PL	A
tend to/definitely welcome such a measure						
1991		13		22	32	8
1992	25		18	24	40	
1993	19		20			
1994	17		24	27	28	
1995	15		21	25	29	
tend to/definitely reject it						
1991		41*)		65	64	90
1992	74		79	73	54	
1993	78		78			
1994	81		73	69	68	
1995	85		79	70	66	

Source: 'New Democracies Barometer' (1991-1995).
Note: percent remainder = no response.
*) high rate of no response (47%).

6.4. Spread of Antidemocratic and/or Antipluralist Orientations

Antidemocratic orientations are encountered most frequently in Hungary and in the Slovak Republic. In both countries, one in six respondents supports the demand for a restoration of communist rule – at least verbally. In the Czech Republic and in Poland, only one in ten respondents expresses the desire to return to the "old" regime. Meanwhile, the "hard core" of nostalgics who yearn for communist rule has diminished drastically. There is also no support for or acceptance of army rule or military coups in any of the postcommunist societies surveyed. But "strong leaders" who might reach decisions quickly and implement them without consulting parliament are another matter. The desire for a strong order-keeping force is most prevalent in Poland, where in 1995 roughly one third of respondents valued efficient political action more highly than parliamentary legitimation. The same year, one in five Hungarians and one in six Slovaks expressed a preference for 'strong leadership'. And even though Czechs' calls for a strong leader became markedly weaker during the period surveyed, 14 percent of those polled in 1995 still favored a strong leadership, i.e., one no longer accountable to parliament. In the Russian Republic, 39 percent of respondents favored such a solution to their country's problems (Weil, 1993: 211). The call for a "strong man" and for clear and seemingly transparent structures of decision making is by no means restricted to postcommunist societies. Twenty-two percent of Austrians polled in 1991 also expressed their preference for a strong leader (Plasser and Ulram, 1993a: 46). This verbal endorsement of authoritarian rule should not, however, be taken literally, as it seems to indicate a diffuse dissatisfaction with current practices of decision making. "People may be upset that 'democracy' has not produced more, but that does not mean that they want to eliminate free press, free speech, competitive elections, and other democratic rights" (Gibson, 1995: 87). Widespread discontent with the ability of incumbent governments to make policy choices and implement them – particularly with regard to economic policy – is also at the root of a strong desire for experts to make such decisions in lieu of elected representatives. This indicator, too, primarily gauges dissatisfaction with, and criticism of, the economic performance of incumbent leaders. For the majority of citizens in reform countries, poor performance meant new socioeconomic risks, declining real incomes, and frustrated expectations regarding consumer affluence and welfare. (See Table 13)

Empirical studies of democratic consolidation processes in Southern Europe similarly indicate a sharp increase in political dissatisfaction and disappointment during the first years following a change in government, intensified by economic recessions and social as well as economic crises of adaptation. "Accordingly, frustration, disillusionment and disenchantment were widespread during those first years. Nonetheless, negative perceptions of democratic efficacy did not affect the level of legitimacy to the same extent" (Morlino and Montero, 1995: 243). The consequences of social, political and economic ruptures during the transformation period did, however, have an obviously negative impact on democratic confidence and pride. This took the form of "dissatisfaction in the workplace, threats to professional and personal plans, experience with inadequate public reaction to antidemocratic politics, material and spiritual poverty that dimmed outlooks, and insufficient information combined with training for one job to the exclusion of alternative qualifications, all of which, in turn, tended to promote attitudes, expectations, and behavior patterns untouched by or even hostile to the spirit of democracy" (Claußen, 1996: 535).

Table 13: Antidemocratic orientations (1993-1995)

Affirmative answers in percentage.	CZ	SK	H	PL
The former communist regime ought to be restored.				
1993			16	
1994	7	15		15
1995	9	17	16	9
The army ought to govern the country.				
1993			2	
1994	2	5		10
1995	2	0	3	4
We don't really need Parliament; we need a strong leader who can make decisions quickly and implement them.				
1993	22	19	18	39
1994	17	25		34
1995	14	17	20	32
The most important matters of economic policy should be decided by experts in the field, not by the government.				
1993			79	
1994	80	88		59
1995	70	79	69	59

Source: 'New Democracies Barometer' (1993-1995).

Despite some latent antidemocratic reservations, antipluralist gut reactions, and widespread political economic dissatisfaction, the process of democratic consolidation – the dissemination and deepening of democratic attitudes – has come a long way from what it was only recently. In this same context, Linz and Stepan have identified a "surprisingly high degree of political support for the new political regime (political regime, not necessarily political *incumbents*), despite economic hardship" (1996b: 445). In each of the five reform countries surveyed, an overwhelming majority of the population rejects antidemocratic forms of government. In both Poland and the Czech Republic, public opinion strongly opposes any idea of returning to the old order. Even in Hungary and Slovenia, more than three quarters of respondents clearly have no desire whatsoever to revive communist regime practices. For the process of democratic consolidation in Southern Europe, too, it has been possible to identify a blend of pronounced political dissatisfaction, highly critical attitudes toward the political elite, and diffuse democratic support. From this, Morlino and Montero (1995: 253) conclude that "the present level of democratic legitimacy has its origin not so much in a cluster of positive attitudes but rather in the intensity of the rejection of the authoritarian past."

Table 14: Rejection of antidemocratic and/or antipluralist forms of government (1995)

Percentage of respondents who reject the statement	CZ	SK	H	PL	SLO
The former communist regime should be restored.	91	83	78	91	78*)
The army should govern the country.	97	95	95	96	88
We don't really need parliament; we need a strong leader who can make decisions quickly and implement them.	87	83	77	68	64
The most important matters of economic policy should be decided by experts in the field, not by the government.	30	21	18	40	35

Source: 'New Democracies Barometer' (1995).
*) relatively high "no response" rate in Slovenia.

A comparative survey of selected indicators of democratic support in 1997 showed once again just how far these postcommunist democracies have come on the road toward democratic consolidation. Our data indicate that basic democratic principles are already firmly anchored in Slovakia despite a degree of political dissatisfaction that appears alarmingly high compared to that of the Czech Republic. The Slovak figures also lend perspective to the political dissatisfaction in Hungary, where democratic attitudes and principles have become anchored among and internalized by the majority of citizens, albeit less firmly than in the Czech and Slovak Republics. The same is true of Poland, which has also enjoyed the concomitant benefit of moderate satisfaction with both democracy and the political system. A continuous unfolding of democratic attitudes can be shown for the Czech Republic: only here do we find evidence of *linear* dynamics of democratic consolidation. In the Slovak Republic, in contrast, there is evidence of *abrupt* alterations caused by exacerbated economic or domestic crises. Meanwhile, however, a solid majority of the population has come to accept democratic attitudes and the basic rules of the game. Hungary has also seen a steady rise in democratic support over the period studied, even though it remains lower on the whole. The same, finally, holds true for Poland, despite scattered and temporary setbacks.

The strength and determination of diffuse democratic support as well as the extent to which democratic attitudes are anchored in a society manifestly correlate with social and economic conditions (Tóka, 1995). The perceived consequences of regime change are even more decisive for the acceptance and support of democracy. Individuals whose original optimistic expectations in system change have more or less been fulfilled display an exceptional commitment to democracy in all five countries. Those who count themselves among the winners of market economic transformation are quite obviously happier with the rules and procedures of democracy than are people whose hopes have been disappointed. Finally, we find democratic support to be weakest among individuals who have been afraid of system change and its impact on their lives from the very inception. Self-defined losers of the transformation process view the democratic system with wariness and/or outright hostility. They also tend to be nostalgic about the old regime or to seek refuge in nationalist-populist political figures who offer apparently simple palliatives to economic and social distress.

Our attempt to explain the tensions and contradictions within the political cultures of postcommunist societies leads to the identification of three underlying cleavages (Plasser and Ulram, 1996: 6f.):

1) between (self-defined) winners and losers of the transformation process
2) between proponents of a competitive market economy and supporters of a strong paternalistic state
3) between persons with active, individualistic orientations (with the emphasis on self reliance and subjective efficacy), and those with more passive, collectivist orientations who seek the conformity, subordination and protection of groups.

Figure 4: Model of underlying tensions in the political culture of postcommunist societies.

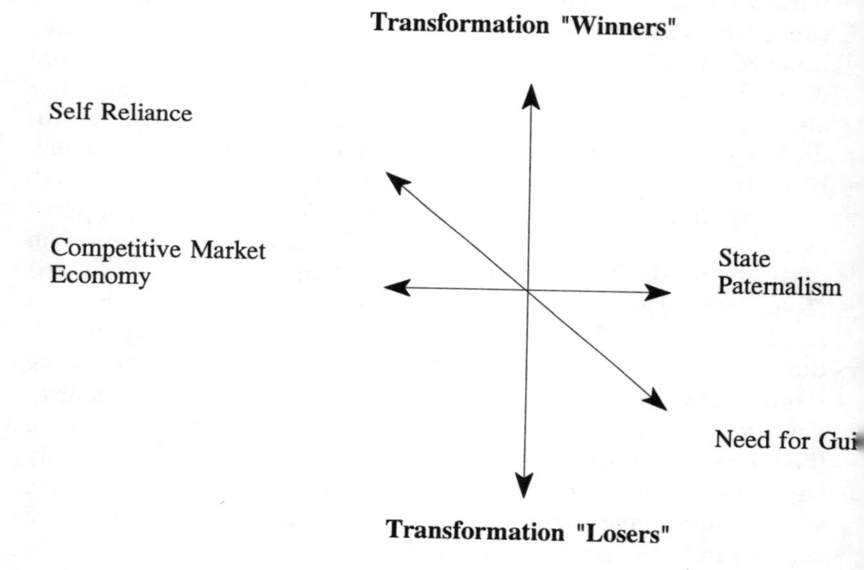

The obvious correlation between perceived socioeconomic status, prospects for improvement and diffuse support for democracy shows the potentially explosive nature of the cleavage between the self-declared winners and losers of transformation, despite the tendency of theorists of economic modernization to underestimate it. This correlation can clearly be interpreted as a challenge to examine the "unintentional" consequences of social dynamics which endanger consolidation from a sociological perspective (see Müller, 1995: 49).

6.5. Concepts and Extent of Legitimacy in Comparison

We chose the following indicators to gauge the intensity of diffuse system support in East-Central Europe and contrasted them with Austrian data collected during a representative survey in 1996:

1) Functional legitimacy of the political system (satisfaction with social and economic development or, in Austria, with the performance of democracy)
2) Diffuse legitimacy of the regime (preference for democracy as a form of government)
3) Procedural legitimacy of the democratic system (preference for a multi-party system).

Table 15: Diffuse legitimacy of democratic systems compared (1997)

Percentage of respondents who	CZ	SK	H	PL	SLO	A	USA
are satisfied with the performance (the development) of democracy in their country (**functional** legitimacy)	38	21	21	43	36	61	71
prefer democracy to dictatorship under any circumstances (**diffuse** legitimacy)	66	68	65	65	59*)	90	n.a.
favor a multi-party system, so that diverse opinions could be represented (**procedural** legitimacy)	94	84	72	67	78	97	n.a.

Sources: For functional legitimacy, see 'Central and Eastern Eurobarometer' (7/1997); for diffuse and procedural legitimacy, see 'Politischer Kulturwandel' (1990-997); Austrian figures in 'Politischer Kulturwandel in Österreich' (1996); The National Election Study (NES) 1996.
*) relatively high 'no response' rate.

The attitudes of Austrians and East-Central European postcommunist societies differ mainly in the extent of their functional legitimacy. Austrians are far more satisfied with the performance of their democracy than are East Europeans with the development of theirs.

This is hardly surprising, since the indicator specifically targets criteria such as the performance and "efficiency" of governments. The gap between Austrian and East European figures for diffuse legitimacy is considerably narrower. Finally, a look at the procedural legitimacy of democratic systems shows that Austrian, Czech and Slovak data are quite similar.

6.6. Typology of Democratic Orientations in International Comparison

While the East European general elections of 1989 and 1990 were primarily anticommunist plebiscites, the results of the subsequent round of elections (1990 in Poland, 1992 in Czechoslovakia) already indicated the disintegration of anticommunist coalitions. This fragmentation of the party spectrum was particularly extreme in Poland, where 29 parties held seats in parliament. In Hungary, a similar process of erosion or rearrangement split the parties represented in parliament and proved especially divisive for incumbents. Of all the Czech democratic parties, only the governing ODS succeeded in consolidating its position and setting up at least semi-stable structures of organization. In East-Central Europe, we generally find "floating party systems" which are neither functionally differentiated nor anchored at the grass roots level. This is especially evident in the relatively low level of party identification in Poland and Hungary (see Plasser and Ulram, 1996). Politics in East-Central European societies is also characterized by an "intermediary vacuum" impeding citizens' integration into what are still rudimentary and unstable political structures. This has made it possible for political debate to remain at a highly intellectual level, but unfortunately also one so far removed from the real concerns of society that it has contributed substantially to the rise of populist leaders.

These features of East-Central European party systems, in addition to the economic, social and psychological upheavals of transformation, have reinforced antiparliamentary and antiparty prejudices. In Hungary and Slovakia, the small percentage of respondents seriously considering a dissolution of parliament and political parties is increasing slowly but steadily. In Poland, the trend toward authoritarian solutions which peaked in 1992 has been ebbing away since late 1993. The general trend, however, is still significant and may be found across the range of population sectors and electoral choices, this being a specific and unique trait of Polish political culture. In 1995, more than half of all Polish voters believed that a move toward authoritarianism was within the realm of possibility.

Table 16: Authoritarian trends in East-Central Europe (1991-1995)

Percentage of respondents who	CZ		SK	H	PL
consider the dissolution of parliament and political parties likely or possible					
1991		21		25	53
1992	35		33	25	67
1993	28		31		
1994	28		33	27	53
1995	19		33	25	59
would welcome the dissolution of parliament and political parties					
1991		13		22	32
1992	25		18	24	40
1993	19		20		
1994	17		24	27	28
1995	15		21	25	29

Source: 'New Democracies Barometer' (1991-1995).

Following Rose's and Haerpfer's schematic opposition of regime support vs. regime subversion, more than two thirds of Czech citizens, as well as 6 out of 10 Slovaks and Hungarians, may be classified as "confident democrats".[3] This group, which not only rejects authoritarianism but also considers its advent unlikely, has been growing over the past four years in the Czech Republic and has remained stable in both Slovakia and Hungary. "Anxious democrats" who reject but dread authoritarian trends are a shrinking group, as are "hopeful authoritarians", who would welcome and are confidently awaiting authoritarianism; in the Czech Republic, for instance, they comprise less than 10 percent of the population. "Dejected authoritarians" who yearn for authoritarianism but know their hopes are futile are equally few in number. The case is slightly different, however, in Poland, where only three out of ten respondents can be classified as confident democrats and one third as anxious democrats. The sizes of both groups have increased at the expense of the numbers of both hopeful and dejected authoritarians. Compared to other East-Central Europeans, however, Poles are still relatively volatile in their political preferences (see Plasser and Ulram, 1994b: 370f.) and more sensitive to struggle or conflict between the institutions of the president and parliament.

Table 17: Confident and anxious democrats (1992/93-1995)

In percentage	CZ			SK			H			PL		
	92/93	94	95	92/93	94	95	92	94	95	92	94	95
Confident democrats	57	65	71	61	57	59	64	61	65	33	41	33
Anxious democrats	21	17	13	19	17	19	11	9	9	24	30	34
Hopeful authoriarians	15	12	9	13	16	15	13	18	16	35	23	27
Dejected authoritarians	7	6	7	6	7	7	12	11	8	8	5	5

Source: Rose and Haerpfer (1993); 'New Democracies Barometer' (1994); Plasser and Ulram (1994b); Rose and Haerpfer (1996: 86).

6.7. Trust in Institutions

Trust in institutions is first and foremost an indicator of *specific support* (Listhaug and Wiberg, 1995). Levels of trust in individual institutions may differ greatly even in consolidated democracies, both traditional and postauthoritarian. Trust is based on two factors: whether an institution's public profile is primarily corporate or predominantly centered around a leader or representative (Fuchs, 1989: 116; Klages, 1990: 56); and whether it is seen as a competitive (hence contentious and partial) or "neutral" and "allencompassing" body (Plasser and Ulram, 1993b: 137ff.).[4]

Trust in institutions, however, is also of crucial importance for any analysis of *diffuse* system support:

- The overall level of institutional trust would seem to indicate the extent of diffuse political support. But a high level of trust in some institutions may also either compensate for low or declining confidence in others, or cushion and blunt the effect of their temporarily deficient credibility.[5]

- If the level of confidence in predominantly hierarchic and authoritarian institutions (e.g., armed forces) differs greatly from that in institutions of political control and/or pluralist politics, liberal-democratic consensus is likely to be shaky.[6]

- Different levels of confidence in non-competitive executive institutions on the one hand, and government and/or parliament on the other, indicate similarly divergent patterns of functional and/or attitudinal democratic consolidation.[7]

- No full assessment of levels of trust is possible unless we understand the dynamics and development of trust in each particular institution, as well as confidence in each institution relative to each of the others.

For these reasons, we do not limit our analysis of trust in institutions in East-Central Europe to political institutions in the narrower sense, i.e., to institutions which compete in elections and have, directly or indirectly, acquired democratic legitimacy in the process. We also include executive institutions, as well as other associations which, taken together, constitute societal and political pluralism.

Political institutions and institutions of political pluralism/ competition

Confidence in East-Central European presidents depends to considerable degree on his (or, in theory, her) institutional role. If the chief executive's position is strong and powerful, as in Russia or, to a certain extent, in Poland, we find a lack of trust. If, conversely, the president is primarily a moral and balancing agent, if his executive position is weak and he remains above daily political bickering, as is the case in Hungary and the Czech Republic, trust is very high and matches West European standards.[8] Government and parliament generally enjoy much less public confidence, and political parties as well as old trade unions formerly associated with communist parties are seen as least trustworthy. The case is somewhat different in the Czech Republic,[9] where explicit trust in the government and even in political parties exceeds not only that of its East-Central European neighbors, but also that of some consolidated Western European democracies.[10] This is the result not merely of government performance, but also of systematic institutional and organizational partybuilding across the political spectrum.

Institutions of societal pluralism

Poles express a high level of confidence in the Catholic church (53 percent trust, 28 percent distrust, 19 percent neutral) based in large measure on its traditional role as, among other things, a seat and vehicle of national identity and on its deep structural roots in the population. More than 90 percent of Poles claim to be devout Catholics, and nearly two out of three attend Mass regularly. In other countries, the share of confessionally committed respondents is much smaller. Here, too, the Czech Republic marks the other extreme: it also shows the lowest level of trust in religious institutions. Environmentalist groups, examples of new political actors with no direct ties to parties or ideologies, enjoy high levels of trust which generally exceed those of competitive political organizations. The same holds true for the media, which are considered relatively untrustworthy only in Russia, the former GDR, and, more recently, also in the Czech Republic.[11]

Executive and judiciary

Trust in administrative institutions, as well as, in some cases, in courts of law and police forces – precisely those institutions which citizens most frequently encounter – is remarkably low. This is especially true of the Czech Republic, and to a lesser degree of Hungary and Slovakia. East-Central Europeans are generally much more wary of the state authority figures than Austrians, West Germans or even East Germans, who are now emulating their compatriots' faith in the judiciary. "As a result of this latter development, the structures of trust in institutions are becoming more similar in East and West Germany. Beneficiaries of this trend have been first and foremost the executive and judiciary. By contrast, all institutions which represent interests, with the sole exception of trade unions, have suffered from declining trust" (Gabriel, 1996b: 31). Obviously, East-Central Europeans' past experiences with officials and the judiciary play an important role in this, as do functional deficiencies, doubts concerning the present claim to impartiality, and the widespread conviction that bureaucracies have been left more or less unaffected by transition. As in Western Europe, trust in the executive and judiciary generally exceeds trust in competitive political institutions, but as a rule, East-Central Europe has no basis for trust in the network of state institutions[12] which could, if it existed, absorb legitimacy crises of particular political institutions or compensate for their still rather fragile foundations. The low levels of trust in East-Central Europe appear less dramatic, however, when compared to those which prevail in Russia. Here, only the armed forces' public standing seems in any way balanced, while the administration, police and judiciary are subject to much more severe criticism than their East-Central European equivalents. Among East-Central Europeans, there seems to be no consensus on whether or not to trust the armed forces. The two extremes are Poland, where nearly three quarters of respondents declare their confidence in the national army (17 percent expressing distrust), and the Czech Republic, where distrust is predominant (27 percent trust, 46 percent distrust). (See Table 18)

The patterns of the development and dynamics of institutional trust in East-Central Europe show great divergence. Public confidence in Hungary's political institutions began to wane as early as 1989 and continued in this vein for at least three more years (Bruszt and Simon, 1991; Ilonszki and Kurtán, 1992). Following the parliamentary elections of 1993, executive institutions improved their standing somewhat, only to lose it again in 1997. Churches and the army continued to lose credibility. In Poland, the armed forces and police were discredited as "henchmen of the old guard" in the wake of the change of regime, while the churches and new democratic institutions enjoyed a surge of popularity. Soon, however, the latter had all but used up their bonus of confidence: political and pluralist institutions were increasingly judged by their often poor performance during the first years of transformation and consequently suffered a "punitive" withdrawal of trust. In turn, army and police forces re-emerged in the public consciousness as supposedly neutral agents of order and security. Even trade unions affiliated with the former Communist Party were considered more trustworthy than Solidarity in 1992 – a trend which, however, proved short-lived. Courts of law, the civil service sector and the media consistently improved their confidence ratings, as did the Catholic church and

Table 18: Comparison of trust in institutions (1994-1997)

Percentage of those who gave grades of 5, 6 or 7 on a scale of 1 (no trust) to 7 (complete trust)	CZ 97	SK 97	H 97	PL 97	SLO 95	RUS 94	EG 95	WG 95	A 96
President	74	31	46	44	57	24	n.a.	n.a.	51
Government	39	25	17	27	43	18	36	41	30
Parliament	24	19	19	24	25	12	39	46	31
Political parties	17	14	9	14	12	14	n.a.	n.a.	14
New, independent trade unions	16	17	14	26	22				
						}14	}41	}34	}29
Old, formerly party-affiliated trade unions	8	13	10	14	30				
Church(es)	23	38	36	53	25	n.a.	n.a.	n.a.	28
Environmentalist associations*)	(54)	(54)	(35)	(41)	(41)	n.a.	n.a.	n.a.	n.a.
Media	32	36	39	40	51	30	30	33	21
Government authorities and civil service	27	26	27	30	38	18	n.a.	n.a.	46
Courts of law	30	35	34	39	43	25	45	50	60
Police	25	30	31	38	39	21	n.a.	n.a.	62
Army	27	55	37	63	45	50	44	46	44

*) 1995

Source: 'Politischer Kulturwandel' (1995 and 1997); Plasser and Ulram (1996: 18) for Russia; Gabriel (1996b) for East and West Germany; 'Politischer Kulturwandel in Österreich' (1996).

Note: EG = East Germany, WG = West Germany.

independent unions.[13] Trust in parliament and government is still low, but somewhat higher than in 1991.

In Slovakia, levels of trust in institutions have tended to shift and fluctuate. Once independence was attained, there was a dramatic improvement in the reputations of the institutions which symbolized the new nation state, such as the armed forces and the government. The administrative bureaucracy, the police and the judiciary were largely unaffected, and trust in political and political-pluralist institutions continued to decline. Church(es) and the media have yet to recover from the loss of confidence they suffered once the initial enthusiasm for transition had waned. A surge of confidence in the government only lasted a few months and never extended to the parties. Today, nearly all Slovak institutions command less trust than they did in 1991, with political and executive institutions, judiciary and the media primarily bearing the brunt of the general chagrin.

In contrast to this scenario, Czech confidence in institutions has remained stable over a long period. The only exceptions are the churches and the army, whose reliability is being questioned by an ever-increasing number of citizens. In 1997, however, against the backdrop of slowing economic growth, austerity measures and fierce conflict within the government, trust in institutions eroded for the first time. The media, government, political parties, trade unions and security forces have served as targets of discontent, while President Vaclav Havel has managed to strengthen his position as a moral authority and stable force in the face of political strife. The salient role accorded to the president forms an obvious link with the democratic traditions of inter-war Czechoslovakia.

In all four countries, trade unions with no party affiliation are winning employees' loyalty at the expense of unions associated with communist successor parties. Another shared trait is the fact that the media enjoy increasing confidence, Slovakia being the notable exception. Finally – and despite all the differences – the Polish, Hungarian, Slovak and Czech Republics are all characterized by a low level of confidence in political parties, most of which rank below other institutions of political pluralism. There is an important difference between this democratic consolidation and that in Austria and Italy (see Ulram, 1990), as well as a loose analogy to post-Franco Spain (see Morlino, 1995): the role of political parties as agents of democratization is relatively limited, while that of civil society is correspondingly strong.

Table 19: Development of institutional trust (1991-1997)

Sums of grades 5, 6 and 7 on a scale of 1 = no trust to 7 = high trust in percentage	Czech Republic						Slovak Republic					
	91	92	93	94	95	97	91	92	93	94	95	97
President	n.a.	n.a.	n.a.	68	66	74	n.a.	n.a.	n.a.	61	37	31
Government	50	48	48	56	45	39	23	49	33	31	29	25
Parliament	32	19	25	32	25	24	34	24	20	22	24	19
Political parties	22	20	20	24	24	17	20	20	12	15	15	14
New independent trade unions	}35	}24	}21	20	26	16	}39	}31	}21	22	29	17
Old, formerly party-affiliated trade unions				11	12	8				12	12	13
Churches	27	33	27	28	25	23	21	45	39	45	35	38
Media	42	40	41	43	59	32	47	39	39	38	39	36
Government authorities and civil service	25	27	24	27	24	27	28	30	26	26	22	26
Law courts	39	38	32	40	34	30	39	37	29	33	32	35
Police	33	36	36	36	32	25	35	35	31	31	28	30
Army	52	42	40	39	33	27	31	52	44	47	44	55

Sums of grades 5, 6 and 7 on a scale of 1 = no trust to 7 = high trust in percentage	Hungary					Poland					East Germany		
	91	92	94	95	97	91	92	94	95	97	91	93	95
President	n.a.	n.a.	n.a.	55	46	n.a.	n.a.	19	29	44	n.a.	n.a.	n.a.
Government	26	16	21	19	17	26	22	25	23	27	}36	25	36
Parliament	29	20	23	21	19	18	12	24	25	24		27	39
Political parties	16	10	11	10	9	7	8	8	8	14	19	18	n.a.
New independent trade unions	20	16	23	23	14	29	9	14	20	26	}39	}40	}41
Old, formerly party-affiliated trade unions	18	20	14	14	10	9	21	13	9	14			
Churches	46	42	39	34	36	50	41	36	47	53	23	25	n.a.
Media	40	34	30	45	39	30	35	34	44	40	n.a.	18	30
Government authorities and civil service	33	24	33	29	27	19	23	24	26	30	24	21	n.a.
Law courts	44	40	46	43	34	30	32	34	38	39	44	36	45
Police	43	34	45	44	31	30	46	41	38	38	37	36	n.a.
Army	47	40	44	40	37	53	63	59	54	63	35	39	44

Source: 'Politischer Kulturwandel' (1991-1997); Gluchowski and Zelle (1992, 1993); Gabriel (1996) for Eastern Germany.

Notes

1. With just 59 per cent, support for the system in Slovenia is markedly lower than in any of the other four countries discussed here. Since no trend data are available, it is impossible to know anything about changes and developments within the period under scrutiny. For details on instrumental acceptance of democracy in Slovenia, see Bernik, Malnar and Tós, 1996.

2. See Gibson (1995) for details on empirical trends of democratic orientation in Russia and Ukraine.

3. Rose and Haerpfer (1993) define "confident democrats" as individuals who reject the dissolution of parliament and think it unlikely to ever happen. "Anxious democrats" also reject the dissolution of parliament and political parties, but are less confident in the resilience of these institutions. "Hopeful authoritarians" favor the dissolution of parliament and consider a concomitant outlawing of parties a likely probability. "Dejected authoritarians", finally, would like to see parliament done away with, but have little hope of ever seeing their wish come true. Note that "confident democrats" here are not identical with "confident democrats" in the typology developed by Linz and Stepan (1996b).

4. By way of example, we might mention politicians and civil servants versus courts of law, or the government versus the president (in most Western European countries.)

5. A current example of this is Italy, where the political crisis reached a climax at the beginning of this decade. A profound and growing lack of confidence in politicians and the administration contrasted starkly with increased levels of confidence in (parts of) the judiciary (Nelken, 1996).

6. On the importance of *rechtsstaat* and fundamental principles of social and political pluralism for the consolidation of liberal democracies, see Diamond (1996) and Linz and Stepan (1996b).

7. Cf. the different levels of trust in parliament found in Switzerland and in the postauthoritarian democracies of (West) Germany and Austria (Plasser and Ulram, 1993b).

8. Due to a prolonged struggle between the president and prime minister plus government and parliamentary majority, the Slovak Republic is an exception to this rule. Trust in the president declined dramatically between 1994 and 1995.

9. Slovenian figures on trust in government show a drastic change between 1994 and 1995. Since we lack data covering a sufficiently long period, no interpretation is warranted.

10. Austrian figures on trust in government seem to be a negative exception within Western Europe. Only Italy has experienced a comparable, near-endemic rejection of parties and criticism of the political class, both of which have increased steadily for more than a decade. Cf. Plasser and Ulram, 1993b.

11. East German views on the media seem to have approached the negative image characteristic of Western Europe (Gabriel, 1996b). As a rule, East-Central European trust in the media far exceeds that of Western Europe, even Austria.

12. Thus in both Germany and Austria, a public increasingly disgruntled with politicians and parties has, for some time now, also shown less and less confidence in political institutions. In the same period, public trust in civil servants, the executive and the judiciary has only been marginally affected.

13. Both have proved much more attractive than liberal-conservative parties as a forum of opposition to the government in power, which was led by a communist-successor party between 1993 and 1997.

7

Evaluation of the Communist Regime

Eight years after the old regimes were ousted – either through pacted transitions retroactively ratified in elections or "velvet revolutions" – communism in East-Central Europe is generally seen as having had both its good and bad sides. Only a minority of respondents in the reform countries see communism as having been mainly positive (Hungary, Slovenia) or negative (Slovakia, Poland, Czech Republic). In the older postauthoritarian democracies of Southern and West Central Europe, there is much stronger emphasis on the negative sides of the authoritarian past. Furthermore, authoritarian (Austria, Portugal) and fascist regimes (Spain, Italy) are judged much more mildly than totalitarian ones (National Socialism in Austria and Germany).[1] In Austria and the former West Germany, a relatively high percentage of respondents nevertheless believe, in retrospect, that National Socialism had its "good sides".[2] Studies, especially those carried out in West Germany during the first post war years, likewise indicate that predominantly negative views of the Nazi regime's totalitarian practices were slow in coming (see Table 20).

Two factors are decisive in evaluating the past regimes of East-Central Europe. The first is ideological proximity: the closer individuals place themselves to the far left end of the political spectrum, the more positive their assessment of communism is. With the exception of Poland, respondents with distinct leftist leanings do not unambiguously condemn communism. Conversely, the further to the right of the political spectrum people are, the more critical their views of the political past. Those who declare their intention to vote for communist or radical leftist parties have a correspondingly positive view of the old regime. This is less true, however, of former members of the (Communist) Party or any of its sub-organizations. In Hungary, for instance, there is no discernible difference between the views of former Communists and non-Communists. This reveals

Table 20: Assessment of authoritarian regimes in postauthoritarian democracies

In Percentage	CZ 97	SK 97	H 97	PL 97	SLO 95	D-W 89	A/1 96*)	A/2 96**)	I 85	SP 85	P 85	GR 85
Only bad / Primarily bad	25	7	4	14	7	21 / 36 }57	22 / 31 }53	12 / 26 }38	37	28	30	59
Good and bad	67	83	78	79	69	36	43	35	43	44	42	31
Primarily good / (Almost) only good	7	9	13	4	19	1	1 / 0 } 1	4 / 0 } 4	7	17	13	6
No answer	1	0	5	2	5	-	3	23	13	11	15	4

Source: 'Politischer Kulturwandel' (1995, 1997); 'Politischer Kulturwandel in Österreich' (1996); Plasser and Ulram (1993b: 39); Linz and Stepan (1996b: 153).
* A/1 = National Socialism
** A/2 = Austrian "Ständestaat" (authoritarian regime between 1934 and 1938).

Table 21: Evaluations of communism in East-Central Europe (1995)

In Percentage	CZ			SK			H			PL		
	-	0	+	-	0	+	-	0	+	-	0	+
Left/Right-self-positioning*)												
- Left	-	94	6	-	65	35	-	59	41	5	88	7
- Center Left	5	89	6	3	89	8	4	78	18	5	88	6
- Center	9	88	2	10	86	5	3	79	17	12	83	4
- Center Right	39	59	2	19	77	4	10	74	14	23	73	3
- Right	53	46	1	38	59	3	19	81	-	30	66	2
Communist party affinity												
- CP member under the old regime	13	82	6	6	75	19	1	80	19	7	89	4
- Party preference for CP or radical Left	4	88	7	8	68	25	-	66	34	*	*	*
Expectations of system change												
- Fulfilled/ exceeded	42	57	1	17	81	1	12	74	12	27	71	1
- Rather disappointed	12	86	2	12	84	4	4	79	16	13	81	4
- Seriously disappointed	9	86	5	12	75	13	3	73	24	7	88	5
- Negative expectations**)	4	82	14	5	76	18	2	75	23	6	88	5
national average	23	74	3	12	81	7	4	76	18	15	79	4

Source: 'Politischer Kulturwandel' (1995).
Note:
'-' = communism was all or mostly bad
'0' = communism had its good and bad sides
'+' = communism was all or mostly good
*) Self-positioning on a scale of 1 to 11.
**) Respondents with negative expectations of system change who have not altered their view.

not only a distinct distancing or dissociation from the past former regime, but also considerable conformity, ranging from voluntary to enforced, which was more important than ideological conviction in motivating people to join the party.[3] The second major factor in evaluations of the old regime is personal experience with the process of transformation. The following graphic shows the extent to which the hopes and expectations originally associated with the establishment of a democratic regime were fulfilled. This link was most direct in the Czech Republic (see Table 21).

Retrospective assessment of communism has remained stable in the Czech Republic and Poland over the period surveyed. In Slovakia, changes were insignificant. Hungarians assessed the defunct communist regime more positively in 1997 than in 1991, but only a diehard minority continued to see it as exclusively positive. The time series of 'New Democracies Barometer' lead to a similar conclusion: in 1991, Hungarians ranked the former communist regime as inferior to the government in place that year. Since 1992, the communist regime's ratings have been on the rise. In fact, in 1995, respondents were more positive about the old regime than about the one expected to be in place by the year 2000. To some extent, this may have to do with the relative liberality of Hungarian communism starting in the 1960s as compared to communist repression in the former Czechoslovakia, as well as with Hungary's having a better supply of material goods than Poland. It is also clearly related to the economic difficulties (relatively low economic growth rates since 1991, sharply falling real incomes) and to pessimistic forecasts for present and short term developments.[4] Because the present is so gloomy, the past now appears brighter than it did then. Even a differentiated and retrospectively nostalgic view of the communist era does not mean, however, that people hope for a return of the former regime. In 1995, the lowest point of morale in Hungary, only 19 percent of those asked favored a return to communism (Rose and Haerpfer, 1996).

Table 22: Evaluations of communism in East-Central Europe (1991-1997)

a) All things considered, communism had... (In Percentage)	Czech Republic					Slovak Republic					Hungary				Poland			
	91	92	93	95	97	91	92	93	95	97	91	92	95	97	91	92	95	97
- mostly or only bad sides.	29	25	28	23	25	15	15	14	12	7	8	5	4	4	17	16	15	14
- good and bad sides.	68	72	69	74	67	80	78	78	81	83	85	89	76	78	76	72	79	79
- mostly or only good sides.	3	2	2	3	7	3	6	7	7	9	5	4	18	13	4	8	4	4
- No answer	1	1	1	-	1	1	1	0	-	0	3	2	1	5	3	4	2	2

b) Positive evaluation of the former communist regime (scale of +100 to -100)	Czech Republic				Slovak Republic				Hungary				Poland			
	91	92/93	94	95	91	92/93	94	95	91	92/93	94	95	91	92/93	94	95
(In Percentage)	23	29	23	25	44	48	50	45	51	68	58	62	34	42	37	23

Source: 'Politischer Kulturwandel' (1991-1997); 'New Democracies Barometer' (1991-1995).

Notes

1. For an in-depth discussion of the situation in Southern Europe, see Morlino and Montero (1995), Linz and Stepan (1996b) and further reading quoted there.

2. Austrian evaluations of national socialism were more critical in 1996 than in 1989 (see Plasser and Ulram, 1993b: 45).

3. A phenomenon also rather well-known in Austria under National Socialism. In 1986, one third of all respondents who said that either they or members of their family had been members of the Nazi Party deny ever having believed in National Socialism (Fessel+GfK, 'Österreichbewußtsein', 1987).

4. The damage done to the collective psyche by Hungary's losing its "pioneering" role in economic transformation to Poland and Czechia should not be underestimated.

8

Political Participation and Integration

8.1. Patterns of Political Communication

Since the regime changes in the new democracies of Eastern Europe, there have been profound changes not only in political and economic structures, but also in the mass media, which have been transformed beyond recognition (Milton, 1997; O'Neil, 1997; Kleinwächter, 1996). Like their counterparts in traditional, Western democracies, political elites have rapidly adapted to the power of the mass media in framing and shaping politics (Jakubowicz, 1996).[1] In Hungary, attempts to instrumentalize the media and control the editorial content of political reporting resulted in fierce conflict and an openly waged power struggle in 1993. In Slovakia, similar skirmishes are still going on (Hallenberger and Krzeminski, 1994). Workable and acceptable rules of communication are being established to settle such issues as the state's potential to interfere with the editorial content of news reporting and the opposition's right to equal access to and fair representation in the media (Downing, 1996). In this section, we concentrate on three questions:

1. Are there country-specific differences in the *use* of political sources of information?
2. How *intensively* are each of these sources used?
3. What is the subjective *credibility* of mass media?

In all five countries studied, television is by far the most important source of political information. Roughly 70 percent of Czech, Hungarian and Polish citizens get most of their political news from TV. Television is slightly less dominant only in Slovakia, where 18 percent of those asked said they listen to the radio for political information. Only 20 percent of respondents in all countries gave newspapers as their primary source of political knowledge.

Table 23: Primary source of political information (1995)

Where do you get most of your information on political developments in your country? In Percentage	CZ	SK	H	PL	SLO
Television	70	54	71	70	62
Daily newspaper	20	23	24	20	20
Radio	7	18	2	7	12
Conversation	2	5	2	2	3

Source: 'Politischer Kulturwandel' (1995).

Statistics on the frequency of recourse to particular sources of information show more accentuated country-specific differences. Roughly 60 percent of Czech and Hungarian respondents say they watch the evening news on television (nearly) every day. In Slovakia, Poland and Slovenia, the corresponding figure is 45 percent. These rates are more or less equivalent to percentages polled in Austria and West Germany. Czechs and Hungarians are the most adamant followers of political news reported in daily papers: approximately 30 percent claim they read reports on domestic affairs (nearly) every day. In contrast, only ten percent of Poles do so; this is by far the lowest percentage of all the East-Central European countries polled. About one third of Austrian and East German respondents said they rely on newspapers for information on national and local politics. Only one in four West Germans regularly reads the domestic politics pages.[2]

Table 24: Sources of political information (1995)

Percentage of those who ... (nearly) every day	CZ	SK	H	PL	SLO
Watch the evening news on TV	61	42	62	48	45
Read about domestic politics in a daily newspaper	30	27	34	10	20

Source: 'Politischer Kulturwandel' (1995).

Everywhere but in the Slovak Republic, television is considered by far the most *trustworthy* source of information. Two thirds of Hungarian and Polish respondents regard television as their most reliable source, compared to only 36 percent in Slovakia, where 31 percent consider daily newspapers particularly trustworthy. Figures for Slovenia are by and large identical with those for Austria.

Table 25: Most trustworthy source of political information (1995)

What is your most reliable source of information on political topics? In Percentage	CZ	SK	H	PL	SLO	A
Television	48	36	62	67	51	53
Radio	6	15	10	8	12	13
Daily newspaper	31	31	11	11	19	13
Political magazines	7	5	6	5	5	6
Conversation with relatives/friends	8	14	9	7	1	10

Source: 'Politischer Kulturwandel' (1990-1995); 'Politischer Kulturwandel in Österreich' (1996).

The mass media play an especially important role in the consolidation process because the confidence gaps which exist between citizens and political institutions are often wide, the structures of political integration are deficient, and the need for orientation is acute. The mass media construct political reality through their reporting; they supply situational interpretations and provide insights into the practice of democratic competition, for example the acceptance of democratic rules and conventions by competing elites. The mass media are therefore decisive in shaping citizens' conceptions of politics and democracy. Their capacity for political and democratic socialization largely depends on whether or not citizens trust them. In the countries surveyed, trust in the media varies considerably, and this allows for (indirect) conclusions regarding the autonomy and efficacy of mass media systems.

Table 26: Trust in mass media (1995-1997)

Percentage of those who trust the mass media (answers of 5, 6 or 7 on a scale of 1-7)		
	1995	1997
1. Czech Republic	59	32
2. Slovenia	51	-
3. Hungary	45	39
4. Poland	44	40
5. Slovak Republic	39	36

Source: 'Politischer Kulturwandel' (1995-1997).

In the Czech Republic and in Hungary, the mass media hold top positions in the hierarchy of institutional trust. In these countries, trust focuses on the media, which in turn must compensate for the lack of confidence in central democratic institutions such as the parliament or political parties. In the Slovak Republic and Slovenia, on the other hand, there is significantly less trust in the media. Restrictions based on power politics and attempts by governing elites to manipulate the media seem to have limited its compensatory potential.[3] Such practices can also destroy trust, an underdeveloped and largely untapped resource in postcommunist democracies (Sztompka, 1995). In the former East Germany, for instance, the mass media – and particularly television – enjoyed an unusually high reputation for credibility at the height of reunification. Gabriel has since reported (1996: 261) a dramatic loss of media reputation following an onslaught of criticism very similar to that in West Germany and Austria. The latest trend data indicate further widespread losses of confidence in the mass media. In the Czech Republic, only 32 percent of respondents indicated their trust in the media in 1997, and palpable skepticism *vis-à-vis* the media has also been on the increase in Hungary and Poland.

8.2. Getting Involved in the Political Process: Interest and Participation

Interest in politics – as an indicator of citizens' cognitive involvement in the political process – is allocated a key role in empirical theories of democracy which assume that a democracy "can only work if its citizens have a keen interest in politics, a high level of information and a highly developed capacity for judgement" (Gabriel, 1994b: 101). Analyses and data series culled in Western democracies, however, do not produce a uniform pattern of political involvement. "The empirical evidence shows that there are widely divergent levels of political interest between countries and that the level of interest within countries changes between time points" (Gabriel and Deth, 1995: 410). The situation is similarly inconsistent and contradictory in postcommunist democracies. After a phase of extraordinary mobilization, there is now a marked tendency towards demobilization; after an unusual activation of political attention to regime change, interest in politics is now either sharply declining (the Czech Republic and Slovakia) or stagnating at an already low level (Hungary and Poland) (see Table 27).

About half of all Czechs, Slovaks and Hungarians either keep their distance from politics or show no interest. In Poland, the share of politically disinterested individuals is 45 percent; in Slovenia, 41 percent. Political interest in East Germany is much stronger in comparison: the 1995 figure, in fact, is only slightly below that of West Germany. Austria's share of politically disinterested individuals was 28 percent in 1996.[4] Declining political interest has also meant a concomitant decline in citizens' willingness to take action. In the four postcommunist societies studied, participation rates have been falling sharply since 1991. That year, 35 percent of respondents in the Czech Republic said they had recently attended a political meeting, but the figure fell to 15 percent in 1995. There has also been a corresponding decline in participation in citizens' groups. In 1991, 36 percent of Czech respondents had worked with others to solve problems in their local communities, while only 15 percent had done so in 1995. A similar decline in participation is also evident in the Slovak Republic. In Hungary, on the other hand, activity rates remained stable throughout the time period studied, and participation in protests such as demonstrations actually increased. Poland's already low level of political activism continued to decline after 1991. Participation in Slovenia is lower than in the other four countries, with the exception of local initiatives in which 16 percent of the population took part in 1995 (see Table 28).

Table 27: Political interest (1990-1995)

Interest in politics, in percentage	CZ	SK	H	PL
Very keen or keen interest				
1990	39	34		
1991	26	23	14	12
1992	19	18	7	12
1993	22	22		
1994	11	10	11	12
1995	9	10	19	12
Moderate interest				
1990	41	40		
1991	57	52	40	35
1992	57	53	34	34
1993	54	53		
1994	44	45	37	31
1995	43	42	30	42
No or hardly any interest				
1990	20	26		
1991	17	23	43	51
1992	24	29	59	51
1993	22	25		
1994	34	35	52	56
1995	48	48	52	45

Source: 'Politischer Kulturwandel' (1990-1995).

A comparison of levels of political participation in the new democracies with those in Austria, West Germany and Switzerland tends to relativize the impression of widespread cognitive exhaustion and weariness in postcommunist societies (Plasser and Ulram, 1993b). The rates of political participation in the Czech Republic, Slovakia and Hungary largely correspond to those of consolidated democracies. In 1989, personal contact with politicians was the only form of participation more common in the German-speaking nations than in the new East-Central European democracies. Given postcommunist societies' comparatively deficient structures of participation, political actors' inability to deal with political integration, and their traditional cultures of participation that for decades followed the rules of "democratic centralism", however, the degree and intensity of political participation in those countries do not indicate a retreat from political realities. In his trend analyses of the former East German participatory orientations, Gabriel (1996) arrived at a similar conclusion, namely that "minor differences between East and West notwithstanding, patterns of participation primarily resemble each other. Since 1991, there has been no evidence of widening gaps anywhere" (ibid.: 287f.).

Table 28: Development of political participation (1991-1995)

Percentage of those who	CZ		SK		H		PL		SLO
	91	95	91	95	91	95	91	95	95
Attended a political meeting	35	15	29	17	17	18	13	7	9
	-20		-12		+1		-6		*
Cooperated with other citizens to solve local problems	36	15	30	17	20	16	13	6	16
	-21		-13		-4		-7		*
Took part in a political rally	27	15	23	10	5	11	9	3	5
	-12		-13		+6		-6		*
Contacted politicians in order to discuss political issues	9	4	7	7	8	9	5	3	6
	-5		+-0		+1		-2		*
Did volunteer work for the election campaign of a party or candidate	9	4	8	5	6	8	5	1	3
	-5		-3		+2		-4		*
Were involved in a confrontation with the police	3	1	2	2	1	4	3	1	2
	-2		+-0		+3		-2		*

Source: 'Politischer Kulturwandel' (1990-1995).

Table 29: Participation in political activities by country

Percentage of those who have participated in the past or who "often" or "sometimes" participate by	CZ	SK	H	PL	SLO	A	D-W	CH
	95	95	95	95	95	96	89	89
Attending a political meeting	15	17	18	7	9	13	19	11
Cooperating with other citizens to solve problems of the local community	15	17	16	6	16	14	20	17
Contacting politicians in order to discuss political issues	4	7	9	3	6	12	11	15
Working as a volunteer in the election campaign of a party or candidate	4	5	8	1	3	4	8	5

Source: 'Politischer Kulturwandel' (1990-1995); Plasser and Ulram (1993a: 20); Austrian data in 'Politischer Kulturwandel in Österreich' (1996).
Note: D-W = West Germany

8.3. Political Efficacy and Civic Orientations

Orientations toward the input structures of the political system are an important part of a country's political culture. Attitudes towards participatory aspects of politics concern, among other things, "the self-image of citizens as active and influential participants in the political process (internal efficacy) and the belief in the openness and accountability of political leaders toward the population (external efficacy)" (Gabriel, 1994a: 118f.; 1994b: 36f.). Studies on the initial stages of democratic transformation and current data both show that citizens' participatory orientations and their belief in their own civic competence are still underdeveloped in the new democracies. "The spirit of dawning democracy stands in stark contrast to the apathy, resignation, exhaustion and feelings of powerlessness which dominate the political-psychological climate in the new democracies" (Plasser and Ulram, 1992a: 18). 'Times Mirror' data from 1991 confirm the existence of a strong, widespread conviction in East-Central Europe that the individual has no power or political influence. This belief is clearly stronger than anything comparable in traditional democracies (Kaase, 1994a: 98f.). Subsequent studies also confirmed the prevalence of despondent self-images and predominantly passive role conceptions among citizens of new democracies. Data indicate overwhelming feelings of political inefficacy which are in turn related to passivity, a lack of civic engagement and a disinterest in politics (Plasser and Ulram, 1993a: 38f.). The image which emerges is that of a demobilized society (Rose, 1995), although comparisons with relevant data on participative orientation in traditional democracies soften the image somewhat.

On the basis of data taken from 'Politischer Kulturwandel in Ost-Mitteleuropa' (PKOM), it is now possible to analyze the development of civic orientations between 1991 and 1995. The following section focuses on three questions:

1. Have active participatory orientations become stronger or weaker in the time period studied?

2. Have evaluations of the responsiveness of political elites and authorities become more positive or more negative over time?

3. Have the differences between the dominant civic orientations of consolidated democracies and those of new democracies narrowed, or has the subjective political 'competence gap' widened over time?

In *Civic Culture,* their classic comparative study of political culture, Almond and Verba created a now-famous indicator to measure external efficacy, i.e., subjective evaluations of political competence. We used it to measure the degree to which respondents feel that they could influence the actions and decisions of governing elites. The following table gives the percentages of individuals whose responses indicated active civic orientations.

External efficacy has become weaker over time in all the countries for which we have trend data except Poland. Compared to 1991, feelings of political powerlessness have increased particularly in Hungary, Slovakia and the former East Germany. Even the modest increase in Poles' sense of political competence remains *de facto* within the margin of statistical error. The situation seems relatively stable in the Czech Republic, where external efficacy is stronger than in the other four new democracies surveyed. Again, however, a comparison of these findings with those for Western democracies tends to put the data into perspective (see Table 31).

Table 30: Trends in external political efficacy (1991-1996)

Rejection of the statement: "People like me have no influence on what the government does."						
In Percentage	CZ	SK	H	PL	SLO	D-East
1991	22	20	19	11		23
1992	24	23	10	8		
1993	23	22				
1995	20	14	12	14	13	20
1996						17
PPD (1991-1995/96)	-2	-6	-7	+3	*	-6

Source: 'Politischer Kulturwandel' (1990-1995). East German data (1991-1996) in Gabriel (1996: 282).
Note: PPD = percentage point difference

In the United States and Switzerland, both "classic" democracies with specific mentalities and traditions of civic culture, active civic orientation is taken for granted. It is by no means widespread everywhere else, not even in most countries of Western Europe. In spite of social and economic welfare, exceptional education resources, and a wealth of opportunities to wield influence and participate, only certain segments of the populations of the highly industrialized information societies of Western Europe consider themselves involved citizens who have a real impact on the political process. In comparison, the figures on external efficacy in the former East Germany and the Czech Republic do not appear as low as the percentages initially suggest. There is more cause for concern in the increasing political resignation and passivity of Slovaks and Hungarians, since this trend points to *latent* tensions, conflicts and barriers between the political culture and the political structures in place. A comparison of additional indicators of civic orientation reveals one problem specific to the transformation of political culture in Hungary: only 22 percent of Hungarians (compared to an average of 50 percent in other reform nations) believe that they have a good understanding of the important problems of their country. In Austria, where the political culture has traditionally been characterized by a lack of active civic orientations (Plasser and Ulram, 1993a), the figure was 55 percent in 1996 (see Table 32).

Table 31: External political efficacy in international comparison

Rejection of the statement: "People like me have no influence on what the government does."		
1. Switzerland	46	(1992)
2. USA	46	(1996)
3. Netherlands	38	(1988)
4. West Germany	33	(1995)
5. Austria	32	(1996)
6. East Germany	20	(1995)
7. Czech Republic	20	(1995)
8. Slovak Republic	14	(1995)
9. Poland	14	(1995)
10. Slovenia	13	(1995)
11. Hungary	12	(1995)

Source: 'Politischer Kulturwandel' (1995); 'Politische Resonanz' (1995); 'Politischer Kulturwandel in Österreich' (1996); Plasser and Ulram (1993b); Gabriel (1996); The National Election Study (1996).

There are fewer and smaller discrepancies in evaluations of people's subjective view of their qualification to participate in the political process. Only 20 percent of the citizens of reform countries consider themselves sufficiently well informed and knowledgeable to participate. In comparison, the Austrian figure was 43 percent in 1996. In 1995, barely one in three Slovenes and Slovaks, one in five Czechs and Poles, and one in six Hungarians considered themselves capable of holding a political position. Again in comparison, 36 percent of Austrians felt that they could meet the challenge of professional politics. In juxtaposing East-Central European and Austrian data, it becomes clear that the citizens of postcommunist societies cannot be expected to fulfill the normative requirements of "civic competence" when even the citizens of traditional Western democracies, with the exception of Denmark and Luxembourg, still fall short of meeting these demanding criteria.

Table 32: Civic orientations compared (1995)

Agreement in percentage	CZ	SK	H	PL	SLO	A
I believe I have a good understanding of my country's problems.	45	42	22	48	45	55
I consider myself sufficiently qualified to take part in the political process.	20	20	20	24	20	43
I think I could do well in a political position.	20	30	16	20	31	36
I believe that I am better informed than most people about current political matters.	17	21	18	22	19	27

Source: 'Politischer Kulturwandel' (1995); 'Politischer Kulturwandel in Österreich' (1996).

An overview of select indicators of democratic support and civic orientation in the five reform countries points to different dynamics of political culture in each of them. Over the period studied, civic orientations among Czech citizens were already clearly approaching those empirically verified in Austria, and other key civic orientations also more or less matched Western European averages. The exceptions were diffuse support for democracy as a form of government and external political efficacy, both of which were weaker in the Czech Republic than in Austria. Slovak civic orientations were likewise moving toward the norms of the Western democracies despite obvious contradictions and some signs of attrition. The same can be said of Slovenia, though not without substantial further qualification. Polish civic orientations became more widespread or at least more stable over time, whereas Hungarian trends indicated a gradual weakening of active civic participation potential and resources in a political culture overshadowed by resignation and reluctance (see Table 33).

The input dimension of political culture includes not only the awareness of external efficacy, which is based on respondents' subjective evaluations of their potential to influence politics and the opportunities they have taken to do so, but also perceptions of elite responsiveness. While questions about responsiveness often stimu-

Table 33: Indicators of civic orientation in comparison (1995)

In Percentage	CZ	SK	H	PL	SLO	A
a) Preference for a multiparty system	94	87	72	73	78	97
b) Preference for democracy as a form of government	74	66	67	65	59	90
c) Interest in politics	52	52	49	54	58	71
d) Positive evaluation of own insight into political matters	45	42	22	48	45	55
e) Competent participatory orientation	20	20	20	24	20	43
f) Subjective political competence	20	14	12	14	13	32

Source: 'Politischer Kulturwandel' (1995); 'Politischer Kulturwandel in Österreich' (1996).

late latent frustrations because of their loaded wording, over time they nevertheless provide input on the development of anti political stereotypes. For decades, cycles of disgruntlement with parties or politicians and sweeping criticism of political elites have been mainstays of political reality in Western democracies. It is therefore hardly surprising that these negative factors are now also discernible in postcommunist democracies. In this context, Kaase (1994a) refers to the "political folklore" which appears to be an integral part of the complex practices of decision-making in democratic systems. "Still, it may make quite a difference whether such orientations exist in a firmly established democratic polity or in one that is just beginning to seek public support" (ibid.: 99).

Our data indicate a sharp rise in anti political sentiment in Hungary and an increasingly critical attitude toward elites in Poland, both starting from an already high level. "Political folklore" or disappointment with elites has spread in every reform country except the Czech Republic, where criticism of elite responsiveness remained relatively moderate and stable over the period studied. A similar pattern emerges in evaluations of the responsiveness of members of parliament: the image is that of a general mood of resignation also evident in Austria and, to a lesser extent, in Germany (Plasser and Ulram, 1993b) (see Table 35).

Table 34: Criticism of elite responsiveness (1991-1995)

Percentage of those who agree with the statement: "Politicians don't really care what people like me think."	CZ	SK	H	PL	SLO	A
1991	68	83	67	82	-	-
1995/6	68	84	83	89	85	67
PPD (1991-1995)	+-0	+1	+16	+7	-	-

Source: 'Politischer Kulturwandel' (1990-1995); 'Politischer Kulturwandel in Österreich' (1996).
Note: PPD = percentage point difference

Democratic consolidation in Southern Europe during the early 1980s followed a similar pattern. In Spain, Portugal and Greece, there was growing general support for the democratic system, and prodemocratic attitudes became more widespread. "At the same time, we also find pervasive feelings of political alienation and cynicism, an intense distrust of elites, and limited legitimacy of parties, together with a low level of sympathy for them, in spite of the acknowledgment of their role in politics" (Morlino and Montero, 1995: 259).

8.4. Party Identification and Networks of Political Integration

In the new democracies, the phase immediately following regime change was characterized by "floating" and shapeless party systems, scant party affiliations, a fundamental inability of collective actors such as unions or associations to integrate and mobilize, and, finally, by exceptionally low levels of trust in central institutions of the political system.

> The current dearth of diffuse trust in democratic institutions is also due in part to the absence of workable intermediary

Table 35: Indicators of political efficacy in comparison (1995/96)

In Percentage	CZ		SK		H		PL		SLO		D-E		D-W		A		USA	
	+	-	+	-	+	-	+	-	+	-	+	-	+	-	+	-	+	-
Internal efficacy																		
"People like me have no influence on government."	80	20	86	14	87	12	85	14	86	13	75	20	64	33	68	32	43	46
"Sometimes politics is so complicated that people like me can hardly understand what is going on."	79	21	77	23	77	22	83	16	78	21	58	36	57	39	58	42	60	30
External efficacy																		
"Members of Parliament quickly lose touch with their constituents."	85	14	90	10	87	11	88	10	86	10	68	19	69	24	85	13	n.a.	n.a.
"Politicians don't really care what people like me think."	68	31	84	16	83	16	89	10	85	12	68	24	66	28	67	26	n.a.	n.a.

Source: 'Politischer Kulturwandel' (1995); 'Politische Resonanz' (1995); 'Politischer Kulturwandel in Österreich' (1996); Gabriel (1996); The National Election Study (1996).
Note: '+' = agreement; '-' = rejection.
D-E = East Germany, D-W = West Germany

> mechanisms. The new democracies suffer from an intermediary vacuum: parties are still not firmly established in the society; organized interests are weak; and networks, both those of integration and those which represent of societal concerns, have no clear profile. The overwhelming majority maintains a skeptical or distant attitude toward parties and the choices they offer (Plasser and Ulram, 1992b: 399).

Three years later, little had changed (Rose, 1995).[5] The affiliations between voters and parties were still loose and fragile, and there were no reserves of affective loyalty to mitigate disappointment and frustration. The overwhelming majority of citizens in the new democracies must be considered "non-aligned voters" (Plasser and Ulram, 1994b; Wyman *et al.*, 1995: 538f.)

Table 36: Trends in party identification (1991-1995)

Percentage of those who identity with a particular party or political movement	CZ	SK	H	PL	SLO
1991	31	25	25	15	
1992	36	35	23	13	
1993	36	31			
1994	38	30	22	15	
1995	30	35	18	18	15

Source: 'Politischer Kulturwandel' (1991-1995).

Party identification, the long-term affective proximity or affiliation with a particular political party, gradually increased in the Czech Republic between 1991 and 1994 before falling to previous levels the following year, when only 30 percent of Czech voters had emotional leanings toward any particular party. Trends in Slovakia have been more discontinuous and volatile: a distinct increase in party identification between 1991 and 1992 was followed by a two-year slump. Between 1994 and 1995, the figures rose once again, this time to 35 percent. In Poland, the low level of party identification changed very little throughout the period surveyed, while in Hungary it has weakened steadily since 1991. Party identification was lowest of all in Slovenia, where in 1995 only 15 percent of respondents had emotional ties with a particular political party. Although most Western democracies have experienced a constant erosion of affective ties to parties, there are still significant differences in their levels of party identification.

Table 37: Party identification in international comparison

Percentage of respondents with party identification		
1. West Germany	68	(1994)
2. East Germany	59	(1994)
3. Austria	57	(1996)
4. Slovak Republic	35	(1995)
5. Czech Republic	30	(1995)
6. Russian Republic	25	(1994)
7. Poland	18	(1995)
8. Hungary	18	(1995)
9. Slovenia	15	(1995)

Source: 'Politische Einstellungen und politische Partizipation im vereinigten Deutschland' (1994); 'Politischer Kulturwandel' (1990-1995); 'Politischer Kulturwandel in Österreich' (1996); Russian data in Plasser and Ulram (1996b).

There has also been little change in the percentages of party members over the period studied. Poland and Hungary show the lowest levels of party-political organization, while figures for the Czech Republic, Slovakia, and Slovenia exceed even those of East and West Germany. Austria is a special case: despite continuous erosion, party membership figures are still exceptionally high (see Table 38).

From an analytical perspective, it is interesting to compare the organization cultures of the 'old' communist regimes (in retrospect) to those of the new democratic systems. In the five reform countries surveyed, 10 to 13 percent of respondents (only 6 percent in Poland) admitted to having been members of the former Communist Party. If we include family members who, according to the respondents, were also in the Party, then the share of former Party members in the new democracies surveyed ranges from one fifth (Poland) to more than one third (Slovakia) of the population.

Table 38: Party membership in comparison

Percentage of those who are members of a political party or movement		
1. Austria	14	(1996)
2. Slovak Republic	7	(1995)
3. Czech Republic	6	(1995)
4. Poland	6	(1995)
5. Slovenia	4	(1994)
6. West Germany	3	(1994)
7. East Germany	3	(1995)
8. Hungary	2	(1995)

Source: 'Politische Einstellungen und politische Partizipation im Vereinigten Deutschland' (1994); 'Politischer Kulturwandel' (1990-1995); 'Politischer Kulturwandel in Österreich' (1996).

Table 39: Former Communist Party membership, countries compared

In Percentage	CZ	SK	H	PL	SLO
Respondent was a Party member	12	13	12	6	10
Family members were Party members	21	24	11	14	19

Source: 'Politischer Kulturwandel' (1995).

An analysis of these data reveals the continuity of state socialist cultures of organization (Rose, 1995; Kopecky, 1995). Even in the new democracies, former Communist Party members are much more likely to join a party than respondents who had no previous Communist Party affiliation. "In other words, it is largely the same people active in politics now as were active in the communist period" (Wyman *et al.*, 1995: 539). Thus, most party members in the Czech and Slovak Republics are recruited from the ranks of former Communist Party members, while this pattern is much less obvious in Hungary and Slovenia and barely perceptible in Poland.[6]

Of the five countries surveyed, Poland has by far the weakest structures of political integration. Strong allegiance to the Catholic Church (56 percent attend Mass regularly) and to the evening news on television (almost 48 percent watch it daily) have so far compensated for modes of integration which political parties, interest groups and trade unions normally provide. Structures of political integration are similarly deficient and rudimentary in Hungary, where televised newscasts (viewed almost daily by 62 percent of respondents) and unions (though with significantly less contact) are also the main sources of political orientation and integration. In Slovenia, too, political integration comes mostly from the mass media and – to a much greater extent than in Poland or Hungary – from trade unions. In the Slovak Republic, more and more people are already taking advantage of the integrative structures offered by political parties and unions. Ties to the Catholic Church are also traditionally strong in Slovakia, whereas only seven percent of Czechs profess church affiliation. Today, the main factors of political integration in East-Central Europe include exceptionally high exposure to TV news, relatively strong union membership, and still-moderate party affiliations.

Table 40: Continuity in cultures of organization (1995)

Percentage of party members	CZ	SK	H	PL	SLO
Of all respondents	6	7	3	2	6
Of former Party members	22	23	8	4	15
Of non-Party members	3	6	2	2	6
Share of current party membership who are former Communist Party members	69	53	43	26	36

Source: 'Politischer Kulturwandel' (1995).

Table 41: Indicators of political integration in comparison

In Percentage	CZ	SK	H	PL	SLO	A
a) Party identification	30	35	18	18	15	57
b) Strong party identification	5	8	3	4	4	18
c) Party membership	6	7	3	2	6	13
d) Union membership	25	33	19	9	32	22
e) Strong ties to Church	7	29	10	56	14	18
f) Regular viewing of TV news	61	42	62	48	45	47

Source: 'Politischer Kulturwandel' (1990-1995); 'Politischer Kulturwandel in Österreich' (1996).

*) Respondents who say they attend religious services (nearly) every week.

Structures of political integration in an established democracy are, on the other hand, much more differentiated and heterogeneous. In Austria, for example, the most common links are emotional affinity to a particular political party and strong affective and/or organizational ties to parties or unions. Religious networks of social and political integration are comparatively insignificant. For many Austrians, institutional ties provide a source of information which balances out the symbolic second-hand reality presented by the mass media.

Notes

1. Ágh (1996b) describes three types of attitude characteristic of East-Central European party elites: "(1) The new party leaders were intellectuals and they had an extreme sensitivity and vanity concerning the press, the opinions of their former colleagues and those of their own former socio-cultural milieu. (2) The new parties were engaged in a cultural war among themselves because of their vague and over-ideologized programs and 'tribal', subcultural political profiles. In this cultural war, the media was extremely important for them. (3) The intensive media contacts compensated the party leaders for the organizational deficit and for the weakness of the national organization with its missing communicational channels within the party. In fact the media messages substituted for the regular party meetings" (1996b: 251).

2. German data from 'Politische Einstellungen und politische Partizipation im Vereinigten Deutschland' (1994). Austrian figures taken from 'Politischer Kulturwandel in Österreich' (1996).

3. With regard to the realities of media politics in German-speaking democracies, Pöttker (1996) argues that "parties' intensive efforts to use public broadcasting for their own purposes (...) contribute to the declining image of politics" (1996: 156).

4. East and West German data from the study 'Politische Resonanz' (1995). 1996 data on Austria from 'Politischer Kulturwandel in Österreich' (1996). See also list of empirical sources.

5. On structural and formation difficulties in postcommunist party systems, see, among others, Segert and Machos (1995); Wightman (1995); Lewis (1996); and *Party Politics*, Special Issue on 'Party Politics in Eastern Europe', no. 4/1995. Nohlen and Kasapovic (1996) and Merkel and Sandschneider (1997) offer a survey of electoral systems in new Eastern European democracies.

6. On ideological attitudes and orientations of former Communist Party supporters in reform countries, see Evans and Whitefield (1995a).

9

Societal and Political Cleavages

The founding elections of 1989 and 1990 were primarily anticommunist plebiscites. In the Czech and Slovak Republics and Poland, though not in Hungary, they introduced the second stage of party building: the organizational differentiation of ideologically heterogeneous and hitherto largely unstructured "civic movements" (Mangott, 1992: 104). Despite the crystallization of milieu parties, especially among Catholic subcultures (Enyedi, 1996), most political parties were weakly rooted in society and suffered from internal factionalization. Party systems were, on the whole, highly fragmented (Segert and Machos, 1995). Riviera (1996) tested the two hypotheses of party building in postauthoritarian systems: the "defreezing" of earlier, fundamental societal cleavages latent or frozen under the communist regime *vs.* "modes of transition" away from authoritarian systems. He concluded that both factors were less important in East-Central Europe than in Western and Southern Europe. "Rather it is the legacy of the communist authoritarian period – the command economy, the decomposition of civil society and the imposition of one-party rule – that seems to have the greatest effect on the early stages of party formation" (ibid.: 195). Kitschelt (1995a, b) developed a multifactor model for ideal typical conflict configuration in the various postcommunist societies. In the following section, our goal is to arrive at an empirical identification of the societal and political cleavages which prevail in East-Central Europe. To do so, we proceeded in two consecutive steps:

1. On the basis of interviews with experts, we assigned the parties of each country to "party families" according to their programmatic orientation; specifically, communist or radical Left, social democratic or socialist, liberal, conservative/Christian democratic, (majoritarian) nationalists and minority parties.[1] In a few cases (the HZDS in Slovakia or the Peasant Party of Poland)

this was not possible, so those parties are handled separately. For Poland, it was also appropriate to distinguish between social democrats of the postcommunist SLD and those of the former opposition, the UP.

2. We then compared the electorates of each party family with regard to organizational or attitudinal continuities between the old and the new regimes, images of democracy, ideological and political orientations, and distinctive sociodemographic features. If respondents indicated either no party preference or preference for one of the parties excluded under point 1, we also excluded them from this analysis. In each of the four countries, these respondents comprised about one fourth of the representative sample. As a further qualification, we would add that the sample sizes only allow for tentative conclusions, especially concerning sociodemographic variables.[2]

9.1. The Heritage of the Communist Past

The history of party formation – in particular, the creation of some parties as the successors of earlier communist or communist satellite parties and others as the successors of the opposition or dissident movements – has left its mark on the electorates of East-Central European parties or party families (Wightman, 1995). The constituencies of each of the communist successor parties studied[3] contain an unusually high percentage of former CP or communist suborganization members. Conversely, the share of former Party members in other parties does not exceed the population average.[4] Those who vote for communist successor parties (with the exception of Hungarian social democrats) generally have a more positive view of the old system in retrospect. Not surprisingly, this tendency is much stronger among supporters of communist or radical Left parties than among those who vote for communist successor parties now turned socialist or social democratic. Supporters of conservative, Christian democratic or liberal parties are far more critical of the old regime. A similar pattern is repeated in the assessment of system change: in comparison to other parties, the communist successor parties have a significantly higher proportion of voters who are very disappointed with system change or who never expected anything good to come from it, Hungarian social democrats again being the exception.[5] Just the opposite is true of conservative,

Christian democratic and liberal parties: they attract fewer thoroughly disillusioned voters (see Table 42).

9.2. Patterns of Ideological and Social-Political Cleavages

Organizational continuity and historical memories are factors which divide the voters of former communist parties from those of other political groups. In contrast, the line between unconditional supporters of pluralist democracy and those whose attitudes toward it are ambivalent or negative, separates partisans of communist or radical Left groupings from supporters of all other political associations. In Hungary, the Czech Republic and the Slovak Republic, fewer than half of the supporters of communist successor parties are committed democrats. In Hungary and Slovakia, where the former Communists split into two parties, one communist and one social democratic, a majority of social democrats embrace democracy and the multiparty system. It is also evident, however, that unconditional support of democracy is strongest among conservative/Christian democratic (the Czech Republic, Hungary) and liberal (Poland, Slovakia) voters.

In the Czech Republic, the gap between egalitarian and state-centered sociopolitical orientations puts communists and social democrats on one side and conservatives and Christian democrats on the other, with liberals somewhere in the middle. Religious cleavages divide polities along similar lines. An ideological self-positioning of party voters forms a left-to-right spectrum (communists, social democrats, liberals, conservatives/Christian democrats) equivalent to that in Western Europe.[6] In Slovakia, the sphere of conflict is multidimensional: state-interventionist and egalitarian orientations are dominant among communist voters and, to a lesser degree, among social democrats and HZDS supporters.[7] Conversely, individualist orientations prevail among conservative/Christian democratic and liberal voters as well as among nationalists, i.e., they are less likely to accept the dominant role of the state. The process of Slovak nation building is a second major area of conflict: hard-core nationalists and, to a lesser extent, HZDS and communist party supporters, defend a concept of nation which is based on a common language and therefore excludes minorities. The diametrically opposed concept of a pluralistic nation state[8] is most frequently en-

Table 42: Communist Party membership, evaluations of communist regimes and system change; parties or party families in East-Central Europe (1995)

PPD (percentage point difference to respective national average)	Former Party members	CP regime evaluation		Very disappointed about regime change or had no positive expectations
		pos.	neg.	
Czech Republic				
CP/radical Left*)	+21	+4	-19	+20
Social Democrats	-1	0	-17	-2
Liberals	-4	-3	+2	0
Conservatives/Christian Democrats	-5	-2	+15	-17
Slovak Republic				
CP/radical Left*)	+20	+18	-4	+4
Social Democrats*)	+21	+3	-5	+9
HZDS	-2	+1	-3	-1
Liberals	-3	-7	+3	-10
Conservatives/Christian Democrats	-10	-4	+13	-17
Nationalists	-1	-2	+6	-3

PPD (percentage point difference to respective national average)	Former Party members	CP regime evaluation		Very disappointed about regime change or had no positive expectations
		pos.	neg.	
Hungary				
CP/radical Left*)	+13	+16	-4	+12
Social Democrats*)	+11	+2	-1	-6
Liberals	-1	-2	-3	+1
Conservatives/Christian Democrats	-4	-4	+7	-11
Nationalists	-6	+1	0	+4
Poland				
Social Democrats (SLD)*)	+6	+2	-6	+14
Social Democrats (UP)	+4	-1	-3	+7
Peasant Party (PSL)*)	0	+5	-9	-3
Liberals	-2	-3	+9	-12
Conservatives/Christian Democrats	-2	-1	+4	-5
Nationalists	-1	-2	+5	-5

Source: 'Politischer Kulturwandel' (1995).

* Indicates party immediately succeeding the former Communist Party or one of its satellites.

countered among national minority (especially Hungarian) party voters. Communists, social democrats, and HZDS and liberal supporters, finally, exhibit a markedly secular political orientation, whereas conservatives and Christian democrats naturally tend to the opposite view.

There are majoritarian nationalist parties of relevant size and impact in Slovakia, Hungary and Poland (McIntosh, Abele McIver and Abele, 1996). Both Slovak and Hungarian hard-core nationalists are among the economic losers in the transformation process. Belief in an exclusive concept of nation is also more widespread among Hungarian nationalists than among Hungarian voters at large.[9] Hungarian and Polish nationalists display a pronounced law and order orientation, whereby the lines which separate these groups from their conservative and Christian democratic counterparts are less clear than comparable lines in Slovakia. When asked about their socio-economic orientations and ideological self-descriptions, supporters of expressive (majoritarian) nationalism in Poland and Slovakia place themselves tend towards near the right end of the political spectrum; in Hungary, in the center (see Figure 5).

In Poland and Hungary, conservative and Christian democratic voters show strong statist and egalitarian orientations similar to those of social democrats. Liberals, with their individualistic and market orientation, take the opposing standpoint. Political secularism is most marked among communists in Hungary and social democrats (SLD and UP) in Poland; the same applies to church attendance. In both countries, the political sphere is multidimensional, with an axis of socioeconomic conflict and a cleavage between religious and secular approaches to politics.

PKOM's findings concerning social political and ideological orientations on the level of party families generally confirm Kitschelt's typology (1995a, b):

- In the Czech Republic, there is a single, largely uniform and dominant axis of conflict which corresponds to the left-right dichotomy.

- In Poland and Hungary, there are at least two such axes, i.e., one between statist-egalitarian and liberal-individualist orientations, and another between secular and religious or traditionalist orientations.

Figure 5: Hard-core nationalists in East-Central Europe (1995)

Dominant or outstanding characteristics	SK	H	PL
Personal economic situation since the beginning of system change	Worse	Worse	*
Concept of nation	Common language	Common language	Nation state
Ideological self-positioning	Right	Middle of the road (*)	Right
Socioeconomic orientation	Individualistic, market oriented	* *	Individualistic *
Concept of society (law and order)	*	Rigid	Rigid
Sociodemographics of the electorate	Young Poorly educated Male	Older Poorly educated Male	Young * Male

Source: 'Politischer Kulturwandel' (1995).
*) No significant deviation from respective national average.

- In Slovakia, ethnic conflict has become a third major cleavage line. It must be added, however, that the HZDS, which competes with communists and social democrats for credibility in the field of "economic populism", cannot be considered a postcommunist successor party.

On the level of parties, the pattern is more diversified. This can be attributed to the "heritage" of parties dating back to communist rule and to strategic political decisions by party elites (i.e., "social democratization" versus adherence to a communist or radical left identity in CP successor parties). In the case of Slovakia, the specific conditions of nation building have been important in shaping the new political landscape. Thus the HZDS's special position derives,

Table 43: Ideological and social-political cleavages – parties and party families in East-Central Europe (1995)

a) = in percentage b) = mean average ($\bar{x}$ 1-5) c) = mean average ($\bar{x}$ 1-11)		Church attendance (a):		Sociopolitical orientations (b):			
	Committed democrats (a)	Regular	Never/no religious affiliation	Secular[**)]	Egalitarian[**)]	Egalitarian[**)]	Left to right self-positioning (c)[***)]
Czech Republic							
CP/radical left[*)]	48	6	68	1.9	2.6	2.0	4.9
CP/radical left	73	4	71	1.9	2.6	1.9	5.5
Social Democrats	71	7	63	1.9	2.9	2.4	7.2
Liberals	84	14	58	2.3	3.3	2.5	7.8
Conservatives/Christian Democrats	71	10	62	2.2	2.9	2.2	6.7
CZ total							
Slovak Republic							
CP/radical left[*)]	44	25	31	1.6	2.5	1.6	4.5
Social Democrats[*)]	60	29	37	1.6	2.8	1.7	4.1
HZDS	59	32	17	1.7	2.7	1.7	6.3
Liberals	74	40	25	2.0	3.2	2.1	6.5
Conservatives/Christian Democrats	66	58	16	2.8	3.3	2.1	7.4
Nationalists	71	34	26	2.0	3.1	2.1	6.6
SK total	61	36	31	2.0	2.9	1.9	6.1
Hungary							
CP/radical Left[*)]	30	8	46	2.3	2.6	2.2	5.1
Social Democrats[*)]	58	18	36	2.6	2.9	2.4	4.6
Liberals	61	12	36	2.6	3.3	2.4	5.8
Conservatives/Christian Democrats	68	34	15	3.1	2.7	2.3	6.2
Nationalists	51	17	24	2.7	2.9	2.3	5.6
total	57	17	30	2.6	2.9	2.3	5.6

a) = in percentage b) = mean average ($\bar{x}$ 1-5) c) = mean average ($\bar{x}$ 1-11)		Church attendance (a):		Sociopolitical orientations (b):			
	Committed democrats (a)	Regular	Never/no religious affiliation	Secular**)	Egalitarian**)	Egalitarian**)	Left to right self-positioning (c)***)
Poland							
Social Democrats (SLD)*)	51	63	6	2.0	2.6	2.0	4.4
Social Democrats (UP)	50	64	6	2.0	3.0	1.9	5.8
Peasant Party (PLS)*)	46	87	0	2.4	2.9	2.0	6.1
Liberals	67	70	3	2.5	3.2	2.3	7.4
Conservatives/Christian Democrats	55	84	2	2.8	2.7	2.0	7.7
Nationalists	57	69	0	2.4	3.0	2.1	7.7
PL gesamt	54	74	3	2.4	2.9	2.1	6.5

Source: 'Politischer Kulturwandel' (1995).
*) Successor of former CP or satellites.
**) Political secularism, egalitarianism, statism; the closer to 1.0 on the scale, the stronger the orientation.
***) Scale from 1.0 (=extreme left) to 11.0 (= extreme right).

factors of political contingency aside, from its having been "twice removed" from the center to the periphery (secession of the "Slovak periphery" from the "Czech center", and concentration of HZDS voters in the "periphery" of Central and Eastern Slovakia). In Poland, the cleavage between rural areas and industry is manifested institutionally (and socio-structurally) in the Peasant Party, the PLS (Riviera, 1996).

9.3. Sociodemographic Characteristics of Parties and Party Families

With a few important exceptions, the sociodemographic differences which distinguish the various groups of voters in East-Central

Europe are *less* significant than they are in most of Western Europe. The most striking differences are, as a rule, between those who vote for communist or radical left parties and those who vote liberal or (in the Czech Republic) conservative. Liberal or conservative party preferences are exceptionally well established among entrepreneurs, white collar workers and civil servants; higher incomes and higher education are also indicative of liberal or conservative leanings. These parties (exception: Slovak liberals) have a relatively urban profile and an unusually large following of young voters. Communist parties, on the other hand, find few supporters among professionals and white collar workers; instead, they draw on a considerable reservoir of working class votes in Hungary and Slovakia and tend to attract senior citizens in the Czech Republic. Procommunists are, in other words, an aging population, especially in the Czech Republic. Support for all communist parties generally comes from low income groups and, except in Slovakia, from voters with the least education.

Significant country-specific differences are evident among social democratic voters. This is primarily true of blue collar workers, who constitute a large portion of the social democratic electorate in the Czech Republic and a relatively small one in Hungary and Slovakia. The social democratic parties of Slovakia and Poland already have a relatively large following of white collar workers and are gaining in popularity among average and higher income groups. There are also significant differences in the education levels of social democratic voters: they are above average in Poland (especially among UP voters), only slightly lower in Hungary and distinctly low in Slovakia. With the exception of the UP in Poland, social democratic parties also have an overproportionally high number of older voters, while young voters are underrepresented. Hungarian, Czech and Slovak social democrats tend to have strong links with trade unions.

The Slovakian HZDS draws most of its votes from lower income and lower education strata and from older citizens. As mentioned above, there is a remarkable degree of regional concentration in economically less-developed parts of the country. In Poland, the PSL claims roughly 40 per cent of the agricultural vote; its constituency is therefore clearly defined as coming from the lowest income brackets. Conservative and Christian democratic voters are, in contrast, much more heterogeneous. In Poland, they attract a considerable share of union labor but generally fail to appeal to better-educated voters. In Hungary, this situation is exactly reversed. Slovak Christian democratic voters do not, from a sociodemographic point of view, stand out among the population at large. The majoritarian nationalist vote is invariably male dominated: voters are relatively young in Poland and Slovakia, but older than average in Hungary. With all due caution – in view of the relatively small study samples – we can draw the following conclusions:

- The sociodemographic structures of Czech parties and party families come closest to those of Western Europe.

- Liberal parties find strong support among the current and potential "winners" of transformation (except in the Czech Republic, where the ODS has managed to capitalize on this vote).

- Communists and, to some degree, nationalists predictably attract an exceptionally large share of transformation "losers".

- The characteristics of cleavage structures (at least how patterns of societal conflict relate to party allegiance) are still relatively weak and hard to define.

9.4. Value Orientations and Political Priorities

A longing for material security, social integration and harmony, a strong sense of duty, and an emphasis on personal relationships within a circle of friends and family members: these were central values during the early stages of transformation in East-Central European societies. Throughout the decades of material shortages, restricted personal spheres, and retreat into niches of privacy impervious to ideological and organizational penetration by the Communist regime, there was little scope for hedonism, dynamic lifestyles and ostentatious individualism.

In addition to these common features, there were considerable country-specific differences rooted in social and cultural traditions. The strong religious and traditionalist mold of Polish society, for example, distinguished it from the secularized societies of Hungary and the Czech Republic. The materialistic tendencies, new trends toward individual self-realization, and "familial privatism" of Hungarian society contrasted with the humanist-idealist images of society prevalent in the former Czechoslovakia (Bretschneider, 1991). As advances in economic, social and political transformation were

Table 44: Political issues and problems (1991, 1995)

Political tasks considered most important:... Spontaneous, unprompted answers Total of 1st, 2nd and 3rd responses (in percentage)*	ČSFR Spring 1991		ČSFR Summer 1991		CZ 1995		SK 1995		H 1991		H 1995		PL 1991		PL 1995
• Economy, economic reform	54		39		38		57		39		57		34		
• Unemployment	15	}78	23	}73	9	}53	37	}97	18	}82	45	}125	22	}68	}88
• Inflation	9		11		6		3		25		23		12		
• Living standard, wages and salaries					15		31				36				
• Social problems, material security, health system, problems of social groups		}19		}24	50	}65	48	}79		}23	34	}70		}34	}31
• Crime					41		19				8				
• Corruption, law enforcement		} 4		}11	6	}47	4	}23		} 2	5	}13		} 1	}18
• Democracy, civil rights, political stability, performance of parties and politicians, etc.		12		18		37		38		7		19		9	38
• Environmental issues		-		12		10		3		0		2		1	1
• Foreign policy, international diplomacy		nc.		nc.		9		10		nc.		4		nc.	21

Source: Fessel+GfK, 'Lebensstile in Ost-Mitteleuropa' (1991) for H, PL (1991) and CSFR (Spring 1991); 'Politischer Kulturwandel' (1991, 1995) for CSFR (Summer 1991) and CZ, SK, H, PL (1995).
*) selected problem areas
Note: n.c = not comparable.

made, the set of social or political issues and tasks facing each country became more and more differentiated. In countries already burdened with massive economic and social problems[10] (especially prevalent in Hungary and Slovakia), other issues soon took on new importance. These included political stability, the making of laws, and the performance of parties and politicians. In the Czech and Slovak Republics, rising crime rates and inadequate public safety were added to the list of serious problems (see Table 44).

Pervasive feelings of existential insecurity and imminent danger have certainly had an impact on value priorities. In all the countries surveyed, there is an increasing demand for rights and laws to be respected. In the former Czechoslovakia, there is also a need for security in the most comprehensive sense of the term: cultural change and the collapse of former lifestyles are apparently seen as more serious and dangerous than in Hungary and Poland, where societies enjoyed a degree of cautious and informal pluralism even under the old regime. Because Hungarians and Poles have a different perception of "social dangers" than Czechs and Slovaks, they consistently place a high value on the concept of a "humane society" (see Table 45).

Data taken from 'Vergleichende Nationalismus-Studie' (1995) (cf. Weiss and Reinprecht, 1996) indicate that Poles and Hungarians are more alarmed than Czechs and Slovaks about the levels of social and political conflict in their respective countries.[11]

In view of this attitude, the high degree of rigidity in East Central Europe, i.e., the demand for tough law enforcement policies for serious crimes, is less surprising: two thirds of respondents have an uncompromising *law and order orientation*, while only one fifth have a more tolerant and understanding attitude. State-interventionist attitudes prevail throughout East-Central Europe. The opposite attitude – emphasis on more individual initiative and problem solving – is rarest in Slovakia and most frequent in Hungary. *Egalitarian orientations*, i.e., preference for more equality and justice, if necessary at the expense of individual liberty, are more or less on a par with those in Austria, the neighbor to the west.[12] In absolute terms, however, these orientations are only slightly more prevalent than the opposite preference for more individual liberty at the expense of social equality. The same is true, more or less, of *ethnocentric views*. In Poland and the Czech Republic, the concern that Western businesses, lifestyles and mentalities are already too influential and are threatening familiar ways of life is only slightly

Table 45: Changes in value priorities: East Central Europe (1991-1995)

I wish to live in a society in which... Total of 1st and 2nd responses (in percentage)	CZ 91	SK 91	H 91	PL 91	CZ 95	SK 95	H 95	PL 95	SLO 95	A 96
• law and order are respected.	45	33	45	47	65	58	55	61	35	20
• tradition is valued and respected.	27	25	20	21	58	52	17	25	16	17
• human beings are more important than money.	48	53	49	49	27	36	44	50	30	50
• hard work is rewarded with success.	39	42	39	40	22	27	43	25	52	33
• citizens are involved in all decisions.	23	24	27	24	22	19	27	24	27	29
• there is openness to new ideas and intellectual progress.	16	20	14	11	7	7	13	11	20	20

Note: Figures given = percentage of respondents who ranked this answer either first or second.
Source: 'Politischer Kulturwandel' (1990-1995); 'Politischer Kulturwandel in Österreich (1996).

stronger than its diametrical opposite: the belief that Western modes of thinking and ways of life, and not just Western capital, should play an increasingly important role in the country.

There are also distinct country-specific differences in a number of other sociopolitical orientations. *Political secularism* (operationalized as the reaction to the extensive influence of the Church or churches in public and political matters) predominates in the Czech and Slovak Republics. A majority in Poland also opposes such interference, while protest against the impact of the Church on society is weakest in Hungary. The Polish attitude, although perhaps surprising, can be explained by the fact that nearly three out of four Poles sense (and obviously disapprove of) a high level of conflict between church and state, while this problem is considered much less important in other countries, especially in Hungary (Fessel+GfK, 'Nationalismus in Ost-Mitteleuropa' 1995).

Authoritarianism meets with substantial approval only in Poland. An overwhelming majority of respondents in the three other East-Central European countries and Austria advocates the greatest possible degree of public participation in all political and economic matters. Ecological orientations are rarest in Poland and Hungary, and most frequent in the Czech Republic and Slovakia. This also testifies to the relative importance the public places on environmental issues in the Czechoslovakian successor states. There is, however, no clear data on environmental concerns in East-Central Europe as a whole: the environment, in sharp contrast to all other values and orientations, failed to elicit a concrete response from 41 to 48 percent of all respondents.

In conclusion, the findings on sociopolitical orientations show

- that there are some distinct country-specific differences, i.e., the countries of East-Central Europe do not form a homogeneous cluster.
- that there are, as a rule, either no serious divergences from Austrian patterns or that divergences have no common direction (except for social rigidity), i.e., the figures do not indicate any systematic divergence between East and West Central Europe.

Table 46: Sociopolitical orientations in comparison

Mean average on a scale of 1 to 5	CZ 1995	SK 1995	H 1995	PL 1995	SLO 1995	A 1996
State interventionism (1,00)	2.24	1.91	2.32	2.06	2.07	2.50
Egalitarianism (1,00)	2.93	2.91	2.92	2.86	3.29	2.99
Rigidity (5,00)	3.79	3.73	3.89	3.82	3.46	3.00
Authoritarianism (5,00)	2.09	1.94	2.30	3.22	2.02	2.06
Ethnocentrism (5,00)	3.19	3.03	3.04	3.23	2.72	nc.
Political secularism (1,00)	2.18	2.00	2.63	2.39	1.93	nc.
Environmentalism (5,00)	3.57	3.40	2.83	2.74	2.78	3.06

Source: 'Politischer Kulturwandel' (1995); 'Politischer Kulturwandel in Österreich' (1996).

* Figures in parentheses indicate the position of each item on a five point scale. For details on operationalization, see the documentation of variables in the appendix.

n.c. = not comparable.

Notes

1. Wherever the number of respondents was lower than N=50 for a particular party, i.e., in the case of all national minority parties except in Slovakia, the party was not included in the analysis. The same is true of parties which could not be assigned to any of the above categories.

2. An in-depth sociodemographic analysis would either require a representative sample of several thousand interviewees in each country (since subgroups would otherwise be too small) or at least a cumulation of declared party preferences from several surveys. Unfortunately, no such data were available.

3. Since the Polish Peasant Party had its own organization and members under communist rule, it was – predictably – impossible to establish a correlation.

4. Postcommunist government parties' share of votes amounted to 20.4 percent in Poland (1994) and 33 percent in Hungary (1994). Direct successors of former communist parties received 10.3 percent of the votes in the Czech Republic (1996), 10.4 percent in Slovakia, and 13.6 percent in Slovenia (1992). East Germany's PDS won 19.8 percent of the votes in the "new federal states" (1994).

5. For details on the Hungarian Socialist Party, see Ágh (1996b, c). On communist successor parties in general, see Evans and Whitefield (1995); Ishiyama (1995); and Waller (1995).

6. On the right end of the political spectrum, the dominant party (ODS under V. Klaus) is conservative, not Christian democratic.

7. Hnuti za socialni spravedlnost (Movement for a Democratic Slovakia) under Prime Minister V. Meciar.

8. The concept of nation state is used here to indicate identification with a country regardless of the individual's cultural background or language.

9. Compare this to the existence of strong Hungarian-speaking minorities in the neighboring countries of Romania, Slovakia and Serbia.

10. Differences between countries can be perceived not only in the percentages contained in the following tables, but also in the detailed responses (within each category) not given here for reasons of space. Thus the category of "social problems" in the Czech Republic often yields references to transformation and to relatively specific difficulties of the systems of social and material security; in Hungary and Poland, on the other hand, such references remain on the level of generalities.

11. Fessel+GfK, 'Nationalismus in Ost-Mitteleuropa' (1995); preliminary results of this project were published in Weiss and Reinprecht (1996). In Poland, there is also a close connection between the longing for a "society in which human beings are more important than money" and church attendance or religious orientation. In other words, emphasis on this item increases with exposure to the Catholic faith and the social and political doctrines derived from it.

12. It should be added that egalitarian and state interventionist orientations have lately increased in Austria. This indicates a reversal of the trend of recent years, possibly as a reaction to symptoms of economic crisis and budget cuts. Cf. Ulram (1990) and the latest data of 'Politischer Kulturwandel in Österreich' (1996).

10

Attitudes towards Economic Transformation

The transformation still taking place in the new democracies of East-Central Europe comprises several interwoven and, to some degree, simultaneous processes. Changes have occurred in the political system, and the remodelling of the economic order has also brought about adaptations in social structures. In the case of Slovakia and Slovenia, the establishment of new nation states has meant disentangling national economies from the larger and more or less integrated economic systems which preceded them.

10.1. Point of Departure and Overall Economic Development

Even though all five East-Central European countries studied here were among the most highly developed economies of the former "socialist camp", there are considerable differences between them.[1] Figures for the Czech Republic and Slovenia show that they have the highest levels of economic development, the highest standards of living, and the fewest internal disparities. In general, however, we would like to point out that some of the standard macroeconomic tools used to assess economic power or general economic and social conditions produce inadequate or misleading results. If, for example, we calculate gross domestic product on the basis of exchange rates, the total GDP of Poland, Hungary, Slovenia and the former Czechoslovakia together is roughly that of Austria, a country with only about one eighth the population of the other countries combined. Similarly, if we limit our focus to average income calculated on the basis of exchange rates, we will underestimate standards of living. These statistics fail to take into account the fact that East-Central European households cover large portions of their costs of living by tapping into sources other than regular job earnings.

Table 47: Gross domestic products (GDPs) in comparison

Country	Year	Nominal GDP in billions of US dollars, exchange rate basis	Per capita GDP in thousands of US dollars, exchange rate basis	Per capita GDP in thousands of US dollars, purchasing power parity
Total OECD	1991	17.142	20,3	17,8
OECD-Europe	1991	7.248	17,3	14,7
EU countries	1991	6.271	19,0	16,4
USA	1991	5.611	22,2	22,2
Germany	1991	1.574	24,6	19,5
France	1991	1.199	21,0	18,2
Italy	1991	1.151	19,9	16,9
UK	1991	1.010	17,6	15,7
Switzerland	1991	232	33,8	21,8
Sweden	1991	237	27,5	16,7
Austria	1991	164	21,0	17,3
Spain	1991	525	13,5	12,7
Portugal	1991	69	7,0	9,2
Greece	1991	71	6,9	7,8
Czech Republic	1992	35*)	2,2	5,8-7,0
Slovak Republic	1992		1,9	4,8-5,8
Hungary	1992	37	3,4	5,4
Poland	1992	72	1,9	4,2

Sources: a) Österreichisches Institut für Wirtschaftsforschung, 'WIFO-Monatsberichte', 1993/5 for OECD countries; b) World Bank, 'Alton Project, International Comparison/ICP, EIU' quoted from 'Ost-Wirtschaftsreport', no. 9/30.4.1993, on East-Central Europe; c) *Business Central Europe*, vol. 1/May 1993, for East-Central Europe.
* Official separation of the CSFR into the Czech and Slovak Republics on January 1st, 1991: 70.1 percent of the total GNP was generated by Bohemia and Moravia, 29.9 percent by Slovakia.

A comparison of per capita GDP according to purchasing power parities in the early 1990s shows that the GPD of the Czech

Republic was roughly one third that of Austria; in Poland it was approximately one fourth, and in Hungary and Slovakia, it lay somewhere between the two. Thus the Czech figures are still lower than but comparable to those of economic "latecomers" in the West such as Greece and Portugal.

If we look at household furnishings, we find that while East-Central European homes still have fewer expensive consumer durables than their Western European counterparts, they have achieved a relatively high level of comfort. In many cases, both the quality and quantity of consumer goods have increased sharply in recent years.[2] The overall picture is one of economies not yet wealthy but developed[3], and of standards of living which correspond to those of the European OECD nations during the 1960s and 1970s.

The final decade of "real socialism" was one of severe economic crises: in Poland and Hungary, even official statistics[4] showed declining incomes. The progressive deterioration of living conditions was due at least in part to the rapid decline in the quality of health care systems and the environment (Rupnik, 1989). The nightmare economies inherited from the old system, the virtual collapse of trade with the Eastern bloc following the dissolution of the COMECON trade agreement, and the numerous problems of transition to market economies resulted in drastic drops in GNPs in 1990 and 1991, shrinking real incomes, exponential inflation, and, except in Bohemia and Moravia, sharply rising unemployment. On the macroeconomic level, however, economic reform soon took effect: Poland had already increased its GNP in 1991, and the other three countries followed suit in 1994. Even today, in every country but Poland, the GNP is still lower than it was shortly before the onset of system change.[5] The situation currently seems to be most critical in Hungary, where relatively low growth rates coincide with continuously-falling real incomes, both in part the result of the government's consolidation policy. In Poland and Hungary, inflation was falling and unemployment was stable in 1995, but both remained high (Czachór, 1995; Inotai and Nötzold, 1995). That year, unemployment was low only in the Czech Republic (Handl, Konecný *et al.*, and Poeschl, 1995). Economic transformation has progressed furthest in Poland, the Czech Republic and Hungary (Altmann and Ochmann, 1995). The establishment of market economic institutions is also advancing at a relatively rapid pace.

Slovenia experienced a palpable economic downturn that began immediately following independence in 1991 and lasted until the summer of 1993 (Mencinger and Suppan, 1995). During that period, there was more than 14 percent unemployment and triple-digit inflation. Since 1993, the GNP has again been on the rise, and inflation has fallen rapidly. Unemployment remains high, however, and it will take several more years for real incomes to regain their 1991 levels.

Table 48: Economic indicators: East-Central Europe (1989-1997)

Change from previous year	1989	1990	1991	1992	1993	1994	1995	1996 **)	1997 ***)
Poland									
GDP	+0,2	-11,6	-7,6	+1,0	+3,8	+5,0	+7,0	+4,9	+5,2
Real incomes	+12	-25	0	-3	-3	+1	+4	+3	n.d.
Consumer prices	+251	+586	+70	+43	+35	+32	+29	+21	+18
Unemployment	*	6,3	11,8	13,6	16,4	16,0	14,9	14,0	13,5
Hungary									
GDP	+0,7	-3,5	-11,9	-4,5	-0,8	+2,9	+1,5	+1,5	+3,5
Real incomes	+1	-4	-7	-1	-4	+7	-11	-2	n.d.
Consumer prices	+17	+29	+35	+23	+23	+19	+28	+24	+19
Unemployment	*	1,7	7,4	12,3	12,1	10,4	10,2	10,5	10,2
Slovak Republic									
GDP	+1,4	-0,4	-16,1	-6,0	-4,1	+4,8	+7,0	+5,0	+4,1
Real incomes	+1	-6	-25	+9	-4	+3	+3	+3	n.d.
Consumer prices	+1	+11	+61	+10	+23	+13	+10	+7	+6
Unemployment	*	1,6	11,8	10,4	14,4	14,8	13,1	11,5	10,5
Czech Republic									
GDP	+1,4	-0,4	-14,2	-7,1	-0,9	+2,6	+4,8	+5,0	+4,7
Real incomes	+1	-5	-24	+10	+4	+4	+7	+8	n.d.
Consumer prices	+1	+10	+57	+11	+21	+10	+10	+9	+8
Unemployment	*	0,6	4,1	2,6	3,5	3,2	3,5	3,3	4,0

Source: Wiener Institut für internationale Wirtschaftsvergleiche; Brezinski (1996: 143ff.); The Economist Intelligence Unit.
*) Unemployment rates: percentage, not change.
**) Estimated
***) Expected. n.d. = no data available.

In 1992, the overwhelming majority of citizens in East-Central Europe felt that the economic situation had deteriorated in comparison to the previous year. Three years later, however, 38 percent of Czechs and 34 percent of Poles noticed an improvement, while

Table 49: Assessment of the economic situation and job security: East-Central Europe (1992-1995)

In Percentage	Czech Republic				Slovakia			Hungary				Poland			
	92	93	94	95	92	93	95	92	93	94	95	92	93	94	95
Compared to one year ago, the economic situation is ...															
much better	2	3	2	3	2	0	2	1	0	0	1	1	2	1	2
somewhat better	17	21	24	35	7	5	20	10	8	11	9	7	14	21	32
unchanged	18	21	29	35	11	14	34	12	18	25	17	10	19	24	34
somewhat worse	35	34	27	19	35	45	28	35	35	30	33	26	27	24	15
much worse	21	16	11	5	35	29	12	39	35	28	34	52	32	19	7
No response	7	5	7	5	9	7	4	3	4	6	3	4	6	11	10
Over the next 12 months, there will be...															
much lower unemployment	1	1	0	1	1	0	2	0	1	1	2	1	2	1	2
somewhat lower unemployment	3	5	7	7	5	5	20	0	6	17	9	3	5	11	23
no change in unemployment	11	15	28	52	5	11	39	3	13	25	20	5	9	19	35
somewhat higher unemployment	46	49	42	29	38	47	22	32	46	35	42	34	39	35	15
much higher unemployment	34	21	13	3	42	26	6	59	28	12	16	49	38	20	4
No response	5	9	10	8	9	11	11	6	6	11	10	7	7	14	21

Source: 'Politischer Kulturwandel' (1995); Fessel+GfK, 'Wirtschaftsklima in Ost-Mitteleuropa' (1992-1995).

35 and 34 percent, respectively, saw no change. Only a quarter of respondents in both countries continued to perceive a decline in 1995. While somewhat more cautious in their assessments, Slovaks were clearly more positive in 1995 than they had been three years previously. Hungarians, in contrast, continued to be pessimistic: in 1995, only one in ten respondents saw any improvement in the economic situation, while two in three believed there had been either a slight or sharp decline.

Developments in the labor market have been more promising: in 1992, 90 percent of Hungarians and 80 percent of Poles feared a substantial increase in unemployment, and a majority of Czechs were also uneasy about what the coming year would bring. In the years which followed, however, these attitudes became increasingly positive. In 1995, one in four Polish respondents expected unemployment to decline, as compared to one in five who feared a further rise; in Slovakia, hopes and fears roughly balanced each other out; and in both countries, one third of respondents believed unemployment would continue to be stable. When jobless figures remained consistently low in the Czech Republic between 1992 and 1995, pessimism dropped by half. The exception was once again Hungary: the slightly more hopeful and optimistic mood of 1993 and 1994 reversed itself a year later, when a majority of Hungarians said they expected further increases in unemployment. Even so, their outlook for the future in 1995 was less gloomy in than it had been in 1992.

10.2. Subjective Evaluations of Personal Economic Situations

In times of accelerated economic and social change, macroeconomic data paints an incomplete picture of daily reality because it does not include important information about individuals and families. In 1995, unemployment directly affected three out of ten households in Hungary and Slovenia, one out of four in Poland, one out of three in Slovakia, and one out of five in the Czech Republic. There were similar country-specific differences with regard to the duration of unemployment: in 1995, two thirds of all unemployed Hungarians and 60 percent of Poles and Slovenes were out of work for more than six months. In Slovakia, the average period of unemployment was considerably shorter. The Czech Republic enjoyed the lowest jobless rate of all the countries compared here, and most Czechs who were unemployed found new jobs relatively quickly.[6]

Fear of unemployment is strongest in Hungary and Slovakia: a majority of working people in both countries worry about losing their jobs. Half of all Polish respondents and 40 percent of Czechs admit to feeling threatened by unemployment. The fear of job loss is thus three times higher in the Czech Republic than in neighboring Austria, although the two countries have similarly low unemployment rates. In all East-Central European countries, unskilled workers are among those most threatened by the problems of the labor market. Skilled workers, civil servants, the growing numbers of the self-employed, and the traditionally large group of independent farmers in Poland are significantly less worried about their jobs. In 1993, apprehension about the future reached its peak in East-Central Europe; since then, the number of workers fearful of losing their jobs has fallen in each of the countries studied. The decrease is least noticeable in Hungary, where a relatively large number of the self-employed worry about their livelihood, and where the correlation between being currently unemployed and the fear of future unemployment is the weakest (see Table 50).

Looking back over the years, we can appreciate just how severe – albeit different in each country – the disruption in the economic situation of households has been. With the onset of system change, the financial situation of families deteriorated, first and most drastically in Poland. The Polish population only began to feel a gradual improvement in the macroeconomic situation in 1995. The same is generally true of Slovakia, though to a much lesser extent. Hungarians are most critical of the development of their family income. In the Czech Republic, evaluations of economic development trends are more positive, and for the year 1995, there was even a sense of relative improvement. Nevertheless, more than half a decade after the onset of reform, the financial situation of families was seen as worse or much worse than five years previously. In 1995, 71 percent of Hungarians, 58 percent of Slovaks, 50 percent of Poles, and 40 percent of Czechs declared that they were worse off than before. Only nine percent of Hungarians, 16 percent of Slovaks, 20 percent of Poles and 28 percent of Czechs noticed an improvement in retrospect (see appendix for table).[7]

Many workers find that a steady job does not provide them with enough income to support a family. Even in the two pace-setting reform economies, only 44 percent of Poles and 54 percent

Table 50: Fear of unemployment: East-Central Europe (1991-1995)

Workers' fears about losing their jobs In percentage	Hungary			Poland			ČSFR	Slovakia		Czech Republic		Austria
	91	93	95	91	93	95	91	93	95	93	95	1995*)
Very worried	29	30	25	22	32	15	21	29	15	12	8	(2)
Rather worried	34	33	31	33	25	32	42	44	46	40	33	(12)
Not worried	26	33	44	34	32	51	27	26	38	44	59	(76)
No response	11	1	0	11	11	1	0	1	-	4	-	(9)

Source: Fessel+GfK, 'Vertrauen in Finanzinstitutionen in Ost-Mitteleuropa' (1993); 'Politischer Kulturwandel' (1991, 1995).
*) Different question wording: respondents who fear their job is greatly at risk or somewhat at risk.

of Czechs polled in 1995 said that their regular income was sufficient. The situation is improving somewhat in Poland, but the Czech Republic has been in an economic slump since 1996. Two thirds of all working people in Hungary and Slovakia do not earn enough to make ends meet. They are forced to use their savings, borrow money, work several jobs, or resort to other forms of economic activity (see Plasser and Ulram, 1993a; 1996; Rose and Haerpfer, 1992; 1996)[8]. Of course not all families have these options, so standards of living are deteriorating and poverty is becoming an increasingly widespread phenomenon.[9]

Respondents are, as a rule, very critical when it comes to assessing the economic situation of their own family: eight out of ten Hungarians and nearly two thirds of Slovaks describe it as not very satisfactory or unsatisfactory, and the percentage of extremely dissatisfied Hungarian respondents is remarkably high. Slovaks' views of the family's economic situation have become more critical over time, and Hungarians are particularly depressed about the economy. Corresponding evaluations in the Czech Republic, on the other hand, have been fairly stable and generally positive, with 58 percent describing their family's economic situation as satisfactory. In Poland, there is evidence of an almost linear improvement: between 1991 and 1995, the percentage of "satisfied" respondents doubled, while that of "very dissatisfied" persons dropped by half.

Evaluations of actual standards of living are invariably shaped by an additional subjective component: many people who had high hopes during the initial stages of transition soon found it necessary to modify their expectations and set their sights lower. In the meantime, a majority of respondents in East-Central Europe declare that they have achieved much of what they hoped for in terms of their standard of living, the percentages varying from 53 in Hungary to 71 in the Czech Republic. Responses are very different in the Russian Republic, where most of those polled say that few or none of their expectations have been fulfilled. Over time, there has been more evidence of improvement in standards of living: the predominantly negative assessments of 1991 and 1992 have given way to more positive views in Poland, Slovakia, the Czech Republic, and even in Hungary. Whereas three quarters of all Hungarian respondents complained of unsatisfactory family financial situations in 1991, the number of those who believed few or none of their hopes had been fulfilled had shrunk drastically by 1996.

As to the future, East-Central Europeans polled in 1995 expected the economic situation of their family or household to improve or at least stabilize. The notable exceptions were Hungary, where increasing pessimism about the future hit an all-time low in 1995, and the Czech Republic, where citizens have been exceptionally optimistic from the start. To most people, the future looked brighter in 1995 than it had five years before. The poll showed that 47 percent of Poles, 42 percent of Slovaks and 34 percent of Hungarians expected their family's financial situation to improve within five years, while 29 percent of Hungarians but only 10 percent of Poles, 13 percent of Czechs and 16 percent of Slovaks feared that their standard of living might suffer further decline. The group of resigned individuals who have ceased to believe they will ever attain a level of material comfort has shrunk in all countries except Hungary: in 1995 it consisted of one sixth of Polish and Hungarian, and one tenth of Czech and Slovak respondents. In Slovenia, almost half of all respondents (48 percent) expected their personal economic situation to improve within five years (39 percent expected no change and 13 percent feared a decline), and 31 percent were either already satisfied or hoped to achieve a satisfactory standard of living within that period. Still, one out of five respondents had lost all hope of ever enjoying material security (table see appendix).[10]

For most East-Central Europeans, transition – at least its early stages – has meant considerable economic loss and more worries, especially about jobs, which were more or less guaranteed under the old regime. While various degrees of economic recovery took effect at different times and in specific ways in each country, families did not generally begin to feel it until 1995, and even then only to a limited extent. Everywhere but in the Czech Republic, people still considered the economic situation unsatisfactory, and most Hungarians see it as critical. Again with the sole exception of the Czech Republic, a majority assessed the economic situation of their household as worse in 1995 than shortly before the onset of transition. Macroeconomic data and subjective economic moods alike indicate divergent paths of development in each of the countries of East-Central Europe, and these factors are also reflected in respondents' perception of the future

- In Poland, now that the particularly painful collapse of the early 1990s[11] has been overcome, there is an almost exponential increase of optimism and corresponding improvement in all relevant subjective economic indicators. Expectations for medium-term developments in personal standards of living, however, remain "realistic".

- In Slovakia, patterns of development are less homogeneous. Signs of incipient economic optimism are not as strong there and are subject to frequent setbacks. Hopes for the future are accordingly more cautious.

- In the Czech Republic, the costs of transition have been least palpable. Both the economic conditions and subjective perceptions of them have been more stable, and optimism about the future has tended to be consistently high. Recently, though, the austerity measures of 1997 have clouded the picture, and growth rates for 1997 and 1998 are not likely to meet initial expectations.

- The Hungarian situation is characterized by very slow and lagging macroeconomic recovery. There are also widely held subjective views that the economic situation of families has hardly improved over the years and that economic conditions are stifling and depressing. Economic dissatisfaction is high, and even the future is seen as threatening or uncertain. Hungary is the only country in East-Central Europe in which the number of respondents who expected their personal economic situation to worsen was significantly higher in 1995 than in 1991.

At this point, however, a word of caution against simplifying interpretations of economic and political-cultural attitudinal patterns seems called for. The international comparisons given here should not to be understood as mere "rankings" in which countries, like students, are labeled "gifted", "average", "underachiever", and so on. The real purpose of tracing developments and their heterogeneity is to show how quickly the relative position of each country can change from one year to the next, and how little hastilyapplied labels contribute to an understanding of current situations and perspectives of development.

10.3. Attitudes towards the Economic Order and the Process of Economic Reform

Even in countries with long-established market economies, such as Austria, theoretical reflection and a comprehensive knowledge of how the market works can only provide the basis for an understanding of the economic system. True understanding comes to a large extent from individual, personal experience with the realities of a country's economic system and its effects.[12] At the time when their economies were collapsing, most East-Central Europeans equated the concept of market economy with images of the "rich and successful West" – a stark contrast to the misery of the realities of socialism. The ideological condemnation of capitalism by thoroughly discredited and untrustworthy regimes is also likely to have contributed to the idealization of the market economy, i.e., the tendency to ignore both its drawbacks and its functional prerequisites. In addition, the phase of most radical transition was accompanied by unrealistic expectations[13] of a rapid improvement in individual living conditions.

In the course of economic reform, this understanding of the market economy changed in two important ways. First, individuals experienced market mechanisms and their consequences firsthand, so their own economic system moved into the focus of cognitive reference. Second, the standard of comparison changed, so people no longer judged their own economy only by comparing it to the old system in retrospect; they also judged it on the basis of their original expectations and promises.[14] In 1991, the point of departure for the countries of East-Central Europe was as follows: After a long history of halfhearted attempts at economic liberalization, Hungary had opted for a gradualist course of reform. Poland had a similar history of peremptory economic reform under the old regime, but decided to proceed much more rigorously.[15] The economic transformation which had only recently begun in the former Czechoslovakia was progressing at a different pace in each of the two successor states. East-Central Europeans were generally dissatisfied with the economic system, Slovenes being most critical[16] and Bohemians and Moravians the most positive of all respondents. The emerging economy or economic system fared worse than the previous communist system in popular evaluations in every country except the Czech Republic. At the same time, people placed great hope in the economic system as it would be five years in the future, by which time they expected it to have overcome the present difficulties as well as the deficiencies of the old system (cf. Rose and Haerpfer, 1992).

Table 51: Evaluation of economic systems (1991-1995)

Positive ratings on a scale of -100 to +100 (in percentage)		Czech Republic	Slovakia	Hungary	Poland	Slovenia
a) The communist economy prior to the revolution of 1989	1991	42	61	69	43	39
	1992/93	44	64	75	57	46
	1994	42	74	75	52	48
	1995	52	67	66	34	42
b) The current economic system	1991	57	41	37	31	18
	1992/93	55	34	29	39	36
	1994	66	31	27	50	48
	1995	63	37	26	60	46
c) The economy five years from now	1991	86	77	72	58	75
	1992/93	83	73	69	57	83
	1994	86	73	63	71	73
	1995	82	63	49	80	68
d) PPD* Current system vs. communist economy	1991	+29	-20	-32	-12	-21
	1992/93	+28	-30	-46	-18	-10
	1994	+20	-40	-48	-2	0
	1995	+18	-30	-40	+26	+4
e) PPD* Current system vs. economy five years from now	1991	-29	-36	-35	-27	-57
	1992/93	-28	-39	-40	-18	-47
	1994	-20	-42	-33	-21	-25
	1995	-19	-28	-23	-20	-22
f) PPD* Economy five years from now vs. communist economy	1991	+44	+16	+3	+15	+36
	1992/93	+39	+9	-6	0	+37
	1994	+44	-1	-12	+19	+25
	1995	+30	-2	-17	+46	+26

Source: 'New Democracies Barometer' (1991, 1992/93, 1994, 1995).
*) PPD = percentage point difference.

The social costs of privatization and the all-too-often uncontrolled excesses of capitalism were already obvious in the early 1990s. This was especially true in Poland and Hungary, where criticism was loudest in 1993 despite general support for reform measures (Plasser and Ulram, 1993a). Polish evaluations of the economic system soon showed a remarkable improvement, however, while Hungarian voices became more and more negative. In Poland, the economic past had at first seemed rosier than the present, but the trend reversal which began in 1994 continued the following year. In Hungary and Slovakia, on the other hand, the market economy was still being evaluated much more critically than the old system as late as 1995. In the Czech Republic, the present economic system was judged superior to the previous one throughout the period surveyed. As regards the evaluation of the economic system "five years from now", Poland and Hungary again show diametrically opposed trend patterns. In Hungary, future outlooks are dimming to a point of pessimistic resignation: a past in which "no one had much, but what little they had was theirs" now seems preferable to the present state. In Poland, the outlook for the economic system of the future is so bright that the unlamented past seems even worse than it was. Czechs harbor stable hopes for a better economic future in their republic; the same is true, though to a lesser extent, of Slovenes.

In 1995, the image of the market economy was most positive overall in Poland, while in Slovenia and Slovakia, positive and negative evaluations balanced each other out. According to time series data from the European Union's 'Central and Eastern Eurobarometer' (6/1995), there was increasing Polish criticism of the market economy at first, but assessments subsequently improved. (The 'New Democracies Barometer' also confirmed this.) In other countries, criticism continued to grow. In the Czech Republic, the critical mood of 1995 stands in contrast to the primarily positive view of the current economic system. One explanation for this gap might be that an increasing number of Czechs are finding the reform process too rapid and one-sided. In the spring 1996 elections, the coalition government of Vaclav Klaus lost its absolute majority by a narrow margin, while the number of votes for the Social Democrats increased dramatically. This confirms that many Czechs, unlike their prime minister, would like to see a 'social' modifier added to their market economy.

All across East-Central Europe, market economies and their current workings are generating a fair amount of criticism and dissatisfaction. As in Western Europe, there is a universal longing for a social "shock absorber" to cushion the blow of reform hardship as well as a widespread conviction that the state is fundamentally responsible for the welfare of its citizens (Rose and Haerpfer, 1996: 71; Borre and Scarbrough, 1995). A return to any shape or form of planned state economies is not, however, on the political horizon. It is not on of any government's economic agenda (not even that of Hungary or Poland, where social democratic successors to the former communists were in power until the autumn of 1997), nor does the overwhelming majority of the population wish for it. Admittedly, only a minority advocates an economic system in which the state restricts itself to establishing the economic framework while keeping its distance from sociopolitical issues. Most respondents cherish the ideal of an economic system in which the state and organized interests work together to make important economic policy decisions – a model which they obviously believe is in place in West Central and Northern Europe (Plasser and Ulram, 1993a; 1996).

Table 52: Attitudes towards the market economy (1990-1997)

Creating a market economy an economy largely free of state controls is important (+) or wrong (-) for the future of the country (PPD)	Czech Republic	Slovak Republic	Hungary	Poland	Slovenia
1990	+54	+28	+47	+47	*
1991	+39	+29	+51	+28	*
1992	+23	+15	+39	+33	+36
1993	+15	-4	+21	+29	+2
1994	+11	0	+20	+26	+14
1995	+6	0	+5	+46	+1
1996	+1	-2	+7	+64	+2
1997	-12	-10	-6	+43	±0

Source: 'Central and Eastern Eurobarometer' (1/1990-8/1998).

Notes

1. On difficulties of economic transformation from a macroeconomic point of view, see the articles in Brunner (1996); Knell (1996); Neuhold, Havlik and Suppan (1995). For a theoretical and political analysis, see Balcerowicz (1995). Economic preconditions for EU membership in reform countries are discussed in Weidenfeld (1997). On problems of exogenous strategies of stabilization during transformation processes, see Sand-

schneider (1996).

2. See Fessel+GfK, 'Lebensstile in Ost-Mitteleuropa' (1991, 1996); 'GfK-Zensus' (1991-1996).

3. Cf. also the highly developed educational systems in these countries.

4. Notoriously unreliable because they were systematically manipulated.

5. It should be noted, however, that economic development during the process of transformation is very heterogeneous: for instance, a near-collapse of heavy industry is partially offset by considerable growth rates in the service sector. Brezinski's (1996: 142f) figures for today's GDPs in relation to those of 1989 are: 97 percent in Poland, 94 percent in Slovenia, 86 percent in Hungary, 85 percent in the Czech Republic and 84 percent in Slovakia.

6. Cf. the annual data on the subjective economic situation culled as part of 'New Democracies Barometer' (Rose and Haerpfer, 1996).

7. In some cases, 'New Democracies Barometer' figures for personal economic indicators may be slightly different from those published by Rose and Haerpfer due to the different criteria used.

8. This also explains why the number of incomes per household is high in comparison to Western Europe.

9. Rupnik (1989: 169), however, argues that as early as the 1980s, one quarter of Hungarians subsisted below the poverty line.

10. Cf. Rose and Haerpfer's data in 'New Democracies Barometer' (1995): in the Czech Republic and Slovakia, where, at the beginning of this decade, a majority hoped to succeed in fulfilling their material expectations within the next five years, expectations have since become more pessimistic or, depending on the point of view, more realistic. See also Plasser and Ulram (1993a).

11. This is largely a result of a strategy in economic reform now widely known as "shock therapy".

12. On this point, see Fessel+GfK, 'Wirtschaftspolitische Orientierungen' (1995) for the case of Austria.

13. Not only were unrealistic expectations characteristic of the vast majority of citizens; they were also fed by new Eastern elites and Western politicians (as in the former GDR) for purposes of electoral competition.

14. By way of empirical evidence, the gap between desired and achieved standards of living in the countries studied widened between 1991 and 1992, even though high-quality appliances (increasingly from the West) did find their way into Eastern homes (Plasser and Ulram, 1993a). The enticing world of Western consumerism which lay at their doorstep or filled their living rooms via television turned into a source of sociopsychological stress, since it was omnipresent yet unobtainable for most.

15. On the history of economic reform under the old regime, see, among others, Batt (1991).

16. Not all aspects of the situation in Slovenia, however, can be compared to the situation of other countries. It had only just achieved *de facto* national independence after a brief intervention by the Yugoslav federal army. In addition to war damages, Slovenia also suffered the collapse of its principal market, Yugoslavia.

11

Social Consequences and Evaluations of Regime Change

11.1. Winners and Losers of Transition

System change has not only altered the overall economic situation and subjective economic conditions in East-Central Europe; it has also caused profound changes in social structure. On a macro-societal level, these can be analyzed and described as the emergence of new interest configurations and the dissolution of traditional ones,[1] as increasing societal differentiation or altered relative positions of social groups, and as the development of divergent life-styles and new ways to earn a living. For individuals, this process manifests itself, on the one hand, as a change in their relative social position and the perspectives associated with it, and, on the other hand, as a division of society into "winners" and "losers".

Against the backdrop of an emerging market system and the internationalization of Eastern European economies, it is not surprising that the "winners" include entrepreneurs as well as individuals who have sufficient "cultural capital" to adapt to the new situation (e.g., knowledge of foreign languages). According to conventional wisdom, members of the old nomenclature are also capable of adapting: former managers of state companies are generally considered to have benefited from transformation. To a lesser extent, this also applies to Communist Party functionaries.[2] Also among the winners are civil servants, who are seen as the primary beneficiaries of regime change (especially in the Czech and Slovak Republics) as well as army officers (except in Hungary). In sum, the pillars of the old regime are thought to have secured a place in the sun for themselves, even under the new order.

Conversely, large and important social groups are generally designated as losers of reform; this especially applies to workers, women and retired persons. In considering workers, a clear-cut distinction is usually made between people on public and private payrolls. State workers are counted among the groups who have experienced socioeconomic decline, although only a quarter of them in the Czech and Slovak Republics feel they are now worse off than under the old regime. Private sector employees enjoy a reputation as transformation winners: this attitude is most frequent in the Czech Republic and Poland and least frequent in Hungary, even though a majority there assumes that living conditions have remained stable or improved for workers in the private sector.

As far as subjective self positioning ("people like me") is concerned, there are clearly discernible sociodemographic differences:

- Younger people, those with higher (high school or college) education, urbanites (especially those living in the capitals), white collar workers and civil servants see themselves on the positive side of the scale. The same is mostly true of the self-employed, except for independent farmers in Poland.

- The elderly, retired persons, people living in rural areas and, most of all, blue collar workers believe they are experiencing a significant decline in their social and economic position.

Compared to these stark contrasts, differences of gender are relatively insignificant despite a tendency to count women among transformation losers. Former Communist Party members do not feel that they suffer more social injustice than non-members. Only in the Czech Republic, where "lustration laws" seem to have been implemented more effectively than elsewhere, do former Party members consider their situation exceptionally difficult.

Hungary's group-specific balance of advantages and disadvantages is the most negative overall. In addition, there is a distinct general impression that societal development is uneven and slanted. Two thirds of Hungarian respondents identify a strong tendency toward social injustice, and 55 percent have experienced discrimination as individuals. For the Czech Republic, the figures are 33 and 25 percent, respectively, and Slovakia falls somewhere between the two (Fessel+GfK, 'Nationalismus in Ost-Mitteleuropa', 1995).

Table 53: Winners and losers of system change (1995)

Which of the following groups are better off since the end of communism, and which are worse off? Who are the winners and losers?	Percentage point difference (PPD) Better-worse				
	Hungary	Slovak Republic	Poland	Czech Republic	Slovenia
Private entrepreneurs	+59	+84	+85	+89	+6
People with knowledge of foreign languages	+53	+87	+77	+90	+52
Former managers of state companies	+46	+66	+19	+65	+48
CP functionaries	+26	+32	+8	+24	+4
Civil servants	+19	+72	+28	+74	+46
Army officers	-45	+41	+9	+28	+28
Private sector employees	-5	+4	+29	+42	+6
Employees of state companies	-54	-6	-29	-7	-48
Women	-58	-54	-40	-19	-15
People like myself	-73	-54	-44	-16	-29
Retired persons	-77	-66	-65	-46	-21
Working class people	-92	-86	-76	-51	-78

Source: 'Politischer Kulturwandel' (1995).
*) Difference between figures and 100% = no response or rounded figures. Non-response rates never exceeded five percent except in Slovenia (not included in this table).

11.2. Regime Change: Expectations and Reality

The beginnings of political transformation in 1989 were accompanied by great hopes and expectations that the establishment of democratic order would result in more wealth and social justice, but reality and disillusionment soon set in.[3] As early as 1991, system change had failed to fulfill the hopes of roughly two thirds of East-Central European citizens. Another tenth had never expected anything good to come of it in the first place, and the developments then taking place confirmed their dim prognoses. Those who had supported the Communist Parties and its successor parties were especially bitter,[4] most likely in reaction to the anticommunist plebiscites of the 1989-91 elections and the legitimate vote to relegate the former state parties to opposition benches. Disappointment was highest in all four countries between 1992 and 1993, after which the paths diverged. In Poland, levels of dissatisfaction fell so sharply that in 1997, 37 percent declared that their positive expectations had been fulfilled or even exceeded. The jubilant mood in the Czech Republic in 1995 was crushed by the economic and government crises of 1997. In Slovakia, disappointment was on the rise in 1995 and again in 1997, when only 13 percent of respondents gave a positive overall assessment. In Hungary, finally, there were hardly any changes in the (relatively high) levels of disappointment between 1994 and 1997. In a 1997 poll, only 13 percent of Hungarians and Slovakians declared that their hopes had come true (see Table 54).

The diversification of patterns applies not only to levels of disappointment or fulfilled expectations, but also to group-specific differences of opinion. In 1995, a majority of all Hungarians, regardless of profession, were disappointed or skeptical. In the Czech Republic, divergences according to profession were not only more marked, but also continued to increase over time. Nevertheless, some identical patterns can be discerned across (geographic) borders: the self-employed, skilled workers and civil servants are most likely to believe that their expectations have been fulfilled; to a lesser degree, this is also true of those with a higher education. The percentage of dissatisfied or fundamentally skeptical respondents is the highest of all among blue collar workers. In contrast to this sharp disparity, distinctions along the lines of age and gender are relatively insignificant, although a general sense of disappointment is rarer among the younger generation than among older persons. Finally, there is also an obvious correlation between an individual's perception of his or her own economic situation and social opportunities on the one hand, and his or her level of disappointment on the other: The more negative the perception of the former, the more pronounced skepticism and dissatisfaction is likely to be. This correlation is stronger in the Czech Republic than in any of the other countries studied.[5]

Table 54: Regime change — expectations and reality (1991-1997)

My personal expectations of regime change have been...	Czech Republic						Slovak Republic						Hungary						Poland					
(in percentage)	91	92	93	94	95	97	91	92	93	94	95	97	91	92	93	94	95	97	91	92	93	94	95	97
exceeded or largely fulfilled.	29	26	23	27	40	29	17	18	7	30	14	13	18	9	10	13	10	13	28	13	16	14	27	37
rather disappointed: I expected more.	52	49	54	49	45	50	56	55	46	52	57	55	56	55	42	55	54	53	41	41	38	46	47	41
seriously disappointed: none of my expectations have come true.	10	14	14	13	9	15	19	16	29	11	17	19	13	19	31	17	23	20	19	30	29	24	16	12
confirmed: I was right in never expecting any good to come of it.	8	9	9	10	6	5	8	10	17	6	12	12	11	14	14	11	12	11	10	12	15	15	8	8
No response.	1	1	0	0	0	1	1	1	1	1	0	1	1	2	3	3	1	3	2	4	4	1	2	2

Source: 'Politischer Kulturwandel' (1991-1997).

Notes

1. For instance, the rise of private enterprise, which was previously at best rudimentary.

2. A view generally shared by former Party members.

3. Cf. the change in conceptions of democracy described for the case of Hungary, i.e., the downgrading of "social" components.

4. On average, this group was twice as likely to say they were disappointed or that their negative expectations had been fulfilled than were supporters of other parties in all four countries.

5. For the case of Slovenia, as has been pointed out, we can only draw on the time series data of 'New Democracies Barometer', which indicate an emergent paradoxical development: an increasingly positive evaluation of the current political system coincides with increasing skepticism concerning its future development. Cf. also the analysis in Bernik, Malnar and Tos (1996).

12

Consolidation and Differentiation: a Survey of Trend Patterns

Despite numerous contradictions and inconsistencies, our trend data on the broadening and deepening of democratic orientations in East-Central Europe show how far these countries have progressed toward democratic consolidation in the last eight years. Even with country-specific variations, temporary setbacks and phases of stagnation, trend patterns clearly indicate a rooting of democratic convictions. Although there are no signs of democratic erosion over time in our data, the question of the resilience and strength of prodemocratic attitudes remains to be answered. This will be the task of our final chapter, in which we attempt to explore the typology of core democratic attitudes developed by Morlino and Montero (1995) and Linz and Stepan (1996b) for postauthoritarian democracies of Southern Europe and Latin America.[1]

These authors define *confident democrats* as individuals who prefer democracy to dictatorship as a form of government and who are convinced that democracy is capable of dealing with the problems their country faces. *Worried democrats* have basically prodemocratic attitudes but harbor doubts about the ability of democratic systems to solve problems. *Alienated* individuals are fundamentally indifferent about which type of government rules their country. *Authoritarians* would prefer a dictatorial regime to democracy under certain circumstances (see Figure 6).

Confident democrats constitute a relative majority in each of the East-Central European countries studied: 50 percent in Poland, 48 percent in Slovakia and 43 percent in both the Czech Republic and Hungary. Worried democrats are the second largest group everywhere except in Poland. Predictably, there is evidence of a strong correlation between latent authoritarian or antidemocratic attitudes and skepticism about democratic governments' problem-solving abi-

Figure 6: Typology of democratic legitimacy and efficacy

	Efficacy Indicator	
Legitimacy Indicator	Democracy solves problems	Democracy cannot solve problems
Democracy is preferable.	Confident democrats	Worried democrats
Under certain circumstances an authoritarian government is preferable.	Authoritarians (potential democrats)	Authoritarians (with no positive expectations about democracy)
For someone like me there is no difference.	Alienated (even if democracy works)	Alienated (do not expect democracy to work)

Source: Linz and Stepan (1996b: 228).

lities. The case of East-Central Europe thus proves the validity of Linz and Stepan's conclusion that "preference for the authoritarian alternative is always higher among those not believing in the efficacy of democracy" (1996: 226).

Table 55: Typology of democratic efficacy and legitimacy, countries in comparison (1997)

In Percentage	A	CZ	SK	H	PL
Confident Democrats	70	43	48	43	50
Worried Democrats	21	23	21	25	17
Alienated	4	21	12	14	13
Authoritarian	6	13	19	18	19

*) Percentage of respondents who answered both indicator questions.
Source: Fessel+GfK, 'Politische Kultur in Ost-Mitteleuropa' (1997); Fessel+GfK, 'Politische Indikatoren: Österreich' (1997).

Any changes which occurred in basic democratic orientations remained within the bounds of the extensively defined democratic spectrum or, in rare cases, turned democratic or authoritarian attitudes into alienated ones and *vice versa*. This is a remarkable core finding, given the intense economic situation and the material and social hardships of economic transformation that have long plagued most of the population. The amazing stability of central democratic orientations in East-Central Europe corresponds to empirical findings on the Russian Republic, where economic and social upheaval brought about far more dramatic existential threats, material concessions, and the social marginalization of poorer segments of the population. Yet, "at the level of the aggregate percentages, there is little evidence of a systematic erosion of support for most democratic institutions and processes (...) There were just as many democrats in 1992 as in 1990" (Gibson, 1995: 77).

A differentiated analysis of confident democrats points to three factors related to the spread and intensification of basic democratic orientations in East-Central European countries. The first factor is education: to an exceptional degree, better-educated individuals tend to be prodemocratic. Given the developed systems of education and training in East-Central Europe, the cognitive resources of postcommunist societies represent an important potential support for democracy. A second important factor is the evaluation of the old regime: personal affinity or nostalgic feelings for the Communist regime are a basis for skepticism about democracy as a form of government. This is one of the most important differences between consolidation in the former East Germany and elsewhere: "In two important areas of the relationship between citizens and politics, i.e., support for basic democratic principles and trust in output institutions, whatever links with the GDR remain are either insignificant or have ambivalent effects" (Gabriel, 1996: 277). Evaluations of regime change are the third important factor in democratization: individuals who believe that political and economic system change has largely fulfilled their expectations are much more likely to be prodemocratic than those who are disappointed or disillusioned, or whose expectations were negative from the outset.

It is revealing to juxtapose the share of confident democrats in East-Central Europe eight years after regime change to comparable data culled ten years after the beginning of democratization in Latin America. In the following table, percentages of confident democrats, according to the above-mentioned typology, have been calculated on the basis of representative data sets from postauthoritarian democracies of East-Central Europe (PKOM project), South America and, as an example of a consolidated democracy, Austria (see Table 56).

Having compared the levels of diffuse support for democracy in East-Central Europe, Western Europe, Southern Europe and the postauthoritarian democracies of Latin America, we do not believe that preference for democracy is weak in reform countries. Czech figures, for instance, indicate support levels which are only slightly lower than those of Great Britain or Italy. Figures for Hungary, the Slovak Republic and Poland are similar to those for Spain in 1989. The process of anchoring democracy attitudinally seems to have progressed remarkably far in the four countries studied, especially as compared to the fragility of support for democracy as a form of government in the Russian Republic (50 percent) or Brazil (41 percent).

This is even more apparent if we compare the percentages of authoritarians in these countries. In 1997, 11 percent of Czechs, 17 percent of Hungarians, and 19 percent of Slovaks and Poles fell into this category. In Russia, the corresponding figure was 25 percent in 1994. For Chile and Brazil, Linz and Stepan established a 19 and 25 percent share of authoritarians, respectively, using comparable tools of analysis (1996b: 226f.)[2] (see Table 57).

Table 56: Typologies of confident democrats in East-Central Europe, Austria and Southern Europe compared

Percentage classified as confident democrats, using comparable indicators and dimensions:		
East-Central Europe		
(approx. eight years after regime change)		
Czech Republic	43	(1997)
Slovak Republic	48	(1997)
Hungary	43	(1997)
Poland	50	(1997)
Austria	70	(1997)
South America, from Linz and Stepan (1996)		
(approx. ten years after the onset of democratization)		
Uruguay	57	(1995)
Argentina	55	(1995)
Chile	38	(1995)
Brazil	32	(1995)

Source: 'Politischer Kulturwandel' (1990-1997); Morlino and Montero (1995: 243f.); Linz and Stepan (1996b: 227-230).

Eight years after the collapse of communist regimes and the beginning of unprecedented changes in political, economic and social structures (Brunner, 1996), democratic attitudes have become firmly anchored in a sizable majority of each postcommunist society, albeit with country-specific variations. The dynamics of change in political culture point to a qualitative deepening of democratic attitudes. It is, however, still far from complete, and the political and economic efficacy and performance of democratic governments remain vital to the stability of the new democracies. Positive growth rates, the creation of jobs and the establishment of adequate systems of social welfare will change the attitudes of regime critics and the reluctance of authoritarians. But if qualitative deepening of democratic consolidation is to occur, it will also require more willingness on the part of political elites to engage in responsive politics. This is their only hope of countering vestiges of reactionary attitudes, latent authoritarian tendencies, widespread political rancor, affective disappointment and distrust of institutions. All of these elements are still present in the relatively new democracies, and their potential danger should not be underestimated.[3]

Table 57: Antidemocrats in postauthoritarian democracies compared

Percentage of those who agree with the statement "In some circumstances, an authoritarian government may be preferable to a democratic government"		
Austria	5	(1989)
West Germany	6	(1989)
Italy	13	(1985)
Greece	5	(1985)
Portugal	9	(1985)
Spain	10	(1997)
Czech Republic	11	(1997)
Hungary	17	(1997)
Slovak Republic	18	(1997)
Slovenia	12	(1995)
Poland	18	(1997)
Russian Republic	27	(1994)
Uruguay	8	(1995)
Argentina	11	(1995)
Chile	19	(1995)
Brazil	25	(1995)

Source: 'Politischer Kulturwandel' (1990-1997); data on Austria, West Germany and Italy in Plasser and Ulram (1993: 38); on Greece, Portugal and Spain in Morlino and Montero (1995: 238); on Latin American countries in Linz and Stepan (1996b: 228).

Thus we can now identify the most critical areas of political culture (from today's point of view) in East-Central Europe: *policy culture* and *process culture.* As regards the output dimension of policy culture, evaluations in the Czech Republic are clearly the most optimistic (positive trends in economic development along with impressions of only moderate social injustice), followed by Poland (positive economic development but strong doubts about fair distribution). More pronounced criticism comes from Slovakia and especially Hungary, where cautious (Slovakia) to gloomy (Hungary) evaluations of both overall and personal economic development are combined with a critical to categorically negative perception of social and individual justice.[4] In both countries, there is also clearly less support for the current economic order. Linz and Stepan argue, in this context, that there is no direct linkage between economic development and political legitimacy in the short or medium term. As for the long-term prospects, they "do not believe that such incongruence can last forever" (Linz and Stepan, 1996b: 442).

Criticism of performance is not limited to the socioeconomic domain[5]. In the realm of *process culture,* political competence and the responsiveness of political elites are both assessed lower in East-Central Europe (except the Czech Republic) than in established traditional or postauthoritarian democracies. In countries such as Austria or Italy, disillusionment with politicians and below-average perceptions of subjective political competence are embedded in relatively stable institutional structures. In comparison, actual and attitudinal consolidation on the meso level of East-Central European political systems is much weaker. Indicators of this include low affective identification with political parties, a lack of integration into institutional networks, and the weak intensity of political cleavages. Latent configurations of conflict in society find limited expression in structures of political competition, as evidenced by low levels of trust in competition-oriented political institutions as well as executive or judicial institutions. Low levels of political efficacy and responsiveness, combined with an intermediary vacuum, produce the overall image of an underconsolidated process culture.[6]

Both sets of difficulties were predictable at the start of democratization. Profound economic system change is inevitably linked to high economic and social transformation costs[7]. In addition, poorer societies – and not even the economic disparities among East-Central European countries can conceal the fact that none of them are wealthy – have limited resources with which to cushion the blow of social hardship.[8] Following decades of authoritarian rule, often with totalitarian overtones, a pluralist and democratic process culture will have to evolve step by step. Southern Europe also experienced temporary setbacks and deficits of integration in the early years of consolidation (Morlino and Montero, 1995; Morlino, 1995).[9] Given these obstacles, the process of consolidation in East-Central Europe has been relatively successful, considerable differences between countries[10] notwithstanding. Difficulties on the levels of policy and process have not become apparent on the system level of political culture, not even in countries where the evaluation of output has been temporarily (Poland, Slovakia) or constantly (Hungary) negative, or where the intermediary vacuum is especially strong. There is no doubt, however, that the central tasks in all future consolidation efforts will be to increase material output, establish and expand pluralist institutions, and correct the deficiencies in social and political integration.

Notes

1. Unfortunately, Morlino and Montero (1995) use a different indicator of efficacy than Linz and Stepan (1996b), precluding a direct comparison of figures for East-Central Europe and Latin America with those for Southern Europe.

2. "We will call respondents authoritarian if they gave a positive answer to the statement 'in some circumstances an authoritarian government can be preferable to a democratic government' " (Linz and Stepan, 1996b: 226f.)

3. Despite a primarily optimistic prognosis for the future course of democratic consolidation in East Germany, Gabriel (1996) points to a number of complications in East German citizens' relations to politics. In one form or another, these are also encountered in the new democracies of East-Central Europe: "Among them, we find the markedly lower satisfaction with the performance of the democratic system in the Federal Republic and with the institutions and actors involved in daily politics; dramatically negative and worsening evaluations of the overall economic situation since 1990 and of both individual and collective economic outlooks; the high and ever-increasing approval of socialism, especially its statist-collectivist economic doctrine; and the view that unification has primarily benefited West Germans. It is worth noting, finally, how quickly and how much initial approval of the market economy and of inegalitarian distribution on the basis of individual merit has eroded" (Gabriel, 1996: 311).

4. Compare also the lower overall satisfaction with life – which is, of course, not exclusively dependent on the evaluation of political performance – in Hungary and Slovakia.

5. For instance, with respect to the 'most concrete' indicator of political liberty, namely "living without fear of unlawful arrest", evaluations are much more critical in Slovakia and Hungary than in the Czech Republic and Slovenia (Rose and Haerpfer, 1994). This may well reflect the "milder" regime practices of Hungarian Communism, but no such explanation is plausible for Slovakia. The latter country, in fact, is the only one in East-Central Europe considered a borderline case of democratic minimal criteria as regards as political rights and civil liberties ('Freedom House Study', quoted from Linz and Stepan, 1996b: 447).

6. Country-specific variations are often considerable for each indicator. Case in point: the Czech Republic has relatively high levels of trust in political institutions and a clearly discernible one-dimensional cleavage structure, but low confidence in judicial institutions and no highly integrative societal subcultures. In Poland, trust in political institutions is low, but the integrative performance of the Church is comparatively high. Hungary and Slovakia have only rudimentarily anchored institutions; as in Poland, the field of societal conflict is multidimensional, but the Slovak situation is aggravated by an incomplete process of nation building.

7. Compare the considerable political conflict engendered by recent socioeconomic restructuring and cultural change even in "rich" and established Western democracies (Betz, 1994).

8. For details on the question of resource allocation for social policy purposes, see Offe (1994: 95ff.)

9. In Austria and (West) Germany, phases of totalitarianism were relatively short (1933 or 1938 to 1945), and neither the politicization of civil society nor the destruction of traditional structures of integration proceeded far. Franco's dictatorship lasted several decades, but its penetration of civil society was weaker from the outset: in the last few years prior to the onset of democratization, Spanish economic, social and cultural institutions as well as attitudes began more and more to resemble those of Western Europe (Linz, Stepan and Gunther, 1995: 98ff.)

10. Political traditions also play an important role here. Thus the Czech Republic benefits from the longest pre-authoritarian democratic tradition in East-Central Europe (Plasser and Ulram, 1994b: 1996).

13

Empirical Sources (1990-1997)

1. Czech and Slovak Republics

1.1. Data	**Czechoslovakia (1990)**
Project	'Regimewechsel in der ČSFR' (Regime Change in Czechoslovakia)
Institute	GfK-Czechoslovakia (Prague)
Random sample survey	n = 1000 respondents (aged 14 or older)
Sampling method	stratified multistage clustered random sample
Addresses	voter registration rolls
Mode of interview	face-to-face (in home)
Field work	October – November 1990

1.2. Data	**Czechoslovakia (1991)**
Project	'Demokratie- und Parlamentsverstädnis in Ost-Mitteleuropa' (Conceptions of Democracy and Parliament in East Central Europe)
Institute	GfK-Czechoslovakia (Prague)
Random sample survey	n = 2000 respondents (aged 14 or older)
Sampling method	stratified multistage clustered random sample
Addresses	voter registration rolls
Mode of interview	face-to-face (in home)

Field work	May – June 1991
1.3. Data	**Czechoslovakia (1992)**
Project	'Politische Kultur und Neue Demokratien-Barometer' (Political culture and New Democracies Barometer)
Institute	GfK (Prague)
Random sample survey	n = 1000 respondents (aged 14 or older)
Sampling method	stratified multistage clustered random sample
Addresses	voter registration rolls
Mode of interview	face-to-face (in home)
Field work	November – December 1992
1.4. Data	**Czech and Slovak Republics (1993)**
Project	'Politische Kultur in Tschechien und der Slowakei' (Political Culture in the Czech and Slovak Republics)
Institute	GfK (Prague)
Random sample survey	n = 1000 respondents (aged 14 or older)
Sampling method	stratified multistage clustered random sample
Addresses	voter registration rolls
Mode of interview	face-to-face (in home)
Field work	January – February 1993
1.5. Data	**Czech Republic (1994)**
Project	'Politische Kultur und Neue Demokratien-Barometer' (Political Culture and New Democracies Barometer)
Institute	GfK (Prague)
Random sample survey	n = 1000 respondents (aged 14 or older)
Sampling method	stratified multistage clustered random sample

Addresses	voter registration rolls
Mode of interview	face-to-face (in home)
Field work	January – February 1994
1.6. Data	**Slovak Republic (1994)**
Project	'Politische Kultur und Neue Demokratien-Barometer' (Political Culture and New Democracies Barometer)
Institute	GfK (Bratislava)
Random sample survey	n = 500 respondents (aged 14 or older)
Sampling method	stratified multistage clustered random sample
Addresses	voter registration rolls
Mode of interview	face-to-face (in home)
Field work	January – February 1994
1.7. Data	**Czech Republic (1995)**
Project	'Politische Kultur und Demokratieverständnis in Ost-Mitteleuropa im Trendvergleich' (Trends in East-Central European Political Culture and Conceptions of Democracy Compared)
Institute	GfK (Prague)
Random sample survey	n = 1000 respondents (aged 14 or older)
Sampling method	stratified multistage clustered random sample
Addresses	voter registration rolls
Mode of interview	face-to-face (in home)
Field work	November – December 1995
1.8. Data	**Czech Republic (1997)**
Project	'Politischer Kulturwandel in Ost-Mitteleuropa' (Changes in Political Culture in East Central Europe)

Institute	GfK (Prague)
Random sample survey	n = 1000 respondents (aged 14 or older)
Sampling method	stratified multistage clustered random sample
Addresses	voter registration rolls
Mode of interview	face-to-face (in home)
Field work	January – April 1990

1.9. Data	**Slovak Republic (1995)**
Project	'Politische Kultur und Demokratieverständnis in Ost-Mitteleuropa im Trendvergleich' (Trends in East-Central European Political Culture and Conceptions of Democracy Compared)
Institute	GfK (Bratislava)
Random sample survey	n = 1000 respondents (aged 14 or older)
Sampling method	stratified multistage clustered random sample
Addresses	voter registration rolls
Mode of interview	face-to-face (in home)
Field work	October – November 1995

1.10. Data	**Slovak Republic (1997)**
Project	'Politischer Kulturwandel in Ost-Mitteleuropa' (Changes in Political Culture in East Central Europe)
Institute	GfK (Bratislava)
Random sample survey	n = 1000 respondents (aged 14 or older)
Sampling method	stratified multistage clustered random sample
Addresses	voter registration rolls
Mode of interview	face-to-face (in home)
Field work	January – March 1997

2. Hungary

2.1. Data	**Hungary (1991)**
Project	'Demokratie- und Parlamentsverständnis in Ost-Mitteleuropa' (Conceptions of Democracy and Parliament in East Central Europe)
Institute	GfK-Hungaria (Budapest)
Random sample survey	n = 2000 respondents (aged 14 or older)
Sampling method	random
Addresses	voter registration rolls
Mode of interview	face-to-face (in home)
Field work	June – August 1991

2.2. Data	**Hungary (1992)**
Project	'Politische Kultur und Neue Demokratien-Barometer 1992' (Political Culture and New Democracies Barometer)
Institute	GfK-Hungaria (Budapest)
Random sample survey	n = 1000 respondents (aged 14 or older)
Sampling method	random
Addresses	voter registration rolls
Mode of interview	face-to-face (in home)
Field work	November 1992

2.3. Data	**Hungary (1994)**
Project	'Politische Kultur und Neue Demokratien-Barometer 1994' (Political Culture and New Democracies Barometer)
Institute	GfK-Hungaria (Budapest)
Random sample survey	n = 1000 respondents (aged 14 or older)
Sampling method	random
Addresses	voter registration rolls
Mode of interview	face-to-face (in home)
Field work	January – February 1994

2.4. Data	**Hungary (1995)**
Project	'Politische Kultur und Demokratieverständnis in Ost-Mitteleuropa im Trendvergleich' (Conceptions of Democracy and Parliament in East Central Europe)
Institute	GfK-Hungaria (Budapest)
Random sample survey	n = 1000 respondents (aged 14 or older)
Sampling method	random
Addresses	voter registration rolls
Mode of interview	face-to-face (in home)
Field work	November 1995

2.5. Data	**Hungary (1997)**
Project	'Politischer Kulturwandel in Ost-Mitteleuropa' (changes in East European political culture)
Institute	GfK-Hungaria (Budapest)
Random sample survey	n = 1000 respondents (aged 14 or older)
Sampling method	random
Addresses	voter registration rolls
Mode of interview	face-to-face (in home)
Field work	February – March 1997

3. Poland

3.1. Data	**Poland (1991)**
Project	'Demokratie- und Parlamentsverständnis in Ost-Mitteleuropa' (Conceptions of Democracy and Parliament in East Central Europe)
Institute	GfK-Polonia (Warsaw)
Random sample survey	n = 2000 respondents (aged 14 or older)

Sampling method	random
Mode of interview	face-to-face (in home)
Field work	May – June 1991

3.2. Data	**Poland (1992)**
Project	'Politische Kultur und Neue Demokratien-Barometer' 1992 (Political Culture and New Democracies Barometer)
Institute	GfK-Polonia (Warsaw)
Random sample survey	n = 1000 respondents (aged 14 or older)
Sampling method	random
Mode of interview	face-to-face (in home)
Field work	November – December 1992

3.3. Data	**Poland (1994)**
Project	'Politische Kultur und Neue Demokratien-Barometer 1994' (Political Culture and New Democracies Barometer)
Institute	GfK-Polonia (Warsaw)
Random sample survey	n = 1000 respondents (aged 14 or older)
Sampling method	random
Mode of interview	face-to-face (in home)
Field work	January – February 1994

3.4. Data	**Poland (1995)**
Project	'Politische Kultur und Demokratieverständnis im Trendvergleich' (Trends in Political Culture and Conceptions of Democracy Compared)
Institute	GfK-Polonia (Warsaw)
Random sample survey	n = 1000 respondents (aged 14 or older)
Sampling method	random
Mode of interview	face-to-face (in home)
Field work	November – December 1995

3.5. Data	**Poland (1997)**
Project	'Politischer Kulturwandel in Ost-Mitteleuropa' (Changes in Political Culture in East Central Europe)
Institute	GfK-Polonia (Warsaw)
Random sample survey	n = 1000 respondents (aged 14 or older)
Sampling method	random
Mode of interview	face-to-face (in home)
Field work	February – March 1997

4. Slovenia

4.1. Data	**Slovenia (1995)**
Project	'Politische Kultur und Demokratieverständnis in Ost-Mitteleuropa' (Political Culture and Conceptions of Democracy in East Central Europe)
Institute	Centre for Public Opinion and Mass Communication Research, University of Ljubljana, Faculty of Social Sciences
Random sample survey	n = 1000 respondents (aged 14 or older)
Sampling method	random
Mode of interview	face-to-face (in home)
Field work	November – December 1995

5. Comparable Data for Germany

5.1. code book:	'Politische Einstellungen und politische Partizipation im vereinigten Deutschland' (1994) (n = 4114 respondents) Research

	group: Jürgen Falter, Oscar W. Gabriel, Hans Rattinger and Karl Schmitt.
5.2. code book:	'Politische Resonanz 1995' (n = 2036 respondents) Research group: Oscar W. Gabriel and Max Kaase.

6. Comparable Data for Austria

6.1. Data	**Austria (1996)**
Project	'Politischer Kulturwandel in Österreich' (Changes in Austrian Political Culture)
Institute	FESSEL+GfK (Vienna)
Random sample survey	n = 1000 respondents (aged 14 or older)
Sampling method	stratified multistage clustered random sample
Addresses	voter registration rolls
Mode of interview	face-to-face (in home)
Field work	June – July 1996

6.2. Data	**Austria (1997)**
Project	'Politisch-kulturelle Indikatoren' (Indicators of Political Culture)
Institute	FESSEL+GfK (Vienna)
Random sample survey	n = 1000 respondents (aged 14 or older)
Sampling method	stratified multistage clustered random sample
Addresses	voter registration rolls
Mode of interview	face-to-face (in home)
Field work	January 1997

Appendix of data

Overview

Table A1a: Evaluation of the subjective economic situation: Hungary and Poland (1991-1995/6)

Does your regular job pay you enough to buy what you really need? (Percent of working persons)	Hungary								Poland							
	1991		1992		1994		1995		1991		1992		1994		1995	
More than enough	5	}26	5	}26	5	}29	4	}36	6	}39	6	}34	3	}36	8	}44
Enough	21		21		24		32		33		28		33		36	
Not enough	56	}74	54	}73	39	}67	42	}63	37	}61	39	}65	41	}62	44	}57
Definitely not enough	18		19		28		21		24		26		21		13	
How do you rate your family's economic situation today? (percent of respondents)	**Hungary**								**Poland**							
	1991		1992		1994		1995		1991		1992		1994		1995	
Very satisfactory	1	}24	1	}20	1	}19	1	}21	1	}18	1	}23	1	}24	1	}37
Fairly satisfactory	23		19		18		20		17		22		23		36	
Not very satisfactory	50	}76	47	}80	48	}80	50	}79	56	}82	49	}75	52	}75	49	}63
Very unsatisfactory	26		33		32		29		26		26		23		14	

Comparing actual and desired living standards, (percent of respondents) feel that they	Hungary						Poland						Russia	
	1991		1992		1996		1991		1992		1996		1996	
have achieved all or most of their goals.	22	}55	14	}47	18	}53	10	}41	9	}40	23	}54	11	}42
have achieved many them.	33		33		35		31		31		31		31	
have achieved only a few of them.	21	}43	30	}51	32	}45	42	}57	36	}60	27	}32	36	}58
have achieved hardly any of their goals.	22		21		13		15		24		5		22	

Source: 'New Democracies Barometer' (1991-1995)
*) Fessel+GfK, 'Lebensstile in Ost-Mitteleuropa' (1991, 1992)
*) Fessel+GfK, 'Representative Survey in H, PL, SZ, SK, RUS' (1996)
Percent missing to 100 = rounded or no response.

Table A1b: Evaluation of the subjective economic situation: Slovak and Czech Republic (1991-1995/96)

Does your regular job pay you enough to buy what you really need? (Percent of working persons)	Slovak Republic					Czech Republic				
	1991	1992	1993	1994	1995	1991	1992	1993	1994	1995
More than enough	3 }39	3 }37	3 }35	8 }46	3 }34	6 }46	7 }51	8 }51	12 }56	7 }54
Enough	36	34	32	38	31	40	44	43	44	47
Not enough	33 }61	44 }63	44 }64	35 }52	45 }66	35 }53	33 }47	36 }48	32 }43	36 }46
Definitely not enough	28	19	20	17	21	18	14	12	11	10
How do you rate your family's economic situation today? (percent of respondents)	**Slovak Republic**					**Czech Republic**				
	1991	1992	1993	1994	1995	1991	1992	1993	1994	1995
Very satisfactory	0 }48	2 }49	1 }48	1 }42	1 }37	3 }59	2 }60	2 }60	2 }53	3 }58
Fairly satisfactory	48	47	47	41	36	56	58	58	51	55
Not very satisfactory	42 }52	43 }51	40 }51	41 }58	47 }62	34 }41	34 }39	35 }40	39 }47	35 }42
Very unsatisfactory	10	8	11	17	15	7	5	5	8	7

Comparing actual and desired living standards, (percent of respondents) feel that they	Slovak Republic						Czech Republic					
	1991		1992		1996		1991		1992		1996	
have achieved all or most of their goals.	13	}42	9	}38	24	}67	12	}46	10	}41	28	}71
have achieved many them.	29		29		43		34		31		43	
have achieved only a few of them.	40	}56	39	}61	27	}32	40	}54	42	}59	23	}29
have achieved hardly any of their goals.	16		22		5		14		17		6	

Source: 'New Democracies Barometer' (1991-1995)
*) Fessel+GfK, 'Lebensstile in Ost-Mitteleuropa' (1991, 1992)
*) Fessel+GfK, 'Representative Survey in H, PL, SZ, SK, RUS' (1996)
Percent missing to 100 = rounded or no response.

Table A2: Retrospective evaluation of the subjective economic situation: East Central Europe (1990/91-1995)

a) Compared to the situation 12 months ago, the financial situation of my household has ...(in percent)	Hungary			Poland			Slovak Republic*)			Czech Republic*)		
	improved	stayed the same	become worse	improved	stayed the same	become worse	improved	stayed the same	become worse	improved	stayed the same	become worse
1990	*	*	*	18	34	46	(6)	(27)	(66)	(6)	(27)	(66)
1991	9	24	66	10	25	64	(13)	(20)	(66)	(13)	(20)	(66)
1992	5	23	70	13	26	60	17	19	63	20	29	50
1993	8	23	68	10	32	54	14	26	60	22	33	45
1994	8	24	66	11	32	54	16	31	52	22	37	40
1995	5	18	76	20	43	35	21	37	41	28	43	28

b) Compared to the situation five years ago, the financial situation of most households has...(in percent)	Hungary				Poland				Slovak Republic				Czech Republic			
	improved	stayed the same	become a little worse	become a lot worse	improved	stayed the same	become a little worse	become a lot worse	improved	stayed the same	become a little worse	become a lot worse	improved	stayed the same	become a little worse	become a lot worse
1991	10	23	45	22	18	22	37	23	15	20	37	30	18	29	33	20
1992	7	18	47	27	14	18	35	31	21	19	37	22	22	25	30	21
1993	*	*	*	*	*	*	*	*	17	18	40	24	22	28	32	18
1994	8	18	42	33	17	18	32	31	19	21	35	26	25	26	30	19
1995	9	19	44	27	20	29	34	16	16	26	37	21	28	33	29	11

Sources: a) 'Central and Eastern Eurobarometer' (1/1990-6/1995). b) 'New Democracies Barometer' (1991-1995).
*) a) 1990 and 1991 (Czechoslovakia)

Scaling: a) financial situation of the household has improved/become a little better/stayed the same/become a little worse/become a lot worse. b) household economic situation in the past was much better/a little better/about the same/a little worse/much worse.

Note: presentation of b) has been adapted to that of a)

Table A3: Prospective evaluation of the subjective economic situation: East Central Europe (1990-1995)

a) Percent who believe that the financial situation of their household will ... over the next 12 months	Hungary			Poland			Slovak Republic*)			Czech Republic*)		
	improve	stay the same	become worse	improve	stay the same	become worse	improve	stay the same	become worse	improve	stay the same	become worse
1990	6	18	74	24	31	24	(9)	(17)	(66)	(9)	(17)	(66)
1991	20	31	39	17	33	32	(21)	(37)	(34)	(21)	(37)	(34)
1992	13	27	52	21	30	34	21	21	54	25	37	33
1993	17	28	46	24	37	23	27	26	43	28	37	31
1994	15	23	51	15	37	30	23	39	33	23	43	28
1995	11	19	63	25	39	17	24	38	30	25	43	25

b) Compared to today, the financial economic situation of the household will be ... in five years (in percent)	Hungary				Poland				Slovak Republic				Czech Republic			
	much better	a little better	the same	worse	much better	a little better	the same	worse	much better	a little better	the same	worse	much better	a little better	the same	worse
1991	5	43	28	24	6	36	31	27	5	42	27	25	12	48	24	16
1992	2	41	30	24	4	28	30	31	6	47	22	24	11	44	26	17
1993	*	*	*	*	*	*	*	*	6	43	22	27	10	47	26	15
1994	4	39	33	20	5	37	33	15	8	41	26	24	7	48	30	14
1995	3	32	33	29	6	41	39	10	4	38	41	16	6	46	35	13

Source: a) 'Central and Eastern Eurobarometer' (1/1991-6/1996), b) 'New Democracies Barometer (1991-1995)
*) a) 1990 and 1991 (Czechoslovakia)

Scaling: a) expect the financial situation of household will be much better/get a little better/stay the same/get a little worse/get a lot worse. b) financial situation of the family will be much better/a little better/about the same/a little worse/a lot worse.

Table A4: Winners and Losers of System Change (1995)

Which of the following groups have fared better since the end of communism and which have fared worse? Who are the winners and losers? (in percent)	Hungary			Slovak Republic			Poland			Czech Republic		
	better	same as before	worse	better	same as before	worse	better	same as before	worse	better	same as before	worse
Private entrepreneurs	72	11	13	89	6	5	88	6	3	92	4	3
People with knowledge of foreign languages	63	22	10	88	11	1	79	16	2	91	7	1
Former managers of state-owned companies	58	24	12	72	22	6	41	34	22	70	24	5
CP functionaries	40	41	15	48	36	16	38	29	30	41	41	17
Civil servants	44	26	25	76	20	4	44	37	16	77	19	3
Army officers	9	33	54	48	45	7	30	45	21	41	44	13

Which of the following groups have fared better since the end of communism and which have fared worse? Who are the winners and losers? (in percent)	Hungary			Slovak Republic			Poland			Czech Republic		
	better	same as before	worse	better	same as before	worse	better	same as before	worse	better	same as before	worse
Private sector employees	33	27	38	44	17	40	54	18	25	61	18	19
Employees of state-owned companies	10	23	64	27	33	40	17	34	46	24	44	31
Women	3	26	68	6	34	60	12	33	52	16	48	35
People like me	4	18	77	9	28	63	13	28	57	24	36	40
Retired persons	6	9	83	8	16	76	9	14	74	17	20	63
Workers	1	5	93	2	10	88	5	13	81	11	26	62

Source: Fessel+GfK, 'Politischer Kulturwandel in Ost-Mitteleuropa' (1995).
*) percent missing to 100: no response or rounded.

No-response rates do not exceed five percent except in Slovenia (not included in this table).

Bibliography

Ackerman, Bruce (1993) *Ein neuer Anfang für Europa* (Berlin).

Ágh, Attila (1993) "The Comparative Revolution and the Transition in Central and Southern Europe", in *Journal of Theoretical Politics* no. 2.

Ágh, Attila (1994a) (ed.) *The Emergence of East Central European Parliaments: The First Steps,* Budapest: Hungarian Centre of Democracy Studies Foundation.

Ágh, Attila (1994b) "The Social and Political Actors of Democratic Transition" in Attila Ágh (ed.) *The Emergence of East Central European Parliaments: The First Steps,* Budapest: Hungarian Centre of Democracy Studies Foundation.

Ágh, Attila (1995a) "The Legislative Activity of the First Parliament" in Attila Ágh and Sándor Kurtán (eds) *Democratization and Europeanization in Hungary: The First Parliament (1990–1994),* Budapest: Hungarian Centre for Democracy Studies.

Ágh, Attila (1995b) "The Role of the First Parliament in Democratic Transition" in Attila Ágh and Sándor Kurtán (eds) *Democratization and Europeanization in Hungary: The First Parliament (1990–1994),* Budapest: Hungarian Centre for Democracy Studies.

Ágh, Attila (1995c) "The Permanent 'Constitutional Crisis' in the Democratic Transition: The Case of Hungary" in Joachim Jens Hesse and Nevil Johnson (eds) *Constitutional Policy and Change in Europe* (Oxford).

Ágh, Attila (1996a) "Political Culture and System Change in Hungary" in Fritz Plasser and Andreas Pribersky (eds) *Political Culture in East Central Europe* (London).

Àgh, Attila (1996b) "The Development of the East Central European Party Systems: From 'Movements' to 'Cartels' in Hungarian Political Science Association" (ed.) *The Challenge of Europeanization in the Region: East Central Europe* (Budapest).

Ágh, Attila (1996c) "From Nomenclatura to Clientura: The Emergence of New Political Elites in East Central Europe" in Geoffrey Pridham and Paul Lewis (eds) *Rooting Fragile Democracies: Comparing New Party Systems in Southern and Eastern Europe* (London/New York).

Ágh, Attila and Kurtán, Sándor (eds) (1995) *Democratization and Europeanization in Hungary: The First Parliament (1990–1994),* Budapest: Hungarian Centre for Democracy Studies.

Almond, Gabriel A. (1987) "Politische Kultur-Forschung – Rückblick und Ausblick" in Dirk Berg-Schlosser and Jakob Schissler (eds) *Politische Kultur in Deutschland. Bilanz und Perspektiven der Forschung* (Opladen).

Almond, Gabriel A. (1989²) "The Intellectual History of the Civic Culture Concept" in Gabriel A. Almond and Sidney Verba (eds) *The Civic Culture Revisited: An Analytic Study* (Newbury Park/London/New Delhi).

Almond, Gabriel A. (1994) "Forword: The Return to Political Culture" in Larry Diamond (ed.) *Political Culture and Democracy in Developing Countries* (Boulder).

Almond, Gabriel A. and Verba, Sidney (1989²a) *The Civic Culture. Political Attitudes and Democracy in Five Nations* (Newbury Park/London/New Delhi).

Almond, Gabriel A. and Sidney Verba (eds) (1989²b) *The Civic Culture Revisited: An Analytic Study* (Newbury Park/London/New Delhi).

Almond, Gabriel A., Powell, G. Bingham Jr. and Mundt, Robert J. (1993) "Political Socialization and Political Culture" in Gabriel A. Almond, G. Bingham Powell Jr. and Robert J. Mundt *Comparative Politics. A Theoretical Framework* (New York).

Altmann, Franz Lothar and Ochmann, Cornelius (1995) "Mittel- und Osteuropa auf dem Weg in die Europäische Union. Bericht zum Stand der Integrationsfähigkeit" in Werner Weidenfeld (ed.) *Mittel- und Osteuropa auf dem Weg in die Europäische Union* (Gütersloh).

Arato, Andrew and Jean L. Cohen (1992) *Civil Society and Political Theory* (Cambridge, MA/London).

Balcerowicz, Leczek (1995) *Socialism, Capitalism, Transformation* (Budapest/London/New York).

Batt, Judy (1991) *East Central Europe from Reform to Transformation* (London).

Barnes, Samuel H. (1994) "Politics and Culture" in Frederick D. Weil (ed.) *Political Culture and Political Structure: Theoretical and Empirical Studies* (Greenwich/London).

Bartolini, Stefano (1993) "On Time and Comparative Research" in *Journal of Theoretical Politics* no. 2.

Bauböck, Rainer (1996) "Cultural Minority Rights for Immigrants" in *International Migration Review* no. 1.

Beetham, David (ed.) (1994) *Defining and Measuring Democracy* (London/Thousand Oaks).

Bendel, Petra and Kropp, Sabine (1997) "Zivilgesellschaften und Transitionsprozesse im interregionalen Vergleich: Lateinamerika – Osteuropa." *Zentralinstitut für Regionalforschung* (Erlangen-Nürnberg, mimeo).

Berg-Schlosser, Dirk (1994) "Politische Kulturforschung" in Jürgen Kriz, Dieter Nohlen, Rainer Olaf Schultze (eds) *Politikwissenschaftliche Methoden*, Lexikon der Politik, Vol. 2 (Munich).

Berglund, Sten and Dellenbrant, Jan Åke (eds) (1994) *The New Democracies in Eastern Europe: Party Systems and Political Cleavages*, 2nd Edition (Aldershot).

Bermeo, Nancy (1990) "Rethinking Regime Change" in *Comparative Politics* no. 3.
Bernhard, Michael (1993) "Civil Society and Democratic Transition in East Central Europe" in *Political Science Quarterly* no. 2.
Bernik, Ivan, Malnar, Brina and Tos, Niko (1996) "Die Paradoxa der instrumentellen Akzeptanz von Demokratie" in *Österreichische Zeitschrift für Politikwissenschaft* no. 3.
Betz, Hans-Georg (1994) *Radical Right-Wing Populism in Western Europe* (New York.
Beyme, Klaus von (1994a) *Systemwechsel in Osteuropa* (Frankfurt a.M).
Beyme, Klaus von (1994b) "Die politische Kultur Osteuropas im Wandel" in Oskar Niedermayer and Klaus von Beyme (eds) *Politische Kultur in Ost- und Westdeutschland* (Berlin).
Beyme, Klaus von and Offe, Claus (eds) (1995) *Politische Theorien in der Ära der Transformation, Politische Vierteljahresschrift Sonderheft* no. 26.
Borre, Ole and Scarbrough, Elinor (eds) (1995) "The Scope of Government" in *Beliefs in Government*, Vo. 3 (Oxford/New York).
Bozóki, András (1994a) "Party Formation and Constitutional Change in Hungary", in *The Journal of Communist Studies and Transition Politics* no. 3.
Bozóki, András (1994b) (ed.) *Democratic Legitimacy in Post-Communist Societies* (Budapest).
Bretschneider, Rudolf (1991) "Die Zeichen des Wandels. Lebensstile, Wünsche, Hoffnungen – ein empirisches Psychogramm" in GfK-Nürnberg *Zwischen Frust und Hoffnung – Osteuropa auf dem Weg in die Konsumgesellschaft*, GfK-Conference Report of 14.6.1991 in Nuremberg.
Brint, Steven (1994) " Sociological Analysis of Political Culture: An Introduction and Assessment" in Frederick D. Weil and Mary Gautier (eds) "Political Culture and Political Structure: Theoretical and Empirical Studies". Vol. 2 of *Research on Democracy and Society* (Greenwich).
Brokl, Lubomír and Mansfeldová, Zdenka (1992) "Von der 'unpolitischen' zur 'professionellen' Politik, Aspekte der politischen Kultur der CSFR in der Periode des Systemwechsels" in Peter Gerlich, Fritz Plasser and Peter A. Ulram (eds) *Regimewechsel. Demokratisierung und politische Kultur in Ost-Mitteleuropa* (Vienna/Cologne).
Brunner, Georg (ed.) (1996) *Politische und ökonomische Transformation in Osteuropa* (Berlin).
Bruszt, László and Simon, János (1991) "A 'választások éve' a közvéleménykutatások tükrében" (The Elections in Public Opinion) in Sándor Kurtán, Sándor Peter and László Vass *Magyarország Politikai Évkönyve 1991 (Politisches Jahrbuch Ungarns)* (Budapest).
Bruszt, László and Simon, János (1992) "The Great Transformation in Hungary and Eastern Europe. Theoretical Approaches and Public Opinion about Capitalism and Democracy" in György Szoboszlai (ed.)

Flying Blind. Emerging Democracies in East-Central Europe, Budapest: Hungarian Political Science Association.

Bunce, Valerie (1995a) "Comparing East and South" in *Journal of Democracy* no. 3.

Bunce, Valerie (1995b) "Should Transitologists Be Grounded?" in *Slavic Review* no. 1.

Bunce, Valerie (1995c) "Paper Curtains and Paper Tigers" in *Slavic Review* no. 4.

Bunce, Valerie and Csanádi, Mária (1992) "A Systematic Analysis of a Non-System: Post-Communism in Eastern Europe" in György Szoboszlai (ed.) *Flying Blind. Emerging Democracies in East-Central Europe,* Budapest: Hungarian Political Science Association.

Burton, Michael G. and Higley, John (1987) "Elite Settlements" in *American Sociological Review* no. 2.

Burton, Michael, Gunther, Richard and Higley, John (1992a) "Introduction: Elite Transformations and Democratic Regimes" in John Higley and Richard Gunther (eds) *Elites and Democratic Consolidation in Latin America and Southern Europe* (New York).

Burton, Michael, Gunther, Richard and Higley, John (1992b) "Elites and Democratic Consolidation in Latin America and Southern Europe: An Overview" in John Higley and Richard Gunther (eds) *Elites and Democratic Consolidation in Latin America and Southern Europe* (New York).

Casper, Gretchen and Taylor, Michelle M. (1996) *Negotiating Democracy. Transitions from Authoritarian Rule* (Pittsburgh, Pa).

Chinn, Jeff and Truex, Lise A. (1996) "The Question of Citizenship in the Baltics" in *Journal of Democracy* no. 1.

Chorrin, Chris (1993) "People and Politics" in Stephen White, Judy Batt and Paul G. Lewis (eds) *Developments in East European Politics* (Durham).

Claußen, Bernhard (1996) "Politisches System als strukturgeflechtliche Bezugsgröße politischer Sozialisation" in Bernhard Claußen and Rainer Geißler (eds) *Die Politisierung des Menschen. Instanzen der politischen Sozialisation* (Opladen).

Collier, David and Levitsky, Stephen (1995) *Democracy "With Adjectives": Finding Conceptual Order in Recent Comparative Research.* University of California, Berkeley: Department of Political Science, typescript.

Collier, David and Mahon, James E. (1993) "Conceptual 'Stretching' Revisited: Adapting Categories in Comparative Analysis" in *American Political Science Review* no. 3.

Colomer, Josep M. (1995) "Strategies and Outcomes in Eastern Europe" in *Journal of Democracy* no. 2.

Cotta, Maurizio (1992) "Elite Unification and Democratic Consolidation in Italy: An Overview" in John Higley and Richard Gunther (eds) *Elites and Democratic Consolidation in Latin America and Southern Europe* (New York).

Cotta, Maurizio (1994) "Building Party Systems After the Dictatorship: The East European Cases in a Comparative Perspective" in Geoffrey Pridham and Tatu Vanhanen (eds) *Democratization in Eastern Europe. Domestic and International Perspectives* (London).

Cotta, Maurizio (1996) "Structuring the New Party Systems after the Dictatorship. Coalitions, Alliances, Fusions and Splits during the Transition and Post-Transition Stages" in Geoffrey Pridham and Paul Lewis (eds) *Stabilizing Fragile Democracies. Comparing New Party Systems in Southern and Eastern Europe* (London/New York).

Crawford, Beverly and Lijphart, Arend (1995) "Explaining Political and Economic Change in Post-Communist Europe" in *Comparative Political Studies* no. 2.

Crawford, Keith (1996) *East Central European Politics Today: From Chaos to Stability?* (Manchester).

Czachór, Zbigniew (in cooperation with Dieter Bingen) (1995) "Polen" in Werner Weidenfeld (ed.) *Mittel- und Osteuropa auf dem Weg in die Europäische Union* (Gütersloh).

Dahl, Robert (1971) *Polyarchy: Participation and Opposition* (New Haven/London).

Dahl, Robert A. (1992) "Why All Democratic Countries Have Mixed Economies" in John Chapman and Ian Shapiro (eds) *Democratic Community* (New York).

Dahl, Robert A. (1995) "The Newer Democracies: From the Time of Triumph to the Time of Troubles" in Daniel N. Nelson (ed.) *After Authoritarism. Democracy or Disorder?* (Westport).

Dalton, Russel J. (1996a) *Citizen Politics. Public Opinion and Political Parties in Advanced Western Democracies* (Chatham N.J.).

Dalton, Russell J. (1996b) "Comparative Politics: Micro-behavioral Perspectives" in Robert E. Goodin and Hans-Dieter Klingemann (eds) *A New Handbook of Political Science* (Oxford).

Dalton, Russell J. (1997) Citizens and Democracy: Political Support in Advanced Industrial Democracies. *CSD Center for the Study of Democracy* (mimeo).

Dawisha, Karen (1997) "Democratization and political participation: research concepts and methodologies' in Karen Dawisha and Bruce Parrott (eds): *The Consolidation of Democracy in East Central Europe* (Cambridge).

Dawisha, Karen and Parrott, Bruce (eds) (1997) *The Consolidation of Democracy in East Central Europe* (Cambridge).

Desfor Edles, Laura (1995) "Rethinking Democratic Transition: A Culturalist Critique and the Spanish Case" in *Theory and Society* no. 3.

Diamond, Larry (1993a) "Introduction: Political Culture and Democracy" in Larry Diamond (ed.) *Political Culture and Democracy in Developing Countries* (Boulder).

Diamond, Larry (1993b) "Causes and Effects" in Larry Diamond (ed.) *Political Culture and Democracy in Developing Countries* (Boulder).

Diamond, Larry (1994) "Toward Democratic Consolidation" in *Journal of Democracy* no. 3.

Diamond, Larry (1995a) "Democracy and Economic Reform: Tensions, Compatibilities, and Strategies for Reconciliation" in Edward P. Lazear (ed.) *Economic Transition in Eastern Europe and Russia. Realities of Reform* (Stanford, California).

Diamond, Larry (1995b) "Democracy in Latin America: Degrees, Illusions, and Directions for Consolidation" in Tom Farer (ed.) *Beyond Sovereignty: Collectively Defending Democracy in a World of Sovereign States* (Baltimore).

Diamond, Larry (1996) "Is the Third Wave Over?" in *Journal of Democracy* no. 3.

Diamond, Larry, Linz, Juan J. and Seymour, Martin Lipset (1995) "Introduction: What Makes for Democracy?" in Larry Diamond, Juan J. Linz and Martin Lipset Seymour (eds) *Democracy in Developing Countries: Persistence, Failure, and Renewal* (Boulder).

Diamond, Larry and Plattner, Marc F. (eds) (1993) *The Global Resurgence of Democracy* (Baltimore/London).

Diamond, Larry and Plattner, Marc F. (eds) (1994) *Nationalism, Ethnic Conflict, and Democracy* (Baltimore/London).

Diamandouros, P. Nikiforos, Puhle, Hans-Jürgen and Gunther, Richard (1995) "Conclusion" in Richard Gunther, P. Nikiforos Diamandouros and Hans-Jürgen Puhle (eds) *The Politics of Democratic Consolidation. Southern Europe in Comparative Perspective* (Baltimore/London).

Di Palma, Giuseppe (1990a) "Parliaments, Consolidation, Institutionalization: A Minimalist View" in Ulrike Liebert and Maurizio Cotta (eds) *Parliament and Democratic Consolidation in Southern Europe: Greece, Italy, Portugal, Spain, and Turkey* (London).

Di Palma, Giuseppe (1990b) *To Craft Democracy. An Essay on Democratic Transition* (Berkeley/Oxford).

Di Palma, Giuseppe (1991) "Legitimation from the Top to Civil Society. Politico-Cultural Change in Eastern Europe" in *World Politics* no. 1.

Di Palma, Giuseppe (1993) "Democratic Transitions: Puzzles and Surprises from West to East" in Frederick D. Weil (ed.) *Democratization in Eastern and Western Europe* (Greenwich/London).

Dowding, Keith (1994) "The Compatibility of Behaviouralism, Rational Choice and 'New Institutionalism'" in *Journal of Theoretical Politics* no. 1.

Downing, John (1996) *Internationalizing Media Theory: Transition, Power, Culture* (Newbury Park).

Duch, Raymond (1995) "Economic Chaos and the Fragility of Democratic Transition in Former Communist Regimes" in *Journal of Politics* no. 1.

Dunn, Chris and Dunn, Elizabeth (eds) (1996) *Civil Society. Challenging Western Models* (London).

Easton, David (1975) "A Re-Assessment of the Concept of Political Support" in *British Journal of Political Science* no. 4.

Easton, David (1979[3]) *A Systems Analysis of Political Life* (Chicago/London).
Eatwell, Roger (ed.) (1997) *European Political Cultures* (London).
Eckstein, Harry (1996) "Culture as a Foundation Concept for the Social Sciences" in *Journal of Theoretical Politics* no. 4.
Edvardsen, Unni (1997) "A Cultural Approach to Understanding Modes of Transition to Democracy" in *Journal of Theoretical Politics* no. 2.
Eisen, Andreas and Kaase, Max (1996) "Transformation und Transition: Zur politikwissenschaftlichen Analyse des Prozesses der deutschen Vereinigung", in Max Kaase et al. *Politisches System* (Opladen).
Elster, Jon (1995) "Transition, Constitution-Making and Separation in Czechoslovakia" in *Archives Européennes de Sociologie* no. 1.
Elster, Jon and Slagstad, Rune (eds) (1988) *Constitutionalism and Democracy* (Cambridge).
Enyedi, Zsolt (1996) "Organizing a Subcultural Party in Eastern Europe. The Case of the Hungarian Christian Democrats" in *Party Politics* no. 3.
European Commission (ed.) (1991) *Central and Eastern Eurobarometer. Public Opinion and the European Union* (4 Countries Survey), (CEEB 1990) (Bruxelles)
European Commission (ed.) (1992) *Central and Eastern Eurobarometer. Public Opinion and the European Union* (11 Countries Survey), (CEEB 1991) (Bruxelles).
European Commission (ed.) (1993) *Central and Eastern Eurobarometer. Public Opinion and the European Union* (18 Countries Survey), (CEEB 1992) (Bruxelles).
European Commission (ed.) (1994) *Central and Eastern Eurobarometer. Public Opinion and the European Union* (18 Countries Survey), (CEEB 1993) (Bruxelles).
European Commission (ed.) (1995) *Central and Eastern Eurobarometer. Public Opinion and the European Union* (18 Countries Survey), (CEEB 1994) (Bruxelles).
European Commission (ed.) (1996) *Central and Eastern Eurobarometer. Public Opinion and the European Union* (19 Countries Survey), (CEEB 1995) (Bruxelles).
European Commission (ed.) (1994) *Eurobarometer 41. Public Opinion and the European Union* (12 Countries Survey) (Bruxelles).
European Commission (ed.) (1995) *Eurobarometer. Public Opinion and the European Union. Trends 1974 – 1994* (Bruxelles).
European Commission (ed.) (1995) *Eurobarometer 43. Public Opinion and the European Union* (15 Countries Survey) (Bruxelles).
European Commissison (ed.) (1996) *Eurobarometer 46. Public Opinion and the European Union (15 Countries Survey)* (Bruxelles).
European Commission (ed.) (1997) *Central and Eastern Eurobarometer. Public Opinion and the European Union (20 Countries Survey)*, (CEEB 1996) (Bruxelles).

European Commission (ed.) (1998) *Central and Eastern Eurobarometer. Public Opinion and the European Union (10 Countries Survey)*, (CEEB 1997) (Bruxelles).

Evans, Geoffrey and Whitefield, Stephen (1995a) "Communist-successor Parties in the Czech Republic, Slovakia and Hungary Compared" in *Party Politics* no. 4.

Evans, Geoffrey and Whitefield, Stephen (1995b) "The Politics and Economics of Democratic Commitment: Support for Democracy in Transition Societies" in *British Journal of Political Science* no. 4.

Fischer, Mary Ellen (ed.) (1996) *Establishing Democracies* (Boulder).

Fishman, Robert (1990) "Rethinking State and Regime. Southern Europe's Transition to Democracy" in *World Politics* no. 3.

Fuchs, Dieter (1989) *Die Unterstützung des politischen Systems der Bundesrepublik Deutschland* (Opladen).

Fuchs, Dieter (1997) "Welche Demokratie wollen die Deutschen? Einstellungen zur Demokratie im vereinigten Deutschland" in Oscar W. Gabriel (ed.) *Politische Orientierungen und Verhaltensweisen im vereinigten Deutschland* (Opladen).

Fuchs, Dieter, Guidorossi, Giovanna and Svensson, Palle (1995) "Support for the Democratic System" in Hans-Dieter Klingemann and Dieter Fuchs (eds) *Citizens and the State, Beliefs in Government* Volume 1 (Oxford).

Fuchs, Dieter and Klingemann, Hans-Dieter (1995) "Citizen and the State: A Relationship Transformed" in Hans-Dieter Klingemann and Dieter Fuchs (eds) *Citizens and the State* (Oxford).

Gabriel, Oscar W. (1994a) "Politische Kultur aus der Sicht der empirischen Sozialforschung" in Oskar Niedermayer and Klaus von Beyme (eds) *Politische Kultur in Ost- und Westdeutschland* (Berlin).

Gabriel, Oscar W. (1994[2]b) "Politische Einstellungen und politische Kultur" in Oscar W. Gabriel and Frank Brettschneider (eds) *Die EU-Staaten im Vergleich. Strukturen, Prozesse, Politikinhalte* (Opladen).

Gabriel, Oscar W. (1995) "Political Efficacy and Trust" in Jan W. van Deth and Elinor Scarbrough (eds) *The Impact of Values. Beliefs in Government* Volume Four (Oxford).

Gabriel, Oscar W. (1996) "Politische Orientierungen und Verhaltensweisen" in Max Kaase et al. *Politisches System* (Opladen).

Gabriel, Oscar W. (ed.) (1997) *Politische Orientierungen und Verhaltensweisen im vereinigten Deutschland* (Opladen).

Gabriel, Oscar W. and Deth, Jan W. van (1995) "Political Interest" in Jan W. van Deth and Elinor Scarbrough (eds) *The Impact of Values. Beliefs in Government* Volume Four (Oxford).

Geddes, Barbara (1995) "A Comparative Perspective on the Leninist Legacy in Eastern Europe" in *Comparative Political Studies* no. 2.

Gensicke, Thomas (1996) "Ostdeutschland 1989-1995 im Wandel. Objektive und subjektive Umbrüche" in *Journal für Sozialforschung* no. 1.

Gerlich, Peter, Plasser, Fritz and Ulram, Peter A. (eds) (1992) *Regimewechsel. Demokratisierung und politische Kultur in Ost-Mitteleuropa* (Vienna/Cologne).

Gibson, James L. (1995) "The Resilience of Mass Support for Democratic Institutions and Processes in the Nascent Russian and Ukrainian Democracies" in Vladimir Tismaneanu (ed.) *Political Culture and Civil Society in Russia and the New States of Eurasia* (New York/London).

Glaeßner, Gert-Joachim (ed.) (1994) *Demokratie nach dem Ende des Kommunismus. Regimewechsel, Transition und Demokratisierung im Postkommunismus* (Opladen).

Glaeßner, Gert-Joachim and Reiman, Michael (eds) (1997) *Systemwechsel und Demokratisierung* (Opladen).

Gluchowski, Peter Michael and Zelle, Carsten (1992) "Demokratisierung in Ostdeutschland. Aspekte der politischen Kultur in der Periode des Systemwechsels" in Peter Gerlich, Fritz Plasser, Peter A. Ulram (eds) *Regimewechsel. Demokratisierung und politische Kultur in Ost-Mitteleuropa* (Vienna/Cologne).

Gluchowski, Peter Michael and Zelle, Carsten (1993) "Vom Optimismus zum Realismus: Ostdeutschland auf dem Weg in das bundesrepublikanische politische System" in Fritz Plasser and Peter A. Ulram (eds) *Transformation oder Stagnation? Aktuelle politische Trends in Osteuropa* (Vienna).

Goodin, Robert E. (1995) "Institutions and their Design" in Robert E. Goodin (ed.) *The Theory of Institutional Design* (Cambridge).

Goutorov, Vladimir, Koryushkin, Alexander and Meyer, Gerd (eds) (1997) *Political Culture and Political Change in Post-communist Societies* (St. Petersburg).

Gunther, Richard, Diamandouros, P. Nikiforos and Puhle, Hans-Jürgen (eds) (1995) *The Politics of Democratic Consolidation. Southern Europe in Comparative Perspective* (Baltimore/London).

Gunther, Richard, Puhle, Hans-Jürgen and Diamandouros, P. Nikoforos (1995) "Introduction" in Richard Gunther, P. Nikiforos Diamandouros and Hans-Jürgen Puhle (eds) *The Politics of Democratic Consolidation. Southern Europe in Comparative Perspective* (Baltimore/London).

Gunther, Richard, Diamandouros, P. Nikoforos and Puhle, Hans-Jürgen (1996) "O'Donnell's 'illusions': A Rejoinder" in *Journal of Democracy* no. 4.

Haerpfer, Christian W. (1995) "Das Neue Demokratien Barometer 1994. Eine 10-Nationen Studie" in *SWS-Rundschau* no. 1.

Hall, Peter A. and Taylor, Rosemary C. R. (1996) "Political Science and the Three New Institutionalisms" in *Political Studies* no. 4.

Hallenberger, Gerd and Krzeminski, Michael (eds) (1994) *Osteuropas Medienlandschaft im Umbruch* (Berlin).

Handl, Vladimír, Konecný, Cestmír et al. and Ploeschl, Josef (1995) "Tschechische Republik" in Werner Weidenfeld (ed.) *Mittel- und Osteuropa auf dem Weg in die Europäische Union* (Gütersloh).

Havel, Václav, Klaus, Václav and Pithart, Petr (1996) "Civil Society After Communism. Rival Visions" in *Journal of Democracy* no. 1.

Hendrych, Dusan (1995) "Constitutionalism and Constitutional Change in Czechoslovakia" in Joachim Jens Hesse and Nevil Johnson (eds) *Constitutional Policy and Change in Europe* (Oxford).

Hesse, Joachim Jens (ed.) (1993) *Administrative Transformation in Central and Eastern Europe* (Oxford).

Hesse, Joachim Jens and Johnson, Nevil (eds) (1995) *Constitutional Policy and Change in Europe* (Oxford).

Higley, John (1992) "Spain: The Very Model of the Modern Elite Settlement" in John Higley and Richard Gunther (eds) *Elites and Democratic Consolidation in Latin America and Southern Europe* (New York).

Higley, John and Burton, Michael G. (1989) "The Elite Variable in Democratic Transitions and Breakdowns" in *American Sociological Review* no. 1.

Higley, John and Pakulski, Jan (1992) "Revolution and Elite Transformation in Eastern Europe" in *Australian Journal of Political Science* no. 1.

Higley, John and Pakulski, Jan (1994) "Elite Transformation in Eastern Europe and Russia". Paper presented at the XVIth World Congress of the International Political Science Association (Berlin).

Holmes, Stephen (1994) "The End of Decommunization. Explaining the Downfall of Historical Justice" in *East European Constitutional Review* no. 3/4.

Huffman, Jeffrey S. and Gautier, Mary L. (1993) "Continuity in Transitions Theory" in Frederick D. Weil, Jeffrey S. Huffman and Mary L. Gautier (eds) *Democratization in Eastern and Western Europe.* Volume 1 of Research on Democracy and Society (Greenwich/London).

Huntington, Samuel P. (1991) *The Third Wave. Democratization in the Late Twentieth Century* (Norman/London).

Huntington, Samuel P. (1996) "Democracy for the Long Haul" in *Journal of Democracy* no. 2.

Huntington, Samuel P. (1997) "The Future of the Third Wave" in *Journal of Democracy* no. 4.

Ilonszki, Gabriella and Kurtán, Sándor (1992) "Traurige Revolution – freudlose Demokratie. Aspekte der ungarischen politischen Kultur in der Periode des Systemwechsels" in Peter Gerlich, Fritz Plasser and Peter A. Ulram (eds) *Regimewechsel. Demokratisierung und politische Kultur in Ost-Mitteleuropa* (Vienna/Cologne).

Inglehart, Ronald (1995^2) *Kultureller Umbruch. Wertwandel in der westlichen Welt,* Studienausgabe (Frankfurt/New York).

Inglehart, Ronald (1997) *Modernization and Postmodernization. Cultural, Economic, and Political Change in 43 Societies* (Princeton).

Inotai, András and Nötzold, Jürgen (1995) "Ungarn" in Werner Weidenfeld (ed.) *Mittel- und Osteuropa auf dem Weg in die Europäische Union* (Gütersloh).

Ishiyama, John T. (1995) "Communist Parties in Transition: Structures, Leaders and Processes of Democratic Democratization in Eastern Europe" in *Comparative Politics* no. 2.

Ishyama, John T. (1997) "The Sickle or the Rose? Previous Regime Types and the Evolution of the Ex-Communist Parties in Post-Communist Politics" in *Comparative Political Studies* no. 3.

Jablonski, Andrzej W. and Meyer, Gerd (eds) (1996) *The Political Culture of Poland in Transition* (Wroclaw).

Jakubowicz, Karol (1996) "Television and Elections in Post-1989 Poland: How Powerful is the Medium?" in David L. Swanson and Paolo Mancini (eds) *Politics, Media, and Modern Democracy* (Westport/London).

Jowitt, Ken (1992) "The Leninist Legacy" in Ivo Banac (ed.) *Eastern Europe in Revolution.* Ithaca/London. Reprinted in Ken Jowitt (1992) *New World Disorder. The Leninist Extinction* (Berkeley/Los Angeles/London).

Kaase, Max (1994a) "Political Culture and Political Consolidation in Central and Eastern Europe" in Frederick D. Weil (ed.) *Political Culture and Political Structure: Theoretical and Empirical Studies* (Greenwich/London).

Kaase, Max (1994b) "Political Culture and Political Consolidation" in Hendrikus J. Blommestein and Bernard Steunenberg (eds) *Government and Markets. Establishing a Democratic Constitutional Order and a Market Economy in Former Socialist Countries* (Dordrecht/Boston/London).

Kaase, Max and Newton, Kenneth (1995) "Political Attitudes and Political Behaviour" in Max Kaase and Kenneth Newton *Beliefs in Government* (= Beliefs in Government Volume Five) (New York).

Karl, Terry Lynn and Schmitter, Philippe C. (1991) "Modes of Transition in Latin America, Southern and Eastern Europe" in *International Social Science Journal* no. 128.

Karl, Terry Lynn and Schmitter, Philippe C. (1995) "From an Iron Curtain to a Paper Curtain: Grounding Transitologists or Students of Postcommunism?" in *Slavic Review* no. 4.

Kasapovic, Mirjana and Nohlen, Dieter (1996) "Wahlsysteme und Systemwechsel in Osteuropa" in Wolfgang Merkel, Eberhard Sandschneider and Dieter Segert (eds) *Systemwechsel 2. Die Institutionalisierung der Demokratie* (Opladen).

Kato, Junko (1996) "Review Article: Institutions and Rationality in Politics – Three Varieties of Neo-Institutionalists" in *British Journal of Political Science* no. 4.

Kitschelt, Herbert (1995a) "Formation of Party Cleavages in Post-communist Democracies: Theoretical Propositions" in *Party Politics* no. 4.

Kitschelt, Herbert (1995b) "Die Entwicklung post-sozialistischer Parteiensysteme. Vergleichende Perspektiven" in Helmut Wollmann, Helmut

Wiesenthal and Frank Bönker (eds) *Transformation sozialistischer Gesellschaften. Am Ende des Anfangs* (Opladen).

Klages, Herbert (1990) "Vertrauen und Vertrauensverlust in westlichen Demokratien" in Peter Haungs (ed.) *Politik ohne Vertrauen?* (Baden-Baden).

Kleinwächter, Wolfgang (1996) "Zwischen Macht und Markt. Rundfunk in Osteuropa auf dem Weg zum dualen System" in Miriam Mechel and Markus Kriener (eds) *Internationale Kommunikation* (Opladen).

Klingemann, Hans-Dieter, Mochmann, Ekkehard and Newton, Kenneth (eds) (1994) *Political Research in Eastern Europe,* InformationsZentrum Sozialwissenschaften (Berlin).

Klingemann, Hans-Dieter and Fuchs, Dieter (eds) (1995) *Citizens and the State. Beliefs in Government* Volume One (Oxford).

Knell, Mark (ed.) (1996) *Economic of Transition. Structural Adjustments and Growth Prospects in Eastern Europe* (Aldershot).

Koelble, Thomas A. (1995) "The New Institutionalism in Political Science and Sociology" in *Comparative Politics* no. 2.

Kommers, Donald P. and Thompson, W.J. (1995) "Fundamentals in the Liberal Constitutional Tradition" in Joachim Jens Hesse and Nevil Johnson (eds) *Constitutional Policy and Change in Europe* (Oxford).

Kopecky, Petr (1995) "Developing Party Organizations in East-Central Europe" in *Party Politics* no. 4.

Kreuzer, Peter (1996) "Plädoyer für eine Renaissance der kulturellen Perspektive in der politikwissenschaftlichen Analyse" in *Politische Vierteljahresschrift* no. 2.

Küchler, Manfred (1992) "The Dynamics of Mass Political Support in Western Europe" in Karlheinz Reif and Ronald Inglehart (eds) *Eurobarometer. The Dynamics of European Public Opinion* (London).

Kymlicka, Will (1995) *Multicultural Citizenship. A Liberal Theory of Minority Rights* (Oxford).

Lagos, Marta (1997) "Latin America's Smiling Mask" in *Journal of Democracy* no. 3.

Lane, Ruth (1992) "Political Culture: Residual Category or General Theory?" in *Comparative Political Studies* no. 4.

Lane, Jan-Erik and Ersson, Svante O. (1996) "Political Culture" in Jan-Erik Lane and Svante O. Ersson *European Politics* (London/Thousand Oaks).

Lauth, Hans-Joachim and Merkel, Wolfgang (1997) "Zivilgesellschaft und Transformation. Ein Diskussionsbeitrag in revisionistischer Absicht" in *Forschungsjournal NSB* no. 1.

Lawson, Stephanie (1993) "Conceptual Issues in the Comparative Study of Regime Change and Democratization" in *Comparative Politics* no. 2.

Lemke, Christiane (1997) "Nachholende Modernisierung. Demokratisierung und politischer Protest in postkommunistischen Gesellschaften" in *Aus Politik und Zeitgeschichte* B 5.

Lewis, Paul G. (1992) (ed.) *Democracy and Civil Society in Eastern Europe.* Selected Papers from the Fourth World Congress for Soviet and East European Studies (Harrogate, New York).

Lewis, Paul G. (1996) (ed.) *Party Structures and Organization in East-Central Europe* (London).

Lewis, Paul, Lomax, Bill and Wightman, Gordon (1994) "The Emergence of Multi-Party Systems in East-Central Europe. A Comparative Analysis" in Geoffrey Pridham and Tatu Vanhanen (eds) *Democratization in Eastern Europe. Domestic and International Perspectives* (London).

Lewis, Paul G. and Gortat, Radzislawa (1995) "Models of Party Development and Questions of State Dependence in Poland" in *Party Politics* no. 4.

Liebert, Ulrike (1995) *Modelle demokratischer Konsolidierung* (Opladen).

Lijphart, Arend (1992) "Democratization and Constitutional Choices in Czecho-Slovakia, Hungary, and Poland, 1989-1991" in György Szoboszlai (ed.) *Flying Blind. Emerging Democracies in East-Central Europe,* Budapest: Hungarian Political Science Association.

Linz, Juan J. (1978) *The Breakdown of Democratic Regimes. Crisis, Breakdown, & Reequilibration* (Baltimore).

Linz, Juan J. (1990) "Transitions to Democracy" in *The Washington Quarterly* no. 3.

Linz, Juan J. and Stepan, Alfred (1989) "Political Crafting of Democratic Consolidation or Destruction: European and South American Comparisons" in Robert A. Pastor (ed.) *Democracy in the Americas: Stopping the Pendulum* (New York).

Linz, Juan J. and Valenzuela, Arturo (eds) (1994) *The Failure of Presidential Democracy.* Comparative Perspectives (Baltimore/London).

Linz, Juan J. and Stepan, Alfred (1996a) "Toward Consolidated Democracies" in *Journal of Democracy* no. 2.

Linz, Juan J. and Stepan, Alfred (1996b) *Problems of Democratic Transition and Consolidation: Southern Europe, South America, and Post-communist Europe* (Baltimore).

Listhaug, Ola and Wiberg, Matti (1995) "Confidence in Political and Private Institutions" in Hans-Dieter Klingemann and Dieter Fuchs (eds) *Citizens and the State, Beliefs in Government* Vol. One (Oxford).

Longchamp, Claude (1993²) "Politisch-kultureller Wandel in der Schweiz" in Fritz Plasser and Peter A. Ulram (eds) *Staatsbürger oder Untertanen? Politische Kultur Deutschlands, Österreichs und der Schweiz im Vergleich* (Frankfurt/Bern).

Luchterhand, Otto (ed.) (1996) *Neue Regierungssysteme in Osteuropa und der GUS* (Berlin).

Mainwaring, Scott (1992) "Transitions to Democracy and Democratic Consolidation: Theoretical and Comparative Issues" in Scott Mainwaring, Guillermo O'Donnell and J. Samuel Valenzuela (eds) *Issues in*

Democratic Consolidation: The New South American Democracies in Comparative Perspective (Notre Dame).

Malova, Darina (1996) "Slovakia" in *European Journal of Political Research* no. 3/4.

Mangott, Gerhard (1992) "Parteienbildung und Parteiensysteme in Ost-Mitteleuropa im Vergleich" in Peter Gerlich, Fritz Plasser and Peter A. Ulram (eds) *Regimewechsel. Demokratisierung und politische Kultur in Ost-Mitteleuropa* (Vienna/Cologne).

March, James G. and Olsen, Johan P. (1989) *Rediscovering Institutions. The Organizational Basis of Politics* (New York).

Mason, James S. (1995) "Attitudes towards the Market and Political Participation in the Post-Communist States" in *Slavic Review* no. 2.

Mason, David S., Nelson, Daniel S. and Szaklarski, Bohdan M. (1991) "Apathy and the Birth of Democracy: The Polish Struggle" in *East European Politics and Societies* no. 2.

McDonough, Peter (1995) "Identities, Ideologies, and Interests: Democratization and the Culture of Mass Politics in Spain and Eastern Europe" in *Journal of Politics* no. 3.

McGregor, James P. (1991) "Value Structures in a Developed Socialist System: The Case of Czechoslovakia" in *Comparative Politics* no. 2.

McIntosh, Mary E. and Abele MacIver, Martha (1992) "Coping with Freedom and Uncertainty: Public Opinion in Hungary, Poland and Czechoslovakia, 1989-1992" in *International Journal of Public Opinion* no. 4.

McIntosh, Mary E., Abele MacIver, Martha, Abele, Daniel and Smeltz, Dina (1994) "Publics Meet Market Democracy in Central and East Europe, 1991-1993" in *Slavic Review* no. 2.

McIntosh, Mary et al. (1996) *The New European Security Architecture: Public Attitudes Toward European Security*. USIA Office of Research and Media Reaction, Washington D.C. (September).

McIntosh, Mary E., Abele MacIver, Martha and Abele, Daniel G. (1996) "Dominant and Majority Exclusive Nationalism in Eastern Europe" in Frederick D. Weil (ed.) *Extremism, Protest, Social Movements and Democracy. Research on Democracy and Society* Vol. 3, (Greenwich, Ct).

Mencinger, Joze and Suppan, Arnold (1995) "Slowenien" in Werner Weidenfeld (ed.) *Mittel- und Osteuropa auf dem Weg in die Europäische Union* (Gütersloh).

Merkel, Wolfgang (ed.) (1994) *Systemwechsel 1: Theorien, Ansätze und Konzeptionen* (Opladen).

Merkel, Wolfgang (1994a) "Restriktionen und Chancen demokratischer Konsolidierung in postkommunistischen Gesellschaften. Ostmitteleuropa im Vergleich" in *Berliner Journal für Soziologie* no. 4.

Merkel, Wolfgang (1994b) "Struktur oder Akteur, System oder Handlung: Gibt es einen Königsweg in der sozialwissenschaftlichen Transformationsforschung?" in Wolfgang Merkel (ed.) *Systemwechsel 1. Theorien, Ansätze und Konzeptionen* (Opladen).

Merkel, Wolfgang (1996a) "Theorien der Transformation: Die demokratische Konsolidierung postautoritärer Gesellschaften" in Klaus von Beyme and Claus Offe (eds) *Politische Theorien in der Ära der Transformation* (Opladen).

Merkel, Wolfgang (1996b) "Institutionalisierung und Konsolidierung der Demokratien in Osteuropa" in Wolfgang Merkel, Eberhard Sandschneider and Dieter Segert (eds) *Systemwechsel 2. Die Institutionalisierung der Demokratie* (Opladen).

Merkel, Wolfgang (1997) "Die Rolle von Eliten und Massen beim Übergang von autokratischen zu demokratischen Herrschaftssystemen" in Jan Wielgohs and Helmut Wiesendahl (eds) *Einheit und Differenz. Die Transformation Ostdeutschlands in vergleichender Perspektive* (Berlin).

Merkel, Wolfgang, Sandschneider, Eberhard and Segert, Dieter (eds) (1996a) *Systemwechsel 2. Die Institutionalisierung der Demokratie* (Opladen).

Merkel, Wolfgang, Sandschneider, Eberhard and Segert, Dieter (1996b) "Einleitung: Die Institutionalisierung der Demokratie" in Wolfgang Merkel, Eberhard Sandschneider, Dieter Segert (eds) *Systemwechsel 2. Die Institutionalisierung der Demokratie* (Opladen).

Merkel, Wolfgang and Sandschneider, Eberhard (eds) (1997) *Systemwechsel 3. Parteien im Transformationsprozeß* (Opladen).

Meyer, Gerd (ed.) (1993) *Die politischen Kulturen Ostmitteleuropas im Umbruch* (Tübingen).

Meyer, Gerd (1994) "Democratic Legitimacy in Post-Communist Societies: Concepts and Problems" in Andras Bozóki (ed.) *Democratic Legitimacy in Post-Communist Societies* (Budapest).

Meyer, Gerd (1996) "Towards a Political Sociology of Postcommunism: the Political Cultures of East Central Europe on the Way to Democracy" in Andrzej W. Jablonski and Gerd Meyer (eds) *The Political Culture of Poland in Transition* (Wroclaw).

Meyer, Gerd (1997) "Zwischen Haben und Sein. Psychische Aspekte des Transformationsprozesses in postkommunistischen Gesellschaften" in *Aus Politik und Zeitgeschichte* B 5.

Miller, Arthur H., Reisinger, William M. and Hesli, Vicki L. (eds) (1993) *Public Opinion and Regime Change: The New Politics of Post-Soviet Societies* (Boulder).

Miller, Arthur H., Reisinger, William M. and Hesli, Vicki L. (1996) "Understanding Political Change in Post-Soviet Societies" in *American Political Science Review* no. 1.

Milton, Andrew K. (1997) "News Media Reform in Eastern Europe. A Cross-National Comparison" in *The Journal of Communist Studies and Transition Politics* no 1.

Mishler, William and Richard Rose, Richard (1996) "Trajectories of Fear and Hope: Support for Democracy in Post-communist Europe" in *Comparative Political Studies* no. 4.

Misztal, Barbara (1996) "Postcommunist Ambivalence: Becoming of a New Formation?" in *Archives Européennes de Sociologie* no. 1.

Montero, José Ramon and Torcal, Mariano (1990) "Voters and Citizens in a New Democracy: Some Trend Data on Political Attitudes in Spain" in *International Journal of Public Opinion Research* no. 2.

Morlino, Leonardo (1994) "Democratic Consolidation: Definition and Models". Manuscript, Florenz, reprint in Geoffrey Pridham (1995) (ed.) *Transitions to Democracy. Comparative Perspectives from Southern Europe, Latin America and Eastern Europe* (Aldershot).

Morlino, Leonardo (1995) "Political Parties and Democratic Consolidation in Southern Europe" in Richard Gunther, P. Nikiforos Diamandouros and Hans-Jürgen Puhle (eds) *The Politics of Democratic Consolidation. Southern Europe in Comparative Perspective* (Baltimore/London).

Morlino, Leonardo and Montero, Jose R. (1995) "Legitimacy and Democracy in Southern Europe" in Richard Gunther, P. Nikiforos Diamandouros and Hans-Jürgen Puhle (eds) *The Politics of Democratic Consolidation. Southern Europe in Comparative Perspective* (Baltimore/London).

Müller, Klaus (1995) "Vom Post-Kommunismus zur Postmodernität? Zur Erklärung sozialen Wandels in Osteuropa" in *Kölner Zeitschrift für Soziologie und Sozialpsychologie* no. 1.

Müller, Wolfgang C. (1993²) "Politische Kultur: Konzept – Forschungsmethoden – Effekte" in Fritz Plasser and Peter A. Ulram (eds) *Staatsbürger oder Untertanen? Politische Kultur Deutschlands, Österreichs und der Schweiz im Vergleich* (Frankfurt/Bern).

Muller, Edward N. and Seligson, Mitchell A. (1994) "Civic Culture and Democracy: The Question of Causal Relationships" in *American Political Science Review* no. 3.

Munck, Gerardo L. (1994a) "Democratic Transitions in Comparative Perspective" in *Comparative Politics* no. 2.

Munck, Gerardo L. (1994b) "Explaining Institutional Choices in Democratic Transitions: Comparative Perspectives on the East European and South American Cases". Paper presented at the XVIth World Congress of the International Political Science Association (IPSA) (Berlin).

Munck, Gerardo L. (1995) "Political Regime, Transition, and Consolidation. Conceptual Issues in Regime Analysis". Paper prepared for presentation at the XIXth International Congress of the Latin American Studies Association (LASA) (Washington, D.C.).

Munck, Gerardo L. (1996) "Disaggregating Political Regime: Conceptual Issues in the Study of Democratization". Manuskript: University of Illinois at Urbana-Champaign, Department of Political Science.

Nelken, David (1996) "A Legal Revolution? The Judges and Tangentopoli" in Stephen Gundle and Simon Parker (eds) *The New Italian Republic. From The Fall of the Berlin Wall to Berlusconi* (London/New York).

Nelson, Daniel N. (1995) "The Rise of Public Legitimation in the Soviet Union and Eastern Europe" in Daniel N. Nelson (ed.) *After Authoritarianism. Democracy or Disorder?* (Westport).

Neuhold, Hanspeter, Havlik, Peter and Suppan, Arnold (eds) (1995) *Political and Economic Transformation in East Central Europe* (Boulder).

Niedermayer, Oskar and Beyme, Klaus von (eds) (1994) *Politische Kultur in Ost- und Westdeutschland* (Berlin).

Niedermayer, Oskar and Westle, Bettina (1995) "A Typology of Orientations" in Oskar Niedermayer and Richard Sinnott (eds) *Public Opinion and International Governance* (Oxford).

Nohlen, Dieter and Kasapovic, Mirjana (1996) *Wahlsysteme und Systemwechsel in Osteuropa* (Opladen).

Nohlen, Dieter (1996) "Wahlsysteme in Osteuropa. Geschichte, Kritik, Reform" in *Zeitschrift für Parlamentsfragen* no. 3.

O'Donnell, Guillermo (1992) "Transitions, Continuities, and Paradoxes" in Scott Mainwaring, Guillermo O'Donnell and J. Samuel Valenzuela (eds) *Issues in Democratic Consolidation: The New South American Democracies in Comparative Perspective* (Notre Dame).

O'Donnell, Guillermo (1993) "On the State, Democratization and Some Conceptual Problems". (A Latin American View with Glances at Some Post-Communist Countries) in *World Development* no. 8.

O'Donnell, Guillermo (1994) "Delegative Democracy" in *Journal of Democracy* no. 1.

O'Donnell, Guillermo (1995) "Do Economists Know Best?" in *Journal of Democracy* no. 1.

O'Donnell, Guillermo (1996a) "Illusions About Consolidation" in *Journal of Democracy* no. 2.

O'Donnell, Guillermo (1996b) "Illusions and Conceptual Flaws" in *Journal of Democracy* no. 4.

O'Donnell, Guillermo, Schmitter, Philippe C. and Whitehead, Laurence (eds) (1986) *Transitions from Authoritarian Rule.* 4 volumes (Baltimore/London).

O'Donnell, Guillermo and Schmitter, Philippe C. (1986) "Transitions from Authoritarian Rule: Tentative Conclusions about Uncertain Democracies". Vol. 4 of Guillermo O'Donnell, Philippe C. Schmitter and Laurence Whitehead (eds) *Transitions from Authoritarian Rule* (Baltimore/London).

O'Neil, Patrick H. (ed.) (1997) *Post-Communism and the Media in Eastern Europe* (London).

Offe, Claus (1994a) *Der Tunnel am Ende des Lichts. Erkundungen der politischen Transformation im neuen Osten* (Frankfurt).

Offe, Claus (1994b) "Designing Institutions for East European Transitions". *Vienna: Institut für Höhere Studien, Political Science Series* no. 19. Reprinted in Robert E. Goodin (ed.) (1995) *The Theory of Institutional Design* (Cambridge).

Olson, David M. and Norton, Philip (eds) *The New Parliaments in Central and Eastern Europe* (London).

Osiatynski, Wiktor (1995a) "A Letter from Poland" in *East European Constitutional Review*, no. 2.

Osiatynski, Wiktor (1995b) "After Walesa" in *East European Constitutional Review* no. 4.

Paletz, David L., Jakubowicz, Karol and Novosel, Pavao (eds) (1995) *Glasnost and after: Media and Change in Central and Eastern Europe* (Cresskill, N.J.).

Parrott, Bruce (1997) "Perspectives on postcommunist democratization" in Karen Dawisha and Bruce Parrott (eds) *The Consolidation of Democracy in East Europe* (Cambridge).

Parry, Geraint and Miran, Michael (eds) (1994) *Democracy and Democratization* (London/New York).

Pasquino, Gianfranco (1990) "Party Elites and Democratic Consolidation: Cross-National Comparison of Southern European Experience" in Geoffrey Pridham (ed.) *Securing Democracy: Political Parties and Democratic Consolidation in Southern Europe*, (London).

Pasquino, Gianfranco (1995) "Executive Legislative Relations in Southern Europe" in Richard Gunther, P. Nikiforos Diamandouros and Hans-Jürgen Puhle (eds) *The Politics of Democratic Consolidation. Southern Europe in Comparative Perspective* (Baltimore/London).

Plasser, Fritz and Pribersky, Andreas (eds) (1996) *Political Culture in East Central Europe* (London).

Plasser, Fritz and Ulram, Peter A. (1992a) "Zwischen Desillusionierung und Konsolidierung. Demokratie- und Politikverständnis in Ungarn, der CSFR und Polen" in Peter Gerlich, Fritz Plasser and Peter A. Ulram (eds) *Regimewechsel. Demokratisierung und politische Kultur in Ost-Mitteleuropa* (Vienna/Cologne).

Plasser, Fritz and Ulram, Peter A. (1992b) "Perspektiven der Demokratisierung in Ost-Mitteleuropa". Vorläufige Anmerkungen in Peter Gerlich, Fritz Plasser and Peter A. Ulram (eds) *Regimewechsel. Demokratisierung und politische Kultur in Ost- Mitteleuropa* (Vienna/Cologne).

Plasser, Fritz and Ulram, Peter A. (eds) (1993) *Transformation oder Stagnation? Aktuelle politische Trends in Osteuropa* (Vienna).

Plasser, Fritz and Ulram, Peter A. (1993a) "Zum Stand der Demokratisierung in Ost-Mitteleuropa" in Fritz Plasser and Peter A. Ulram (eds) *Transformation oder Stagnation? Aktuelle politische Trends in Osteuropa* (Vienna).

Plasser, Fritz and Ulram, Peter A. (1993[2]) "Politischer Kulturvergleich: Deutschland, Österreich und die Schweiz" in Fritz Plasser and Peter A. Ulram (eds) *Staatsbürger oder Untertanen? Politische Kultur Deutschlands, Österreichs und der Schweiz im Vergleich* (Frankfurt/Bern).

Plasser, Fritz and Ulram Peter A. (1993c) "Of Time and Democratic Stabilization." Paper presented at the WAPOR Seminar " Public Opinion and

Public Opinion Research in Eastern Europe", Tallina (June 11-12th, 1993).

Plasser, Fritz and Ulram, Peter A. (1994a) "Monitoring Democratic Consolidation: Political Trust and System Support in East-Central-Europe", Paper Prepared for Presentation at the XVIth World Congress of the International Political Science Association, Berlin (August 21-25).

Plasser, Fritz and Ulram, Peter A. (1994b) "Politische Systemunterstützung und Institutionenvertrauen in den OZE-Staaten" in *Österreichische Zeitschrift für Politikwissenschaft* no. 4.

Plasser, Fritz and Ulram, Peter A. (1996) "Measuring Political Culture in East Central Europe: Political Trust and System Support" in Fritz Plasser and Andreas Pribersky (eds) *Political Culture in East Central Europe* (London).

Plasser, Fritz, Ulram, Peter A. and Waldrauch, Harald (1997) *Politischer Kulturwandel in Ost-Mitteleuropa. Theorie und Empirie demokratischer Konsolidierung* (Opladen).

Pogany, Istvan (1996) "Constitution Making or Constitutional Transformation in Post-Communist Societies?" in *Political Studies*, Special Issue on "Constitutionalism in Transformation: European and Theoretical Perspectives".

Poppovic, Malak and Pinheiro, Paulo Sérgio (1995) "How to Consolidate Democracy? A Human Rights Approach" in *International Social Science Journal* no. 143.

Preuss, Ulrich K. (1995) "Patterns of Constitutional Evolution and Change in Eastern Europe" in Joachim Jens Hesse and Nevil Johnson (eds) *Constitutional Policy and Change in Europe* (Oxford).

Pridham, Geoffrey (1990a) "Political Parties, Parliaments and Democratic Consolidation in Southern Europe: Empirical and Theoretical Perspectives" in Ulrike Liebert and Maurizio Cotta (eds) *Parliament and Democratic Consolidation in Southern Europe: Greece, Italy, Portugal, Spain and Turkey* (London).

Pridham, Geoffrey (1990b) " Southern European Democracies on the Road to Consolidation: A Comparative Assessment of the Role of Political Parties" in Geoffrey Pridham (ed.) *Securing Democracy: Political Parties and Democratic Consolidation in Southern Europe* (London).

Pridham, Geoffrey (1994) "Democratic Transitions in Theory and Practice. Southern European Lessons for Eastern Europe?" in Geoffrey Pridham and Tatu Vanhanen (eds) *Democratization in Eastern Europe. Domestic and International Perspectives* (London).

Pridham, Geoffrey (1995a) "The International Context of Democratic Consolidation: Southern Europe in Comparative Perspective" in Richard Gunther, P. Nikiforos Diamandouros and Hans-Jürgen Puhle (eds) *The Politics of Democratic Consolidation. Southern Europe in Comparative Perspective* (Baltimore/London).

Pridham, Geoffrey (1995b) "Political Parties and Their Strategies in the Transition from Authoritarian Rule: The Comparative Perspective" in Gordon Wightman (ed.) *Party Formation in East-Central Europe. Post-communist Politics in Czechoslovakia, Hungary, Poland and Bulgaria* (Aldershot).

Pridham, Geoffrey and Lewis, Paul G. (1996a) (eds) *Stabilizing Fragile Democracies. Comparing New Party Systems in Southern and Eastern Europe* (London/New York).

Pridham, Geoffrey and Lewis, Paul (1996b) "Introduction. Stabilizing Fragile Democracies and Party System Development" in Geoffrey Pridham and Paul Lewis (eds) *Stabilising Fragile Democracies. Comparing New Party Systems in Southern and Eastern Europe* (London, New York).

Przeworski, Adam (1986) "Some Problems in the Study of the Transition to Democracy" in Guillermo O'Donnell, Philippe C. Schmitter and Laurence Whitehead (eds) *Transitions from Authoritarian Rule: Comparative Perspectives* (Baltimore/London).

Przeworski, Adam (1991) *Democracy and the Market. Political and Economic Reforms in Eastern Europe and Latin America* (Cambridge).

Przeworski, Adam (1994) "Economic and Political Transformations in Eastern Europe: An Update". Paper presented at the XVIth World Congress of the International Political Science Association (Berlin).

Przeworski, Adam, Michael Alvarez, José Antonio Cheibub and Fernando Limongi (1996) "What Makes Democracies Endure?" in *Journal of Democracy* no. 1.

Rau, Zbigniew (ed.) (1991) *The Reemergence of Civil Society in Eastern Europe and the Soviet Union* (Boulder/San Francisco/Oxford).

Reisinger,William H. (1995) "The Renaissance of a Rubric: Political Culture as Concept and Theory" in *International Journal of Public Opinion Research* no. 4.

Remington, Thomas F. (ed.) (1994) *Parliaments in Transition: The New Legislative Politics in the Former USSR and Eastern Europe* (Boulder).

Rieder, Jonathan (1994) "Doing Political Culture: Interpretive Practice and the Earnest Heuristic" in Frederick D. Weil (ed.) *Political Culture and Political Structure: Theoretical and Empirical Studies* (Greenwich/London).

Rivera, Sharon Werming (1996) "Historical Cleavages or Transition Mode? Influences on the Emerging Party Systems in Poland, Hungary and Czechoslovakia" in *Party Politics* no. 2.

Rose, Richard (1994) "Postcommunism and the Problem of Trust" in *Journal of Democracy* no. 3

Rose, Richard (1995) "Mobilizing Demobilized Voters in Post-communist Societies" in *Party Politics* no. 4.

Rose, Richard (1996) *What is Europe? A Dynamic Perspective* (London).

Rose, Richard (1997) "Where are Postcommunist Countries Going?" in *Journal of Democracy no.3.*

Rose, Richard and Haerpfer, Christian (1992) "New Democracies Between State and Market. A Baseline Report of Public Opinion", *Studies in Public Policy* 204, University of Strathclyde (Glasgow).

Rose, Richard and Haerpfer, Christian (1993) "Adapting to Transformation in Eastern Europe", *Studies in Public Policy* 212, University of Strathclyde (Glasgow).

Rose, Richard and Haerpfer, Christian (1994a) "New Democracies Barometer III: Learning from What is Happening", *Studies in Public Policy* 230, University of Strathclyde (Glasgow).

Rose, Richard and Haerpfer, Christian (1994b) "Mass Response to Transformation in Post-communist Societies" in *Europe-Asia Studies* no. 1.

Rose, Richard and Haerpfer, Christian (1996) "New Democracies Barometer IV: A Ten-Nation Study" (*Studies in Public Policy* no. 262).

Rose, Richard and Mishler, William T. E. (1994) "Mass Reaction to Regime Change in Eastern Europe: Polarization or Leaders and Laggards?" in *British Journal of Political Science* no. 2.

Rose, Richard and Seifert, Wolfgang (1995) "Materielle Lebensbedingungen und Einstellungen gegenüber Marktwirtschaft und Demokratie im Transformationsprozeß. Ostdeutschland und Osteuropa im Vergleich" in Helmut Wollmann, Helmut Wiesenthal and Frank Bönker (eds) *Transformation sozialistischer Gesellschaften. Am Ende des Anfangs* (Opladen).

Rüb, Friedbert W. (1996) "Zur Funktion und Bedeutung politischer Institutionen in Systemwechselprozessen. Eine vergleichende Betrachtung" in Wolfgang Merkel, Eberhard Sandschneider and Segert, Dieter (eds) *Systemwechsel 2. Die Institutionalisierung der Demokratie* (Opladen).

Rupnik, Jayues (1989) *The Other Europe. The Rise and Fall of Communism in East-Central Europe* (New York).

Rustow, Dankwart A. (1970) "Transitions to Democracy" in *Comparative Politics* no. 3.

Sandschneider, Eberhard (1995) *Stabilität und Transformation politischer Systeme. Stand und Perspektiven politikwissenschaftlicher Transformationsforschung* (Opladen).

Sandschneider, Eberhard (1996) "Die Europäische Union und die Transformation Mittel- und Osteuropas. Zum Problem exogener Stabilisierungsstrategien in Transformationsprozessen" in *Zeitschrift für Politikwissenschaft* no. 1.

Schedler, Andreas (1995) "Beyond the Prisoners' Dilemma. Some Thoughts on the Games of Institution Building in New Democracies". Paper prepared for presentation at the 91st Annual Meeting of the American Political Science Association (APSA) (Chicago).

Schedler, Andreas (1996) "Credible Change. Exploring the Bases of Institutional Reform in New Democracies" in *Institut für Höhere Studien, Reihe Politikwissenschaft* no. 38 (Vienna).

Schedler, Andreas (1997) "Concepts of Democratic Consolidation.' *Paper presented at the 1997 Meeting of the Latin American Studies Association, Guadalajara, Mexico.*

Schmitter, Philippe C. (1988) *The Consolidation of Political Democracy in Southern Europe. Third revised version.* Stanford University: mimeo.

Schmitter, Philippe C. (1992) 'The Consolidation of Democracy and Representation of Social Groups" in *American Behavioral Scientist* no. 4/5.

Schmitter, Philippe C. (1994) "Dangers and Dilemmas of Democracy" in *Journal of Democracy* no. 2.

Schmitter, Philippe C. (1995) "Organized Interests and Democratic Consolidation in Southern Europe" in Richard Gunther, P. Nikiforos Diamandouros and Hans-Jürgen Puhle (eds) *The Politics of Democratic Consolidation. Southern Europe in Comparative Perspective* (Baltimore/London).

Schmitter, Philippe (1997) "Clarifying Consolidation" in *Journal of Democracy* no. 2.

Schmitter, Philippe C. and Karl, Terry Lynn (1991) "What Democracy Is and What It Is Not" in *Journal of Democracy* no. 3.

Schmitter, Philippe C. and Karl, Terry Lynn (1992) "The Types of Democracy Emerging in Southern and Eastern Europe and South and Central America" in Peter M. E. Volten (ed.) *Bound to Change: Consolidating Democracy in East Central Europe* (New York/Prague).

Schmitter, Philippe C. and Karl, Terry Lynn (1994) "The Conceptual Travels of Transitologists and Consolidologists: How Far to the East Should They Attempt to Go?" in *Slavic Review* no. 1.

Schmitter, Philippe C. and Santiso, Javier (1998) "Three Temporal Dimensions to the Consolidation of Democracy" in *International Political Science Review* no. 1.

Schneider, Ben Ross (1995) "Democratic Consolidations: Some Broad Comparisons and Sweeping Arguments" in *Latin American Research Review* no. 2.

Segert, Dieter and Machos, Csilla (1995) *Parteien in Osteuropa. Kontext und Akteure* (Opladen).

Segert, Dieter, Stöss, Richard and Niedermayer, Oskar (eds) (1997) *Parteiensysteme in postkommunistischen Gesellschaften Osteuropas* (Opladen).

Seifert, Wolfgang and Rose, Richard (1996) "Subjektive Bewertungen der Lebensverhältnisse in den osteuropäischen Transformationsstaaten und in Ostdeutschland" in Wolfgang Glatzer (ed.) *Lebensverhältnisse in Osteuropa. Prekäre Entwicklungen und neue Konturen* (Frankfurt/New York).

Shin, Doh Chull (1994) "On the Third Wave of Democratization: A Synthesis and Evaluation of Recent Theory and Research" in *World Politics* no. 1.

Simon, János (1994) What Democracy Means for Hungarians?, unpublished research paper (Budapest).

Smolar, Aleksander (1996) "From Opposition to Atomization" in *Journal of Democracy* no. 1.

Sokolewicz, Wojciech (1995) "The Relevance of Western Models for Constitution-Building in Poland" in Joachim Jens Hesse and Nevil Johnson (eds) *Constitutional Policy and Change in Europe* (Oxford).

Sparks, Colin and Reading, Anna (1994) "Understanding Media Change in East Central Europe" in *Media, Culture and Society* no. 2.

Sparks, Colin and Reading, Anna (1997) *Communism, Capitalism and the Mass Media* (Thousand Oaks).

Stankovsky, Jan, Plasser, Fritz and Ulram, Peter A. (1998) *On the Eve of EU-Enlargement. Economic Developments and Democratic Attitudes in East-Central Europe* (Vienna).

Szabo, Máté (1996) "Repertoires of Contention in Post-Communist Protest Cultures: An East-Central European Comparative Survey" in *Social Research* no. 4.

Sztompka, Piotr (1995) "Vertrauen: Die fehlende Ressource in der postkommunistischen Gesellschaft" in Birgitta Nedelmann (ed.) *Politische Institutionen im Wandel* (Opladen).

Tarrow, Sidney (1995) "Mass Mobilization and Regime Change: Pacts, Reform, and Popular Power in Italy (1918–1922) and Spain (1975–1978)" in Richard Gunther, P. Nikiforos Diamandouros and Hans-Jürgen Puhle (eds) *The Politics of Democratic Consolidation. Southern Europe in Comparative Perspective* (Baltimore/London).

Thelen, Kathleen and Steinmo, Sven (1992) "Historical Institutionalism in Comparative Politics" in Sven Steinmo, Kathleen Thelen and Frank Longstreth (eds) *Structuring Politics. Historical Institutionalism in Comparative Politics* (Cambridge).

Times Mirror, Center for the People and Press (1991) *The Pulse of Europe. A Survey of Political and Social Attitudes*, (Mimeo).

Thomassen, Jacques (1995) "Support for Democratic Values" in Hans-Dieter Klingemann and Dieter Fuchs (eds) *Citizens and the State* (Oxford).

Tismaneanu, Vladimir (ed.) (1995) *Political Culture and Civil Society in Russia and the New States of Eurasia* (New York/London).

Tóka, Gábor (1995) "Political Support in East-Central Europe" in Hans-Dieter Klingemann and Dieter Fuchs (eds) *Citizens and the State. Beliefs in Government Volume One* (Oxford).

Ulram, Peter A. (1990) *Hegemonie und Erosion. Politische Kultur und Politischer Wandel in Österreich* (Vienna/Cologne).

Valenzuela, J. Samuel (1992) "Democratic Consolidation in Post-Transitional Settings: Notion, Process, and Facilitating Conditions" in Scott Mainwaring, Guillermo O'Donnell and J. Samuel Valenzuela (eds) *Issues in Democratic Consolidation: The New South American Democracies in Comparative Perspective* (Notre Dame).

Vanhanen, Tatu (1997) *Prospects of Democracy. A Study of 172 countries* (London).

Verba, Sidney (1996) "The Citizen Respondent: Sample Surveys and American Democracy" in *American Political Science Review* no. 1.

Waldrauch, Harald (1994a) "Theoretische Erklärungsansätze der Transitionsprozesse der kommunistischen Länder Osteuropas (1988–1990)" in *Österreichische Zeitschrift für Politikwissenschaft* no. 4.

Waldrauch, Harald (1994b) Transitionstheorien zum Regimewechsel in den Ländern Osteuropas (1988–1990) und ihre Anwendung auf Polen und die Tschechoslowakei, University of Vienna (Master-Thesis).

Waldrauch, Harald (1996a) "Was heißt demokratische Konsolidierung? Über einige theoretische Konsequenzen des osteuropäischen Regimewechsels", *Institut für Höhere Studien, Reihe Politikwissenschaft* no. 36.

Waldrauch, Harald (1996b) "Incommensurability? On the Comparison of Southern and Eastern Regime Changes", *Institut für Höhere Studien,* Vienna, Mimeo.

Waller, Michael (1995) "Adaptation of the Former Communist Parties of East-Central Europe: A Case of Social-democratization?" in *Party Politics* no. 4.

Weidenfeld, Werner (ed.) (1997) *Central and Eastern Europe on the Way into the European Union* (Gütersloh).

Weil, Frederick D. (1993) "The Development of Democratic Attitudes in Eastern and Western Germany in a Comparative Perspective" in Frederick D. Weil (ed.) *Democratization in Eastern and Western Europe* (Greenwich/London).

Weil, Frederick D. (ed.) (1994) *Political Culture and Political Structure: Theoretical and Empirical Studies* (Greenwich/London).

Weiss, Hilde and Reinprecht, Christoph (1996) *Österreichs östliche Nachbarn: Nationale Identität und demokratischer Neubeginn. Eine empirische Untersuchung im Rahmen des "Millenniumsprojekts"*, Mimeo (Vienna).

Welch, Stephen (1993) *The Concept of Political Culture* (New York).

Welsh, Helga A. (1994) "Political Transition Processes in Central and Eastern Europe' in *Comparative Politics* no. 4.

Westle, Bettina (1989) *Politische Legitimität – Theorien, Konzepte, empirische Befunde* (Baden-Baden).

Westle, Bettina (1994) "Demokratie und Sozialismus. Politische Ordnungsvorstellungen im vereinten Deutschland zwischen Ideologie, Protest und Nostalgie" in *Kölner Zeitschrift für Soziologie und Sozialpsychologie* no. 4.

Wiatr, Jerzy J. (ed.) (1997) "Elections and Parliaments in Post-Communist East Central Europe" in *International Political Science Review* No. 4.

White, Stephen, Rose, Richard and McAllister, Ian (1997) *How Russia Votes* (Chatham).

Whitehead, Laurence (1989) "The Consolidation of Fragile Democracies: A Discussion with Illustrations" in Robert A. Pastor (ed.) *Democracy in the Americas: Stopping the Pendulum* (New York).

Whitehead, Laurence (1996a) "Comparative Politics: Democratization Studies" in Robert E. Goodin and Hans Dieter Klingemann (eds) *A New Handbook of Political Science* (Oxford).

Whitehead, Laurence (ed.) (1996b) *The International Dimensions of Democratization. Europe and the Americans* (Oxford).

Wightman, Gordon (ed.) (1995) *Party Formation in East-Central Europe. Post-communist Politics in Czechoslovakia, Hungary, Poland and Bulgaria* (Aldershot).

Wolff-Poweska, Anna (1993) "Politische Kultur in den post-kommunistischen Gesellschaften" in Werner Weidenfeld (ed.) *Demokratie und Marktwirtschaft in Osteuropa* (Gütersloh).

Wollmann, Helmut, Helmut Wiesenthal and Frank Bönker (eds) (1995) *Transformation sozialistischer Gesellschaften. Am Ende des Anfangs* (Opladen).

Wyman, Matthew et al. (1995) "The Place of 'Party' in Post-Communist Europe" in *Party Politics* no. 4.

Zagórski, Krzysztof (1994) "Hope Factor, Inequality, and Legitimacy of Systemic Transformations" in *Communist and Post-Communist Studies* no. 4.

Zifcak, Spencer (1995) "The Battle over Presidential Power in Slovakia" in *East European Constitutional Review* no. 3.

Index